Antonio Gavin

A Master-Key to Popery

Antonio Gavin

A Master-Key to Popery

ISBN/EAN: 9783337088194

Printed in Europe, USA, Canada, Australia, Japan

Cover: Foto ©Lupo / pixelio.de

More available books at **www.hansebooks.com**

TO HER
Royal Highneſs
THE
Princeſs of *WALES*.

MADAM,

AS, in this *Maſter-Key to Popery*, I do write nothing but matters of fact, concerning the corruptions and ſecret practices of the *Romiſh* prieſts, (which I hope in God will prove uſeful to all true proteſtants; nay, to the moſt bigoted Romans, if they will but read it impartially) ſo, in this my humble dedication to your highneſs, I do advance nothing but what is plainly demonſtrable; for your agreeableneſs and affability, your natural propenſion to do good,

and

and your piety and zeal for the proteſtant religion, are known to the world, better then the errors of the church of Rome, for the firſt is liable to no diſpute, even amongſt the Romans, by whom the ſecond never was, nor ever will be, own'd without a particular influence of God's grace.

Theſe, Madam, being matters of fact, together with your Highneſs's readineſs to promote and encourage works of this nature, I do humbly put this edition and myſelf under your mighty protection, that the book might ſafely go thro' all ſorts and conditions of men, the author might be ſecur'd from the inhuman attempts of his implacable enemies, and your Highneſs rewarded, for this and other charitable works, by the eternal King, here and hereafter, which ſhall be the continual wiſhes of,

Madam, **Your** *Highneſs's*
Moſt humble, moſt obedient
And moſt devoted ſervant.

ANTHONY GAVIN.

THE
PREFACE.

WHEN I first designed to publish the following sheets, it was a matter of some doubt with me, whether or no I should put my name to them; for if I did, I considered that I exposed myself to the malice of a great body of men, who would endeavour on all occasions to injure me in my reputation and fortune, if not in my life; which last (to say no more) was no unnatural suspicion of a Spaniard, and one in my case, to entertain of some fiery zealots of the church of Rome.

But on the other hand, I foresaw, that if I concealed my name, a great part of the benefit, intended to the public by this work, might be lost. For I have often observed, as to books of this kind, where facts only are related (the truth of which in the greatest measure must depend on the credit of the relater) that wherever the authors, out of caution or fear, have concealed themselves, the event commonly has been, that even the friends to the cause, which the facts support, give but a cold assent to them, and the enemies reject them entirely as calumnies, and forgeries, without ever giving themselves the trouble of examining into the truth of that which the relater dares not openly avow. On this account, whatever the consequences may be, I resolved to put my name to this, and accordingly did so to the first proposals, which were made for printing it.

But, by this means, I am at the same time obliged to say something in vindication of myself from several aspersions which

which I lie under, and which indeed I have already in a great degree been a sufferer by, in the opinion of many worthy gentlemen. The first is, that I never was a priest, because I have not my letters of orders to produce. This, it must be confessed, is a testimonial, without which no one has a right, or can expect to be regarded as a person of that character; unless he has very convincing arguments to offer the world, that, in his circumstances no, such thing could reasonably be expected from him; and whether or no mine are such, I leave the world to judge. My case was this:

As soon as it had pleased God by his grace to overcome in me the prejudices of my education, in favour of that corrupt church, in which I had been bred up, and to inspire me with a resolution to embrace the protestant religion, I saw, that in order to preserve my life, I must immediately quit Spain, where all persons, who do not publicly profess the Romish religion, are condemned to death. Upon this I resolved to loose no time in making my escape, but how to make it was a matter of the greatest difficulty and danger: However, I determined rather to hazard all events, than either to continue in that church, or expose myself to certain death; and accordingly made choice of disguises as the most probable method of favouring my escape. The first I made use of was the habit of an officer in the army: And, as I was sure there would be strict inquiry and search made after me, I durst not bring along with me my letters of orders, which upon my being suspected in any place, for the person searched after, or on any other unhappy accident, would have been an undeniable evidence against me, and consequently would have condemned me to the inquisition. By this means I got safely to London; where I was most civilly received by the late Earl Stanhope, to whom I had the honor to be known when he was in Zaragosa. He told me, that there were some other new converts of my nation in town, and that he hoped, I would follow the command of Jesus to Peter, viz. When thou art converted, strengthen thy brethren.

Upon

Upon this I went to the late Lord Bishop of London, *and by his lordship's order, his domestic chaplain examined me three days together; and as I could not produce the letters of orders, he advised me to get a certificate from my Lord* Stanhope, *that he knew me, and that I was a priest, which I obtained the very same day; and upon this certificate, his lordship received my recantation after morning prayers in his chapel of* Somerset *house, and licensed me to preach and officiate in a* Spanish *congregation composed of my Lord* Stanhope, *several* English *officers, and a few* Spanish *officers, new converts. My first sermon I had the honor to dedicate to my Lord* Stanhope, *and was printed by Mr.* William Bowyer, *and was sold afterwards, by Mr.* Denoyer, *a* French *bookseller, at* Erasmus's *head, in the* Strand. *By virtue of this license, I preached two years and eight months, first in the chapel of* Queen's-square, Westminster, *and afterwards in* Oxenden's *chapel, near the* hay-market. *But my benefactor, desirous to settle me in the* English *church, advised me to go chaplain to the* Preston *man of war, where I might have a great deal of leisure to learn the language; and being presented and approved by the Bishop of* London, *the Lords of the Admiralty granted me the warrant or commission of chaplain. Then his lordship, though he had given me his consent in writing, to preach in* Spanish, *did enlarge it in the warrant of the Admiralty, which license I shall take leave to insert here at large.*

WHEREAS the Reverend Mr. *Anthony Gavin* was recommended to me, by the right honorable Lord *Stanhope*; and by the same, and other English gentlemen, I was certified that the said Reverend Mr. *Gavin* was a secular priest, and master of arts, in the university of the city of *Zaragosa*, in the kingdom of *Aragon*, in *Spain*, and that they knew him in the said city, and conversed with him several times: This is to certify, that the said Reverend Mr. *Gavin*, after having publicly and solemnly abjured the errors of the Romish religion;

ligion; and being thereupon by me reconciled to the church of *England*, on the 3d day of January, 1715-16; he had then my leave to officiate, in the Spanish language, in the chapel of Queen's-square, *Westminster*; and now being appointed chaplain of his Majesty's ship, the Preston, has my license to preach in English, and to administer the sacraments, at home and abroad, in all the churches and chapels of my diocess. Given under my hand, in *London*, the 13th of July, 1720.

Signed, JOHN LONDON.

The certificate, license, and warrant, may be seen at any time, for I have them by me.

After that, the ship being put out of commission, and my Lord Stanhope *being in* Hanover *with the King, I came over to* Ireland *on the importunity of a friend, with a design to stay here 'till my Lord's return into* England : *But when I was thinking of going over again, I heard of my Lord's death, and having in him lost my best patron, I resolved to try in this kingdom, whether I could find any settlement*: *And in a few days after, by the favour of his grace my Lord Archbishop of* Cashel, *and the Reverend Dean* Percival, *I got the curacy of* Gowran, *which I served almost eleven months, by the license of my Lord Bishop of* Ossory, *who afterwards, upon my going to* Cork, *gave me his letters dismissory.*

I was in Cork *very near a year, serving the cure of a parish near it, and the Rev. Dean* Maule *being at that time in* London, *and I being recommended to him, to preach in his parish church of* Shandon, *he went to inquire about me to the Bishop of* London, *who, and several other persons of distinction, were pleased to give me a good character, as the Dean on my leaving him did me the favour to certify under his hand, together with my good behaviour during my stay in* Cork.

Now my case being such, as I have represented it, I freely submit it to the judgment of every gentleman of ingenuity and candour, to determine, whether it could be expected

from

from me, that I should have my letters of orders *to shew; and yet whether there can be any tolerable reason to suspect my not having been a priest. I think it might be enough to silence all suspicions on this account, that I was received as a priest into the church of* England, *and licensed as such, to preach and administer the sacraments both in that kingdom and this: And I hope no one can imagine, that any of the bishops of the best constituted and governed churches upon earth, would admit any person to so sacred a trust, without their being fully satisfied that he was in orders.*

I shall, on this occasion, beg leave to mention what the Bishop of London *said to me, when I told him I had not my* letters of orders, *but that my Lord* Stanhope, *and other gentlemen of honor and credit, who knew me in my native city of* Zaragosa, *would certify, that I there was esteemed and officiated as a priest. Bring such a certificate, said he, and I will receive and license you; for I would rather depend upon it, than any* letters of orders *you could produce, which, for ought I could tell, you might have forged.*

I hope what I have here said may convince even my enemies, of my being a clergyman: And how I have behaved myself as such, since I came into this kingdom, I appeal to those gentlemen I conversed with in Gowran, Gortroe, *and* Cork, *and for this last year and an half, to the officers of Col.* Barrel, *Brigadier* Napper, *Col.* Hawley, *Col.* Newton, *and Col.* Lanoe's *regiments, who, I am sure, will do me justice, and I desire no more of them; and upon an inquiry into my behaviour, I flatter myself, that the public will not lightly give credit to the ill reports spread abroad by my enemies.*

Another objection raised against me is, that I have perjured myself in discovering the private confessions which were made to me. In one point indeed they may call me perjured, and it is my comfort and glory, that I am so in it, viz. That I have broke the oath I took, when I was ordained priest, which was to live and die in the Roman-Catholic *faith. But as to the other perjury charged upon*

B *me,*

me, they lie under a mistake; for there is no oath of secrecy at all administred to confessors, as most protestants imagine. Secrecy indeed is recommended to all confessors by the casuists, and enjoined by the councils and Popes so strictly, that if a confessor reveals (except in some particular cases) what is confessed to him, so as the penitent is discovered, he is to be punished for it in the inquisition; which, it must be owned, is a more effectual way of enjoining secrecy than oaths themselves.

However, I am far from imagining, that because in this case I have broken no oath, I should therefore be guilty of no crime, though I revealed every thing which was committed to my trust as a confessor, of whatever ill consequence it might be to the penitent; no, such a practice I take to be exceedingly criminal, and I do from my soul abhor it.

But nevertheless there are cases where, by the constitution of the church of Rome itself, the most dangerous secrets may and ought to be revealed: Such as those which are called reserved cases, of which there are many; some reserved to the pope himself, as heresy; some to his apostolical commissary or his deputy, as incest in the first degree: Some to the bishop of the diocess, as the setting a neighbour's house on fire. Now in such cases the confessor cannot absolve the penitent, and therefore he is obliged to reveal the confession to the person, to whom the absolution of that sin is reserved; though indeed he never mentions the penitent's name, or any circumstance by which he may be discovered.

Again, there are other cases (such as a conspiracy against the life of the Prince, or a traiterous design to overturn the government) which the confessor is obliged in conscience, and for the safety of the public, to reveal.

But besides all these, whenever the penitent's case happens to have any thing of an uncommon difficulty in it, common prudence, and a due regard to the faithful discharge of his office, will oblige a confessor to discover it to men of experience and judgment in casuistry, that he may have their advice how to proceed in it: And this is what confessors

sors in Spain not only may do, but are bound by the word of a priest to do wherever they have an opportunity of consulting a college of confessors, or (as it is commonly called) a moral academy.

I believe it may be of some service on the present occasion, to inform my readers what those moral academies are, which are to be met with through Spain, in every city and town where there is a number of secular and regular priests: But I shall speak only of those in the city of Zaragosa, as being the most perfectly acquainted with them.

A moral academy is a college or assembly consisting of several Father Confessors, in which each of them proposes some moral case which has happened to him in confession, with an exact and particular account of the confession, without mentioning the penitent's name: And the proponent having done this, every member is to deliver his opinion upon it. This is constantly practised every Friday, from two of the clock in the afternoon, 'till six, and sometimes 'till eight, as the cases proposed happen to be more or less difficult. But when there is an extraordinary intricate case to be resolved, and the members cannot agree in the resolution of it; they send one of their assembly to the great academy, which is a college composed of 16 casuistical doctors, and 4 professors of divinity, the most learned and experienced in moral cases that may be had; and by them the case in debate is resolved, and the resolution of it entered in the books of the academy by the consent of the president and members.

The academy of the holy trinity, founded and very nobly endowed by Archbishop *Gamboa*, is one of the most famous in the city of *Zaragosa*; and of it I was a member for three years. I was very young and unexpert in cases of conscience, when I was first licensed to be a confessor; for the Pope having dispensed with 13 months of the time required by the canons for the age of a Priest (for which I paid 60 pistoles) I was ordained before I was 23 years old, by *Don Antotonio Ibannez de la Rivia de Herrera*, Archbishop of *Zaragosa* and Viceroy of *Arragon*; and at the same time licensed by him

him to hear confessions of both sexes. In order then the better and more speedily to qualify myself for the office, I thought it my prudentest way to apply, as soon as possible, to be admitted into this learned society, and as it happened, I had interest enough to succeed.

Now among many statutes left by the founder to this academy, one is this, *viz.* That every person, who is chosen a member of it, is on his admission to promise upon the word of a priest, to give the whole assembly a faithful account of all the private confessions he has heard the week before, which have any thing in them difficult to be resolved; yet so as not to mention any circumstance by which the penitents may be known.

And for this end there is a book, where the secretary enters all the cases proposed and resolved every *Friday*; and every third year there is, by the consent of the president and members of the academy, and by the approbation of the *great one*, a book printed containing all the cases resolved for three years before, and which is entitled, *compendium casuum moralium academiæ S. S. trinitatis*. The academy of the holy trinity is always composed of 20 members, so that every one may easily perceive, that each of the members may be acquainted in a year or two, with many hundreds of private confessions of all ranks and conditions of people, besides those which were made to themselves: Which remark I only make by the by to satisfy some men, who, I am told, find fault with me for pretending to impose on the public for genuine, several confessions which were not made to myself, and consequently for the reality of which, I can have no sufficient authority.

Now after all that has been said on this head, I believe I need not be at much trouble to vindicate myself from the imputation of any criminal breach of secrecy; for if the reader observes, that on the foregoing grounds, there is no confession whatever which may not lawfully be revealed (provided the confessor doth not discover the penitent) he cannot in justice condemn me for publishing

lishing a few, by which it is morally impossible, in the present circumstances, that the penitents should be known. Had I been much more particular than I am in my relations, and mentioned even the names and every thing else I knew of the persons, there would scarce be a possibility (considering the distance and little intercourse there is between this place and *Zaragosa*) of their suffering in any degree by it: And I need not observe that the chief, and indeed only reason of enjoining and keeping secrecy, is the hazards the penitent may run by a discovery, but I do assure the reader, that in every confession I have related, I have made use of feigned names, and avoided every circumstance by which I had the least cause to suspect the parties might be found out. And I assure him further, that most of the cases, here published by me are, in their most material points, already printed in the *conpendiums* of that *moral academy* of which I was a member.

As for the reasons which moved me to publish this book, I shall only say, that as the corrupt practices, which are the subject of it, first set me upon examining into the principles of the church of *Rome*, and by that means of renouncing them; so I thought that the making of them public might happily produce the same effect in some others.

I did design on this occasion to give a particular account of the motives of my conversion, and leaving *Spain*; but being confined to 300 pages, I must leave that and some other things relating to the sacraments of the church of *Rome*, to a second part, which I intend to print if the public thinks fit to encourage me.

I must beg the readers pardon for my presumption in writing in his own language, on so short an acquaintance as I have with it. I hope he will excuse the many mistakes I may have committed in the book: I shall be very well pleased to be told of, and I shall take the greater care to avoid them in the second part.

A

A MASTER-KEY TO POPERY.

PART I.

Of the Roman-Catholics *Auricular Confession.*

URICULAR confession being one of the five commandments of the *Roman-Catholic* church, and a condition necessarily required, in one of their sacraments ; and being too an article that will contribute very much to the discovery of many other errors of that communion, it may be proper to make use of the *Master-Key*, and begin with it : And first of all, with the Father Confessors, who are the only key-keepers of it.

Though

Though a priest cannot be licens'd, by the canons of their church, to hear men's confessions, till he is thirty years, nor to confess women, till forty years of age, yet ordinarily he gets a dispensation from the bishop, to whom his probity, secrecy, and sober conversation are represented by one of the diocesan (*a*) examinators, his friend, or by some person of interest with his lordship; and by that means he gets a confessor's license, most commonly, the day he gets his letters of orders, *viz.* Some at three and twenty, and some at four and twenty years of age, not only for men, but for women's confessions also. I say, some at three and twenty; for the Pope dispenseth with thirteen months, to those that pay a sum of money; of which I shall speak in another place.

To priests thus licens'd, to be judges of the tribunal of conscience, men and women do discover their sins, their actions, their thoughts, nay, their very dreams, if they happen to be impure. I say, judges of the tribunal of conscience; for when they are licens'd, they ought to resolve any case (let it be never so hard) proposed by the penitent: And by this means it must often happen, that a young man who, perhaps, doth not know more than a few definitions (which he hath learn'd in a little manual of some casuistical authors) of what is sin, shall sit in such a tribunal, to judge, in the most intricate cases, the consciences of men, and of men too that may be his masters.

I saw a reverend father (*b*) who had been eight and twenty years professor of divinity in one of the most considerable (*c*) universities of *Spain*, and one of the most famous men for his learning, in that religion, kneel down before a young (*d*) priest of twenty-four years of age, and

---

(*a*) Those that are appointed, by the bishop, to examine those that are to be ordain'd, or licens'd to preach and hear confessions.

(*b*) Fr. *James Garcia*.

(*c*) The university of *Zaragofa*, in the kingdom of *Arragon*, in *Spain*, which, according to their historians, was built by *Sertorius*.

(*d*) The thing happened to me when I was twenty-four years of age.

and confess his sins to him. Who would not be surprised at them both? A man fit to be the judge to act the part of a criminal before an ignorant judge, who, I am sure, could scarcely then tell the titles of the *Summæ Morales*.

Nay, the Pope, notwithstanding all his infallibility, doth kneel down before his confessor, tells him his sins, heareth his correction, and receives and performs whatever penance he imposeth upon him. This is the only difference between the Pope's confessor, and the confessors of Kings and other persons, that all confessors sit down to hear Kings and other persons, but the Pope's confessor kneels down himself to hear the Holy Father. What, the holy one upon earth humble himself as a sinner? Holiness and sin in one and the same subject, is a plain contradiction in terms.

If we ask the *Roman-Catholics*, Why so learned men, and the Pope, do so? They will answer, that they do it out of reverence to such a sacrament, out of humility, and to give a token and testimony of their hearty sorrow for their sins. And as for the Pope, they say he doth it to shew an example of humility, as Jesus Christ did, when he wash'd the apostles feet.

This answer is true, but they do not say the whole truth in it; for, besides the aforesaid reasons, they have another, as *Molina* tells them, (*e*) *viz*. That the penitent ought to submit entirely to his confessor's correction, advice, and penance, and he accepts no body from this necessary requisite of a true penitent. Who would not be surprised (I say again) that a man of noted learning would submit himself to a young, unexperienced priest, as to a judge of his conscience, take his advice, and receive his correction and penance?

What would a *Roman-Catholic* say, if he should see one of our learned bishops go to the college to consult a young collegian in a nice point of divinity; nay, to
take

(*e*) In his *Moral Summ*. Chap. XVIII. of the requisites of a true penitent.

take his advice, and submit to his opinion? Really the *Romans* would heartily laugh at him, and with a great deal of reason; nay, he could say, that his lordship was not right in his senses. What then can a protestant say of those infatuated, learned men of the church of *Rome*, when they do more than what is here supposed?

As for the Pope (I say) 'tis a damnable opinion to compare him, in this case, with our Saviour Jesus; for Christ knew not sin, but gave us an example of humility and patience, obedience and poverty. He did wash the Apostles feet; and tho' we cannot know by the scripture whether he did kneel down or not to wash them: Supposing that he did, he did it only out of a true humility, and not to confess his sins: But the Pope doth kneel down, not to give an example of humility and patience, but really to confess his sins: Not to give an example of obedience; for, being *supreme pontifex*, he obeys no body, and assumes a command over the whole world; nor of poverty; for Pope and necessity dwell far from one another. And if some ignorant *Roman-Catholic* should say, that the Pope, as Pope, has no sin, we may prove the contrary with *Cipriano de Valera*, (*f*) who gives an account of all the bastards of several Popes for many years past. The Pope's bastards, in *Latin*, are called *nepotes*. Now mind, O reader, this common saying in *Latin*, among the *Roman-Catholics* : *Solent clereci filios suos vocare sobrinos aut nepotes* : That is, The priests use to call their own sons *cousins* or *nephews*. And when we give these instances to some of their learned men (as I did to one in *London*) they say, *Angelorum est peccare, hominumque penitere*; i. e. It belongs to Angels to sin, and to men to repent. By this they acknowledge that the Pope is a sinner, and nevertheless they call him *His Holiness*, and the most *Holy Father*.

Who then would not be surprised to see the most holy Jesus Christ's vicar on earth, and the infallible in whatever

---

(*f*) The lives of the Popes, and the sacrifice of Mass.

ever he says, and doth submit himself to confess his sins to a man, and a man too that has no other power to correct him, to advise and impose a penance upon the most holy one, than what his holiness has been pleased to grant him? Every body indeed that has a grain of sense of religion, and reflects seriously on it.

I come now to their *Auricular Confession*, and of the ways and methods they practice and observe in the confessing of their sins. There is among them two ranks of people, *learned* and *unlearned*. The learned confess by these three general heads, *thought*, *word* and *deed*, reducing into them all sorts of sins. The unlearned confess by the ten commandments, discovering by them all the mortal sins which they have committed since their last confession. I say mortal sins; for as to the venial sins, or sins of a small matter, the opinion of their casuistical authors (g) is, they are washed away by the sign of the cross, or by sprinkling the face with the holy water. To the discovery of the mortal sins the father confessor doth very much help the penitent; for he sometimes out of pure zeal, but most commonly out of curiosity, asks them many questions to know whether they do remember all their sins, or not? By these and the like questions, the confessors do more mischief than good, especially to the ignorant people and young women; for perhaps they do not know What simple *fornication* is? What voluntary or involuntary *pollution*? What impure *desire*? What *sinful motion* of our hearts? What *relapse, reincidence*, or *reiteration* of sins? And the like; and then by the confessors indiscreet questions, the penitents do learn things of which they never had dreamed before; and when they come to that tribunal with a sincere, ignorant heart, to receive advice and instruction, they go home
with

(g) *Perez, Irribarren,* and *Salazar,* in his Compond. Moral. Sect. 12. *de vitiis et peccatis,* gives a catalogue of the venial sins, and says, among others, that to eat flesh in a day prohibited by the church, without minding it, was so. To kill a man, throwing a stone through the window, or being drunk, or in the first motion of his passion, are venial sins, &c.

with light, knowledge, and an idea of sins unknown to them before.

I said, that the **confessors** do ask questions, most commonly out of curiosity, though they are warned by the casuistical authors to be prudent, discreet, and very cautious in the questions they ask, especially if the penitent be a young woman, or an ignorant; for as *Pineda* says (*b*) *It is better to let them go ignorant than instructed in new sins.* But contrary to this good maxim, they are so indiscreet in this point, that I saw in the city of *Lisbon* in *Portugal* a girl of ten years of age, coming from church, ask her mother what deflouring was? For the father confessor had asked her whether she was defloured or not? And the mother, more discreet than the confessor, told the girl, that the meaning was, whether she took delight in smelling flowers or not? And so she stopped her child's curiosity. But of this and many other indiscretions I shall speak more particularly by and by.

Now observe, that as a penitent cannot hide any thing from the spiritual judge, else he would make a sacrilegious confession; so I cannot hide any thing from the public which is to be my hearer, and the temporal judge of my work, else I should betray my conscience: Therefore (to the best of my memory, and as one that expects to be called before the dreadful tribunal of God, on account of what I do now write and say, if I do not say and write the truth from the bottom of my heart) I shall give a faithful, plain account of the *Roman's* auricular confession, and of the most usual questions and answers between the confessors and penitents; and this I shall do in so plain a style that every body may go along with me.

And first of all it is very proper to give an account of what the penitents do, from the time they come into the church, till they begin their confession. When the penitent comes into the church, he takes holy water, and sprinkles his face, and, making the sign of the cross,
says;

(*b*) Tract. de Penit. Sect. 1. sect. vii.

says, *per signum crucis de inimicis nostris libera nos Deus noster: In nomine Patris et Filii, et Spiritus Sancti.* A-men. *i. e.* By the sign of the cross deliver us our God from our enemies, in the name of the Father, and of the Son, and of the Holy Ghost. *Amen.* Then the penitent goes on, and kneels down before the great altar, where the great *host* (of which I shall speak in another place) is kept in a neat and rich tabernacle, with a brass or silver lamp hanging before it, and burning continually, night and day. There he makes a prayer, first to the holy sacrament of the altar (as they call it) after to the Virgin *Mary*, and to the titular saints of the church. Then he turns about upon his knees, and visits five altars, or if there is but one altar in the church, five times that altar, and says before each of them five times, *Pater noster, &c.* and five times *Ave Maria, &c.* with *Gloria Patria, &c.*

Then he riseth, and goes to the confessionary, *i. e.* The confessing place, where the confessor sits in a chair like our hackney chairs, which is most commonly placed in some of the chapels, and in the darkest place of the church. The chairs, generally speaking, have an iron-grate at each side, but none at all before; and some days of devotion, or on a great festival, there is such a crowd of people that you may see three penitents at once about the chair, one at each grate, and t'other at the door, though only one confesseth at a time, whispering in the confessor's ear, that the others should not hear what he says; and when one has done, the t'other begins, and so on: But most commonly they confess at the door of the chair one after another; for thus, the confessor has an opportunity of knowing the penitent: And though many gentlewomen either out of bashfulness, or shame, or modesty, do endeavour to hide their faces with a fan, or veil, notwithstanding all this they are known by the confessor, who if curious, by crafty questions brings them to tell him their names and houses, and this in the very act of confession, or else he examines their faces when the confession

confession is over whilst the penitents are kissing his hand or sleeve; and if he cannot know them this way, he goes himself to give the sacrament, and then every one being obliged to shew his face, is known by the curious confessor, who doth this not without a private view and design, as will appear at the end of some private confessions.

The penitent then kneeling, bows himself to the ground before the confessor, and makes again the sign of the cross in the aforesaid form; and having in his hand the beads, or rosary of the Virgin *Mary*, begins the general confession of sins, which some say in *Latin*, and some in the vulgar tongue; therefore it seems proper to give a copy of it both in *Latin* and *English*.

Confiteor Deo Omnipotenti; beatæ Mariæ semper Virgini, beato Michaeli Archangelo, beato Joanni Baptistæ, sanctis apostolis Petro, et Paulo, omnibus sanctis, et tibi, Pater; quia peccavi nimis cogitatione, verbo, et opere, mea culpa, mea culpa, mea maxima culpa: Ideo precor beatam Mariam semper Virginem, beatem Michaelem Archangelum, beatum Joannem Baptistam, sanctos apostolos Petrum et Paulum, omnes sanctos et te, Pater, orare pro me ad Dominum Deum nostrum. Amen.

I do confess to God Almighty, to the blessed *Mary*, always a Virgin, to the blessed Archangel *Michael*, to the blessed *John Baptist*, to the holy apostles *Peter* and *Paul*, to all the saints, and to thee, O Father, that I have too much sinned by thought, word, and deed, by my fault, by my fault, by my greatest fault: Therefore I beseech the blessed *Mary*, always a Virgin, the blessed Archangel *Michael*, the blessed *John Baptist*, the holy apostles *Peter* and *Paul*, all the saints, and thee, O Father, to pray God our Lord for me. *Amen.*

This done, the penitent raises him from his prostration to his knees, and touching with his lip, either the ear or the cheek of the Spiritual Father, begins to discover his sins by the ten commandments: And here it may be necessary to give a translation of their ten commandments, word for word.

THE

THE commandments of the law of God are ten: The three firſt do pertain to the honor of God; and the other ſeven to the benefit of our neighbour.

The I. Thou ſhalt love God above all things.
II. Thou ſhalt not ſwear.
III. Thou ſhalt ſanctify the holy days.
IV. Thou ſhalt honor father and mother.
V. Thou ſhalt not kill.
VI. Thou ſhalt not commit fornication.
VII. Thou ſhalt not ſteal.
VIII. Thou ſhalt not bear falſe witneſs, nor lie.
IX. Thou ſhalt not covet thy neighbour's wife.
X. Thou ſhalt not covet the things which are another's.

Theſe ten commandments are compriſed in two; viz. to ſerve and love God, and thy neighbour as thyſelf. *Amen.*

Now, not to forget any thing that may inſtruct the public, it is to the purpoſe to give an account of the little children's confeſſions: I mean of thoſe that have not yet attained the ſeventh year of their age; for at ſeven they begin moſt commonly to receive the ſacrament, and confeſs in private with all the formalities of their church.

There is in every city, in every pariſh, in every town and village, a Lent preacher; and there is but one difference among them, viz. that ſome preachers do preach every day in Lent, ſome three ſermons a week; ſome two, viz. on Wedneſdays and Sundays, and ſome only on Sundays, and the holy days that happen to fall in Lent. The preacher of the pariſh pitches upon one day of the week, moſt commonly, in the middle of Lent, to hear the children's confeſſions, and gives notice to the congregation the Sunday before, that every father of a family may ſend his children, both boys and girls, to church, on the day appointed, in the afternoon. The mothers
dreſs

dress their children the best they can that day, and give them the offering money for the expiation of their sins. That afternoon is a holy day in the parish, not by precept, but by custom, for no parishioner, either old or young, man or woman, misseth to go and hear the children's confessions. For it is reckon'd, among them, a greater diversion than a comedy, as you may judge by the following account.

The day appointed, the children repair to church at three of the clock, where the preacher is waiting for them with a long reed in his hand; and when all are together, (sometimes 150 in number, and sometimes less) the reverend Father placeth them in a circle round himself, and then kneeling down (the children also doing the same) makes the sign of the cross, and says a short prayer. This done, he exhorteth the children to hide no sin from him, but to tell him all they have committed. Then he strikes, with the reed, the child whom he designs to confess the first, and asks him the following questions.

Confessor. How long is it since you last confessed.

Boy. Father, a whole year, or the last *Lent*.

Conf. And how many sins have you committed from that time till now?

Boy. Two dozen.

Now the Confessor asks round about.

Conf. And you?

Boy. A thousand and ten.

Another will say a bag full of small lies, and ten big sins; and so one after another answers, and tells many childish things.

Conf. But pray, you say, that you have committed ten big sins, tell me, how big?

Boy. As big as a tree.

Conf. But tell me the sins.

Boy. There is one sin I committed, which I dare not tell your reverence before all the people; for some body here present will kill me, if he heareth me.

Conf.

Conf. Well, come out of the circle, and tell it me.

They both go out, and with a loud voice, he tells him, that such a day he stole a nest of sparrows from a tree of another boy's, and that if he knew it, he would kill him. Then both came again into the circle, and the Father asks other boys and girls so many ridiculous questions, and the children answer him so many pleasant, innocent things, that the congregation laughs all the while. One will say, that his sins are red, another that one of his sins is white, one black, and one green, and in these trifling questions they spend two hours time. When the congregation is weary of laughing, the Confessor gives the children a correction, and bids 'em not to sin any more, for a black boy takes along with him the wicked children: Then he asks the offering, and after he has got all from 'em, gives 'em the penance for their sins. To one he says, I give you for penance, to eat a sweet cake, to another, not to go to school the day following. To another, to desire his mother to buy him a new hat, and such things as these, and pronouncing the words of absolution, he dismisseth the congregation with *Amen*, so be it, every year.

These are the first foundations of the *Romish* religion for youth. Now, O reader! You may make reflections upon it, and the more you will reflect, so much the more you will hate the corruptions of that communion, and it shall evidently appear to you, that the serious, religious instruction of our church, as to the youth, is reasonable, solid, and without reproach. O! that all Protestants would remember the rules they learned from their teachers in their youth, and practise 'em while they live! Sure I am, they should be like angels on earth, and blessed for ever after death in heaven.

From seven till fifteen, there is no extraordinary thing to say of young people, only that from seven years of age, they begin to confess in private, and receive

ceive the sacrament in public. The Confessors have very little trouble with such young people, and likewise little profit, except with a *Puella*, who sometimes begins at twelve years the course of a lewd life, and then the Confessor finds business and profit enough, when she comes to confess. Now I come to give an account of several private confessions of both sexes, beginning from people of fifteen years of age. The confession is a dialogue between the Spiritual Father and the impenitent; therefore I shall deliver the confessions in a way of dialogue. The letter *C.* signifies *Confessor*, and several other letters, the names of the penitent.

The confession of a young woman in Zaragoza, *whom I shall call* Mary. *And this I set down chiefly to shew the common form of their confessing penitents: The thing was not public; and therefore I give it under a supposed name.*

Confessor. HOW long is it since you last confessed?

Mary. It is two years and two months.

Conf. Pray, do you know the commandments of our holy mother the church?

Mary. Yea, Father.

Conf. Rehearse them.

Mary. The commandments of our holy mother, the church, are five. I. To hear Mass on *Sundays* and *holy-days*. II. To confess, at least, once in a year, and oftener, if there be danger of death. III. To receive the eucharist. IV. To fast. V. To pay tithes and *Primitia.* *

Conf. Now rehearse the seven sacraments.

Mary. The sacraments of the holy mother, the church, are seven. I. Baptism. II. Confirmation. III. Penance.

---

* *Primitia* is to pay, besides the tenth, one thirtieth part of the fruits of the earth, towards the repair of the church-vestments, &c.

III. Penance. IV. The Lord's supper. V. Extreme unction. VI. Holy orders. VII. Matrimony. *Amen.*

Conf. You see in the second commandment of the church, and in the third, among the sacraments, that you are obliged to confess every year. Why, then, have you neglected so much longer a time to fulfil the precept of our holy mother?

Mary. As I am young, and a great sinner, I was ashamed, reverend Father, to confess my sins to the Priest of our parish, for fear he should know me by some passages of my life, which would be prejudicial to me, and to several other persons related to my family.

Conf. But you know that it is the indispensable duty of the minister of the parish, to expose in the church, after *Easter*, all those who have not confessed, nor received the sacrament before that time.

Mary. I do know it very well; but I went out of the city towards the middle of *Lent*, and I did not come back again till after *Easter*; and when I was asked in the country, whether I had confessed that *Lent* or not? I said, that I had done it in the city: And when the minister of the parish did ask me the same question, I told him, that I had done it in the country: So, with this lie, I free'd myself from the public censure of the church.

Conf. And did you perform the last penance imposed upon you?

Mary. Yea, Father, but not with that exactness I was commanded.

Conf. What was the penance?

Mary. To fast three days upon bread and water, and to give ten reals of plate, (*i*) & to say five Masses for the souls in purgatory. I did perform the first part, but not the second, because I could not get money for it, unknown to my parents at that time.

C 2 *Conf.*

(*i*) A real of plate is about seven pence of our money in *Ireland*.

Conf. Do you promise me to perform it, as soon as you can?

Mary. I have the money here, which I will leave with you, and you may say, or order another Prieſt to ſay the Maſſes.

Conf. Very well: But tell me now, what reaſon have you to come to confeſs out of the time appointed by the church? Is it for devotion, to quiet your conſcience, and merely to make your peace with God Almighty, or ſome worldly end?

Mary. Good Father, pity my condition, and pray put me in the right way of ſalvation, for I am ready to deſpair of God's mercy, if you do not quiet and eaſe my troubled conſcience. Now I will anſwer to your queſtion: The reaſon is, becauſe a gentleman, who under promiſe of marriage, has kept me theſe two laſt years, is dead two months ago; and I have reſolved in my heart to retire myſelf into a monaſtery, and to end there my days, ſerving God and his holy mother, the Virgin *Mary*.

Conf. Do not take any reſolution precipitately, for, may be, if your paſſion grows cool, you'll alter your mind; and I ſuſpect, with a great deal of reaſon, that your repentance is not ſincere, and that you come to confeſs out of ſorrow for the gentleman's death, more than out of ſorrow for your ſins; and if it be ſo, I adviſe you to take more time to conſider the ſtate of your conſcience, and to come to me a fortnight hence.

Mary. My father, all the world ſhall not alter my mind, and the daily remorſe of my conſcience brings me to your feet, with a full reſolution to confeſs all my ſins, in order to obtain abſolution, and to live a new life hereafter.

Conf. If it is ſo, let us, in the name of God, begin the confeſſion, and I require of you not to forget any circumſtance of ſin, which may contribute to eaſe your conſcience. And, above all, I deſire of you to lay aſide ſhame,

shame, while you confess your sins; for, suppose that your sins exceed the number of stars, or the number of the sands of the sea, God's mercy is infinite, and accepts of the true penitent heart, for he wills not the death of a sinner, but that he should repent and turn to him.

Mary. I do design to open freely my heart to you, and to follow your advice, as to the spiritual course of my life.

Conf. Begin then by the first commandment.

Mary. I do confess, in this commandment, that I have not loved God above all things; for all my care, these two years past, has been to please Don *Francisco*, in whatever thing he did desire me; and, to the best of my memory, I did not think of God, nor of his mother *Mary*, for many months together.

Conf. Have you constantly frequented the assemblies of the faithful, and heard Mass on *Sundays*, and holy days?

Mary. No, Father: Sometimes I have been four months without going to church.

Conf. You have done a great injury to your soul, and you have given great scandal to your neighbours.

Mary. As for the first, I own it; for every *Sunday* and holy day I went out in the morning, and in so populous a city they could not know the church I use to resort to.

Conf. Did it come into your mind all this while, that God would punish you for your sins?

Mary. Yea, Father: But the Virgin *Mary* is my advocate, I keep her image by my bed-side, and used to address my prayer to her every night before I went to bed, and I had always a great hope in her.

Conf. If your devotion to the Virgin *Mary* is so fervent, you must believe that your heart is moved to repentance by her influence and mediation; and I charge you to continue the same devotion while you live, and fear nothing afterwards.

Mary.

Mary. That is my design.

Conf. Go on.

Mary. The second commandment is, *Thou shalt not swear:* I never was guilty of swearing, but I have a custom of saying, *Such a thing is so, as sure as there is a God in heaven:* And this I repeat very often every day.

Conf. That is a sinful custom, for we cannot swear, nor affirm a thing by heaven or earth, as the scripture tells us; and less by him who has the throne of his habitation in heaven: So you must break off that custom, or else you commit a sin every time you make use of it. Go on.

Mary. The third is, *Thou shalt sanctify the holy days.* I have told you already, my spiritual Father, that I have neglected, some time, to go to Mass, four months together; and, to the best of my memory, in these two years and two months, I have missed sixty *Sundays* and holy days going to Mass, and when I did go, my mind was so much taken up with other diversions, that I did not mind the requisite devotion, for which I am heartily sorry.

Conf. I hope you will not do so for the future; and so go on.

Mary. The fourth is, *Thou shalt honor father and mother.* I have father and mother; as to my father, I do love, honor and fear him; as to my mother, I do confess, that I have answered and acted contrary to the duty, respect and reverence due to her, for her suspecting and watching my actions and false steps, and giving me a christian correction, I have abused her, nay, sometimes, I have lift up my hand to threaten her; and these proceedings of mine towards my good mother, torture now my heart.

Conf. I am glad to observe your grief, and you may be sure, God will forgive you these and other sins upon your hearty repentance, if you persevere in it. Go on.

Mary. The fifth is, *Thou shalt not kill.* I have not transgressed

transgressed this commandment effectively and immediately, but I have done it affectively and mediately, and at second hand; for a gentlewoman, who was a great hindrance to my designs, once provoked me to such a pitch, that I put in execution all the means of revenge I could think of, and gave ten pistoles to an assassin to take away her life.

Conf. And did he kill her?

Mary. No, Father, for she kept her house for three months, and in that time we were reconciled, and now we are very good friends.

Conf. Have you asked her pardon, and told her your design?

Mary. I did not tell her in express terms, but I told her that I had an ill will to her, and that at that time, I could have killed her, had I got an opportunity for it: For which I heartily begged her pardon; she did forgive me, and so we live ever since like two sisters.

Conf. Go on.

Mary. The sixth, *Thou shalt not commit fornication.* In the first place, I do confess that I have unlawfully conversed with the said Don *Francisco*, for two years, and this unlawful commerce has made me fall into many other sins.

Conf. Did he promise solemnly to marry you?

Mary. He did, but could not perform it, while his father was alive.

Conf. Tell me, from the beginning, to the day of his death, & to the best of your memory, your sinful tho'ts words, actions, nay, your very dreams, about this matter.

Mary. Father, the gentleman was our neighbour of a good family and fortune, and by means of the neighbourly friendship of our parents, we had the opportunity to talk with one another as often as we pleased. For two years together we loved one another with innocence; but at last he discovered to me one day, when our parents were abroad, the great inclination he had for me; and that having grown to a passion, and this to an inexpressible love, he could no longer hide it from me: That his design was to marry me, as soon as his father should die, and that he was willing to give me all the proofs of sincerity and unfeigned love, I could desire from him. To this I answered, that if it was so, I was ready to promise never to marry another, during his life: To this, he took a crucifix in his hands, and bowing down before an image of the Virgin *Mary*, called the four elements to be witnesses of the sincerity of his vows, nay, all the saints of the heavenly court, to appear against him in the day of judgment, if he was not true in his heart and words; and said, that by the crucifix in his hands, and by the image of the Virgin *Mary*, there present, he did promise and swear never to marry another during my life. I answered him in the same manner; and ever since, we have lived with the familiarities of husband and wife. The effect of this reciprocal promise was the ruin of my soul, and the beginning of my sinful life; for ever since, I minded nothing else, but to please him and myself, when I had opportunity for it.

Conf. How often did he visit you?

Mary. The first year he came to my room every night, after both families were gone to bed; for in the vault of his house, which joins to ours, we dug one night through the earth, and made a passage wide enough for the purpose, which we covered on each side with a large earthen water-jar; and by that means he came to me every night. But my grief is double, when I consider, that, engaging my own maid into this intrigue, I have been the occasion of her ruin too; for by my ill example, she lived in the same way with the gentleman's servant, and I own, that I have been the occasion of all her sins too.

Conf. And the second year did he visit you so often?

Mary. No, father; for the breach in the vault was discovered by his father, and was stopped immediately; but nobody suspected any thing of our intimacy, except

my

my mother, who from something she had observed, began to question me, and afterwards became more suspicious and watchful.

Conf. Did any effect of these visits come to light?

Mary. It would, had I not been so barbarous and inhuman to prevent it, by a remedy I took, which answered my purpose.

Conf. And how could you get the remedy, there being a rigorous law against it?

Mary. The procuring it brought me into a yet wickeder life; for I was acquainted with a Fryar, a cousin of mine, who had always expressed a great esteem for me; but one day after dinner, being alone, he began to make love to me, and was going to take greater liberties than ever he had done before: I told him, that if he could keep a secret, and do me a service, I would comply with his desire. He did promise me to do it upon the word of a priest. Then I told him my business, and the day after he brought me the necessary medicine; and ever since I was freed from that uneasiness, I have lived the same course of life with my cousin; nay, as I was under such an obligation to him, I have ever since been obliged to allow him many other liberties in my house.

Conf. Are those other liberties, he took in your house, sinful or not?

Mary. The liberties that I mean are, that he desired me to gratify his companion too, several times, and to consent that my maid should satisfy his lusts; and not only this, but, by desiring me to corrupt one of my friends, he has ruined her soul; for, being in the same condition I had been in before, I was obliged, out of fear, to furnish her with the same remedy, which produced the same effect. Besides these wicked actions, I have robbed my parents to supply him with whatever money he demanded.

Conf. But as to Don *Francisco,* pray tell me, how often did he visit you since?

Mary.

Mary. The second year he could not see me in private but very seldom, and in a sacred place; for having no opportunity at home, nor abroad, I used to go to a little chapel out of the town; and having gained the hermit with money, we continued our commerce, that way, for six or eight times the second year.

Conf. Your sins are aggravated, both by the circumstance of the sacred place, and by your cousin's being a Priest, besides the two murthers committed by you, one in yourself, and t'other in your friend. Nay, go on, if you have any more to say upon this subject.

Mary. I have nothing else to say, as to the commandment, but that I am heartily sorry for all these my misdoings.

Conf. Go on.

Mary. The seventh, *Thou shalt not steal.* I have nothing to confess in this commandment, but what I have told you already, i. e. that I have stolen many things from my father's house, to satisfy my cousin's thirst of money; and that I have advised my friend to do the same; though this was done by me, only for fear that he should expose us, if we had not given him what he did desire.

Conf. And do you design to continue the same life with your cousin for fear of being discovered?

Mary. No, Father; for he is sent to another convent to be professor of divinity for three years, and if he comes back again, he shall find me in a monastery; and then I will be safe, and free from his wicked attempts.

Conf. How long is it since he went away?

Mary. Three months, and his companion is dead; so, God be thanked, I am without any apprehension or fear now, and I hope to see my good design accomplished.

Conf. Go on.

Mary. The eighth is, *Thou shalt not bear false witness, nor lie.* The ninth, *Thou shalt not covet thy neighbour's neighbour's wife.* The tenth, *Thou shalt not covet the things which are another's.* I know nothing in these three commandments, that trouble my conscience: Therefore, I conclude by confessing, in general and particular, all the sins of my whole life, committed by *thought*, **word** and *deed*, and I am heartily sorry for them all, and ask God's pardon and your advice, penance and absolution. *Amen.*

Conf. Have you transgressed the fourth commandment of the church?

Mary. Yea, Father; for I did not fast as it prescribes, for though I did abstain from flesh, yet I did not keep the form of fasting these two years past; but I have done it since the gentleman's death.

Conf. Have you this year taken the bull of indulgencies?

Mary. Yea, Father.

Conf. Have you visited five altars, the days appointed for his holiness to take a soul out of purgatory?

Mary. I did not for several days.

Conf. Do you promise me, as a minister of God, and as if you were now before the tribunal of the dreadful judge, to amend your life, and to avoid all the occasions of falling into the same or other sins, and to frequent, for the future, this sacrament, and the others, and to obey the commandments of God, as things absolutely necessary to the salvation of your soul?

Mary. That is my design with the help of God, and of the blessed Virgin *Mary*, in whom I put my whole trust and confidence.

Conf. Your contrition must be the foundation of your new life, for if you fall into other sins after this signal benefit you have received from God, and his blessed mother, of calling you to repentance, it will be a hard thing for you to obtain pardon and forgiveness. You see God has taken away all the obstacles of your true repentance; pray ask continually his grace, that you may make good use of these heavenly favours. But you

you ought to consider, that though you shall be freed by my absolution, from the eternal pains your manifold sins deserve, you shall not be free from the sufferings of purgatory, where your soul must be purified by fire, if you in this present life do not take care to redeem your soul from that terrible flame, by ordering some Masses for the relief of the souls in purgatory.

Mary. I design to do it, as far as it lies in my power.

Conf. Now to shew your obedience to God, and our mother, the church, you must perform the following penance. You must fast every second day, to mortify your lusts and passions, and this for the space of two months. You must visit five altars every second day, and one privileged altar, and say in each of 'em five times *pater-noster, &c.* and five times *Ave Mary, &c.* You must say too, every day for two months time, three and thirty times the *creed,* in honor and memory of the three and thirty years that our Saviour did live upon earth; and you must confess once a week; that by the continuance of these spiritual exercises, your soul may be preserved from several temptations, and may be happy for ever.

Mary. I will do all that with the help of God.

Conf. Say the act of contrition, while I absolve you.

Mary. O God, my God, I have sinned against thee, I am heartily sorry, &c.

Conf. Our Lord Jesus Christ absolve thee; and by the authority given me I absolve thee, &c. *Amen.*

The second. A private confession of a woman to a Fryar of the dominican order, laid down in writing before the moral academy, 1710, *and the opinions of the members about it, the person was not known, therefore I shall call her* Leonore.

Leonore did confess to F. *Joseph Riva* the following misdoings.

Leonore

Leonore. MY reverend Father, I come to this place to make a general confeſſion of all the ſins I have committed in the whole courſe of my life, or of all thoſe I can remember.

Conf. How long have you been in preparing yourſelf for this general confeſſion?

Leon. Eight days.

Conf. Eight days are not enough to recollect yourſelf, and bring into your memory all the ſins of your life.

Leon. Father, have patience till you hear me, and then you may judge whether my confeſſion be perfect, or imperfect.

Conf. And how long is it ſince you confeſſed the laſt time?

Leon. The laſt time I confeſſed was the *Sunday* before *Eaſter*, which is eleven months and twenty days.

Conf. Did you accompliſh the penance then impoſed upon you?

Leon. Yea, Father.

Conf. Begin then your confeſſion.

Leon. I have neglected my duty towards God, by whoſe holy name I have many times ſworn. I have not ſanctified his holy days as I was obliged by law, nor honored my parents and ſuperiors. I have many and many times deſired the death of my neighbours, when I was in a paſſion. I have been deeply engaged in amorous intrigues with many people of all ranks, but theſe two years paſt moſt conſtantly with Don *Pedro Haſta*, who is the only ſupport of my life.

Conf. Now I find out the reaſon why you have ſo long neglected to come to confeſs, and I do expect, that you will tell me all the circumſtances of your life, that I may judge the preſent ſtate of your conſcience.

Leon. Father: As for the ſins of my youth, till I was 16 years of age, they are of no great conſequence, and

and I hope God Almighty will pardon me. Now my general confession begins from that time, when I fell into the first sin, which was in the following manner.

The Confessor of our family was a Francifcan Fryar, who was absolute master in our house; for my father and mother were entirely governed by him. It was about that time of my life I lost my mother; and a month after her my father died, leaving all his substance to the Father Confessor, to dispose of at his own fancy, reserving only a certain part which I was to have to settle me in the world, conditionally that if I was obedient to him. A month after my father's death, on pretence of taking care of every thing that was in the house, he ordered a bed for himself in the chamber next to mine, where my maid also used to lie. After supper, the first night he came home, he addrest himself thus to me. My daughter, you may with reason call me your father, for you are the only child your father left under my care. Your patrimony is in my hands, and you ought to obey me blindly in every thing: So in the first place order your maid's bed to be removed out of your own chamber into another. Which being done accordingly, we parted and went each one to our own room; but an hour was scarcely past away, when the Father came into my chamber, and what by flattery and promises, and what by threatnings, he deprived me of the best patrimony, my innocence. We continued this course of life till, as I believe, he was tired of me; for two months after, he took every thing out of the house, and went to his convent, where he died in ten days time; and by his death I lost the patrimony left me by my father, and with it all my support, and as my parents had spared nothing in my education, and I had always been kept in the greatest affluence of every thing, you may judge how I was affected by the miserable circumstances I was then left in, with servants to maintain, and nothing in the world to supply even the necessary expences of my house. This made me the

more

more ready to accept the first offer should be made me, and my condition being known to an officer of the army, he came to offer me his humble services. I complied with his desire, and so for two years we lived together, till at last he was obliged to repair to his regiment at *Catalonia*; and though he left me appointments more than sufficient for my subsistance during his absence, yet all our correspondence was soon broken off by his death, which happened soon after. Then, resolving to alter my life and conversation, I went to confess, and after having given an account to my Confessor of my life, he, asking my name, did promise to come next day to see me, and to put me into a comfortable and credible way of living. I was very glad to get such a patron, and so the next day I did wait at home for him.

The Father came, and after various discourses, he took me by the hand into my chamber, and told me that if I was willing to put in his hands my jewels, and what other things of value I had got from the Officer, he would engage to get a gentleman suitable to my condition to marry me. I did every thing as he desired me, and so taking along with him all I had in the world, he carried them to his cell.

The next day he came to see me, and made me another proposal very different from what I expected; for he told me that I must comply with his desire, or else he would expose me, and inform against me before the holy tribunal of the inquisition: So, rather than incur that danger, I did for the space of six months, in which, having nothing to live upon (for he kept my jewels) I was obliged to abandon myself to many other gentlemen, by whom I was maintained.

At last he left me, and I still continued my wicked life, unlawfully conversing with married and unmarried gentlemen a whole year, and not daring to confess, for fear to go to find the same success in another Confessor.

Conf.

Conf. But how could you fulfil the precept of the church, and not be expofed in the church after *Eafter*, all that while.

Leon. I went to an old eafy Father, and promifed him a piftole for a certificate of confeffion, which he gave me without further inquiring into the matter; and fo I did fatisfy the curate of the parifh with it. But laft year I went to confefs, and the Confeffor was very ftrict, and would not give me abfolution becaufe I was an habitual finner, but I gave him five piftoles for ten Maffes, and then he told me that a Confeffor's duty was to take care of the fouls in purgatory, and that upon their account he could not refufe me abfolution; fo by that way I efcaped the cenfure of the church.

Conf. How long is it fince you broke off your finful life?

Leon. But fix weeks.

Conf. I cannot abfolve you now, but come again next *Thurfday*, and I will confult upon all the circumftances of your life, and then I will abfolve you.

Leon. Father, I have more to fay: For I ftole from the church a chalice, by the advice of the faid Confeffor, and he made ufe himfelf of the money I got for the filver, which I cut in pieces; and I did converfe unlawfully feveral times in the church with him. To this I muft add an infinite number of fins by *thought*, *word*, and *deed*, I have committed in this time, efpecially with the laft perfon of my acquaintance, though at prefent I am free from him.

Conf. Pray give me leave to confult upon all thefe things, and I will refolve them to you the next confeffion; now go in peace.

THE firft point to be refolved was, whether *Leonore* could fue the Francifcan covent for the patrimony left by her father in the Confeffor's hands?

The prefident went through all the reafons *pro* and *con*, and after refolved, that though the faid *Leonore*
was

was never disobedient to her Confessor, she could not sue the community without the lessening of her own reputation, and laying upon the order so black a crime, as that of her confessor; and that it was the common maxim of all Casuists that, *In rebus dubiis, minimum est sequendum,* In things doubtful, that of the least evil consequence is to be pursued; and seeing the losing of her patrimony would be less damage than the exposing of the whole Franciscan order, & her own reputation: It did seem proper to leave the thing as it was.

The second point to be resolved was, Whether *Leonore* was in *proxima occasione peccati,* in the next occasion of sin, with such a confessor the two first months?

Six members of the academy did think that she was; for immediate occasion of sin signifies, that the person may satisfy his passions *toties quoties,* without any impediment, which *Leonore* could do all that while. But the other members of the academy did object against it: That the nature of *occasio proxima,* besides the said reason, implies freedom and liberty, which *Leonore* did want at that time, being as she was young, unexperienced, timorous, and under the Confessor's care and power; so it was resolved, that she was not the first two months in *proxima occasione peccati.*

The third point: Whether she committed greater sin with the second Confessor, who threatened her with the inquisition? And whether she was obliged to undergo all the hardships, nay death itself, rather than comply with the Confessor's desire?

It was resolved *nemine contradicente,* that she was obliged for self-preservation's sake to comply with the Fryar's desire, and therefore her sin was less than other sins.

The fourth: Whether she was obliged to make restitution of the chalice she stole out of the church by the advice of the confessor?

The members could not agree in the decision of this point, for some were of opinion, that both she and the

Fryar were obliged to make restitution, grounded in the moral maxim: *Facientes, et consentientes eadem pæna puniuntur,* those that act & those who consent are to be punished alike. Others said that *Leonore* was only an instrument of theft, and that the Fryar did put her in the way of doing what she never had done, but for fear of him, and that she was forced to do it; therefore that she had not committed sacrilege, nay, nor venial sin by it; and that the Fryar only was guilty of sacrilege and robbery, and obliged to make restitution. Upon this division, the reverend Mr. *Ant. Palomo,* then professor of philosophy, was appointed to lay the case before the members of the great academy, with this limitation, that he should not mention any thing of the Fryar in it; except the members of the academy should ask him the aggravating circumstances in the case.

He did it accordingly, and being asked by the president about the circumstances, it was resolved that *Leonore* was free from restitution, taking a bull of pardons. And as for the Fryar, by his belonging to the community, and having nothing of his own, and obliged to leave, at his death, every thing to the convent, he must be excused from making such restitution, *&c.*

The fifth point: Whether the church was desecrated by their unlawful commerce? And whether the Confessor was obliged to reveal the nature of the thing to the bishop, or not?

As to the first part, all did agree, that the church was polluted. As to the second, four were of opinion, that the thing was to be revealed to the bishop in general terms: But sixteen did object against it, and said, that the dominical, *asperges me Hysopo, & mundabor,* thou shall sprinkle me with Hysop, and I shall be clean, &c. When the priest with holy water and Hysop, sprinkles the church, it was enough to restore & purify the church.

After which, the president moved another question, *viz.* Whether this private confession was to be entered in the academy's book; *ad perpetuam rei memoriam,* in perpetual memory of the thing. And it was agreed to enter the cases and resolutions, mentioning nothing concerning the Confessors, nor their orders. Item, it was resolved that the proponent could safely in conscience absolve *Leonore* the next confession, if she had the bull of indulgences; and promised to be zealous in the correction and penance, which he was to give her, &c. And accordingly he did, and *Leonore* was absolved.

The third private confession proposed in the academy, by father Gasca, *a Jesuit, and member of the academy: Of a woman of thirty-three years of age.*

MOST reverend and learned fathers, I have thought fit not to trouble you with the methodical way of a private confession I heard last Sunday, but to give you only an account of the difficult case in it. The case is this: A woman of thirty-three years of age came to confess, and told me, that from sixteen years of age, till twenty-four, she had committed all sorts of lewdness, only with ecclesiastical persons, having in every convent a Fryar, who, under the name of a cousin, did use to visit her: And notwithstanding the multiplicity of cousins, she did live so poorly, that she was forced to turn procuress at the same time for new cousins; and that she had followed that wicked life till thirty-two years of age: That last year she dreamed that the devil was very free with her, and these dreams or visions continuing for a long while, she found herself with child; and she protests that she knew no man for fourteen months before: She is delivered of a boy, and she says that he is the devil's son, and that her conscience is so troubled about it, that if I do not find some way to quiet her mind, she will lay violent hands upon herself. I asked her leave to consult the case, with a promise to resolve it next *Sunday*. Now I ask your wise advice upon this case.

The president said that the case was impossible, and that

that the woman was mad, and that he was of opinion to send the woman to the physicians to be cured of some bodily distemper she was troubled with. The *Jesuit* proponent replied, that the woman was in her perfect senses, and that the case well required further consideration: Upon which F. *Antonio Palomo*, who was reputed the most learned of the academy, said, that saint *Augustin* treats *de Incubo & Sucubo*, and he would examine the case and see whether he might not give some light for the resolution of the case?

And another member said, that there was in the case something more than apparition and devilish liberty, and that he thought fit that the father *Jesuit* should inquire more carefully into the matter, and go himself to examine the house, and question the people of it:—— Which being approved of by the whole assembly, he did it the next morning, and in the afternoon, being an extraordinary meeting, he came and said,

Most reverend and learned fathers, the woman was so strongly possessed with such a vision, that she has made public the case among the neighbours, and it is spread abroad; upon which the inquisitors did send for the woman and the maid, and this has discovered the whole story, *viz.* That father *Conchillos*, victorian Fryar, was in love with the woman, but she could not endure the sight of him: That he gained the maid, and by that means he got into her house every night, and the maid putting some *Opium* into her mistress's supper, she fell fast asleep, and the said father did lie with her six nights together: So the child is not the son of the devil, but of father *Conchillos*. Afterwards it was resolved to enter the case for a *memorandum*, in the academy's book.

The Fryar was put into the inquisition, for having persuaded the maid to tell her mistress that it was the devil; for she had been under the same fear, and really she was in the same condition. What became of the Fryar I do not know, this I do aver for a truth, that

I spoke with the woman myself, and with the maid; and that the children used to go to her door, and call for the son of the devil: And, being so mocked, she left the city in a few days after, and we were told that she lived after it a retired christian life in the country.

The fourth private confession of a priest, being at the point of death, in 1710. I shall call him Don Paulo.

Don *Paulo.* SINCE God Almighty is pleased to visit me with this sickness, I ought to make good use of the time I have to live, and I desire of you to help me with your prayers, and to take the trouble to write some substantial points of my confession, that you may perform, after my death, whatever I think may enable me in some measure to discharge my duty towards God and men. When I was ordained priest, I made a general confession of all my sins from my youth to that time, and I wish I could now be as true a penitent, as I was at that time; but I hope, tho' it is too late, that God will hear the prayer of my heart.

I have served my parish sixteen years, and all my care has been to discover the tempers and inclinations of my parishioners, and I have been as happy in this world as unhappy before my Saviour. I have in ready money fifteen thousand pistoles, and I have given away more than six thousand. I had no patrimony, and my living is worth but four hundred pistoles a year. By this you may easily know, that my money is unlawfully gotten, as I shall tell you, if God spares my life till I make an end of my confession. There is in my parish sixteen hundred families, and more or less I have defrauded them all some way or other.

My thoughts have been impure ever since I began to hear confessions; my words grave and severe with them all, and all my parishioners have respected and feared me. I have had so great an empire over them, that some of them, knowing of my misdoings, have taken

ken my defence in public. They have had in me a solicitor in all emergencies, and I have omitted nothing to please them in outward appearance; but my actions have been the most criminal of mankind: For as to my ecclesiastical duty, what I have done has been for custom's sake. The necessary intention of a priest, in the administration of baptism and consecration, without which the sacraments are of none effect, I confess I had it not several times, as you shall see in the parish books; and observe there, that all those names marked with a star, the baptism was not valid, for I had no intention: And for this I can give no other reason than my malice and wickedness. Many of them are dead, for which I am heartily sorry. As for the times I have consecrated without intention, we must leave it to God Almighty's mercy, for the wrong done by it to the souls of my parishioners, and those in purgatory cannot be helped.

As to the confessions and wills I have received from my parishoners at the point of their death, I do confess, I have made myself master of as much as I could, & by that means I have gathered together all my riches. I have sent this morning for fifty bulls, and I have given one hundred pistoles for the benefit of the holy *cruzade*, by which his holiness secures my soul from eternal death.

As to my duty towards God, I am guilty to the highest degree: For I have not loved him; I have neglected to say the private divine service at home every day; I have polluted his *holy days* by my grievous sins: I have not minded my superiors in the respect due to them: And I have been the cause of many innocents death. I have procured, by remedies, sixty abortions, making the fathers of the children their murtherers; besides many other intended, though not executed, by some unexpected accident.

As to the sixth commandment, I cannot confess by particulars, but by general heads, my sins. I confess, in the first place, that I have frequented the parish club

twelve

twelve years. We were only six parish priests in it; and there we did consult and contrive all the ways to satisfy our passions. Every body had a list of the handsomest women in his parish; and when one had a fancy to see any woman, remarkable for her beauty, in another's parish, the priest of her parish sent for her to his own house; and having prepared the way for wickedness, the other had nothing to do but to meet her there, and fulfil his desires; and so we have served one another these twelve years past. Our method has been, to persuade the husbands and fathers not to hinder them any spiritual comfort; and to the ladies to persuade them to be subject to our advice and will; and that in so doing, they should have liberty at any time to go out on pretence of communicating some spiritual business to the priest: And if they refuse to do it, then we should speak to their husbands and fathers not to let them go out at all, or, which would be worse for them, we should inform against them to the holy tribunal of the inquisition: And by these diabolical persuasions, they were always at our command, without fear of revealing the secret.

I have spared no woman of my parish, whom I had a fancy for, and many other of my brethren's parishes; but I cannot tell the number. I have sixty *Nepotes* alive, of several women: But my principal care ought to be of those that I have by the two young women I keep at home since their parents died. Both are sisters, and I have by the eldest two boys, and by the youngest one; and one which I had by my own sister is dead. Therefore I leave to my sister five thousand pistoles, upon condition that she would enter Nun in St. *Bernard's* monastery; and upon the same condition I leave two thousand pistoles a piece to the two young women; and the remainder I leave to my three *Nepotes* under the care of *Mossen John Peralta*, and ordering that they should be heirs to one another, if any of them should die before they are settled in the world, and if all should

die

die, I leave the money to the treasury of the church, for the benefit of the souls in purgatory: *Item*, I order that all the papers of such a little trunk be burnt after my confession is over, (which was done accordingly) and that the holy bull of the dead be bought before I die, that I may have the comfort of having at home the Pope's pass for the next world. Now I ask your penance and absolution for all the sins reserved in all the bulls, from the first Pope; for which purpose I have taken the bull of privileges in such cases as mine. So I did absolve him, and assisted him afterwards, and he died the next day. What to do in such a case, was all my uneasiness after his death; for if I did propose the case before the members of the academy, every body could easily know the person, which was against one of the articles we did swear at our admittance into it: And if I did not propose it, I should act against another article. All my difficulty was about the baptisms which he had administered without intention: For it is the known opinion of their church that the intention of a priest is absolutely necessary to the validity of the sacrament, and that without it there is no sacrament at all. I had examined the books of the parish, and I found a hundred and fifty-two names marked with a star; and examining the register of the dead, I found eighty six of them dead: According to the principles of the church, all those that were alive were to be baptized; which could not be done without great scandal, and prejudice to the clergy. In this uneasiness of mind, I continued till I went to visit the reverend Father *John Gareia*, who had been my master in divinity, and I did consult him on the case, *sub secreto naturali*. He did advise me to propose the case to the assembly, upon supposition, that if such a case should happen, what should be done in it; and he did recommend to me to talk with a great deal of caution, and to insist that it ought to be communicated to the bishop; and if the members did agree with me,

then

then without further confession, I was to go to the bishop, and tell his lordship the case, under secrecy of confession: I did so, and the bishop said he would send for the books, and take a list of all those names; and as many of them as could be found he would send for, one by one, into his own chamber, and baptize them; commanding them under pain of ecclesiastical censure, not to talk of it neither in public or private. But as for the other sins, there was no necessity of revealing them, for by virtue of the bull of *Cruzade* (of which I shall speak in the second chapter) we could absolve them all.

Hear, O heaven! Give ear, O earth! And be horribly astonished! To see the best religion in the world turned into superstition and folly; to see too that those who are to guide the people, and put their flock in the way of salvation, are wolves in sheep's clothing, that devour them, and put them into the way of damnation. O God, open the eyes of the ignorant people, that they may see the injuries done to their souls by their own guides.

I do not write this out of any private end, to blame all sorts of confessors; for there are some who, according to the principles of their religion, do discharge their duty with exactness and purity, and whose lives, in their own way, are unblamable, and without reproach among men. Such confessors as these I am speaking of are sober in their actions: They mortify their bodies with fasting over and above the rules prescribed by the church, by discipline, by kneeling down in their closets six or eight hours every day, to meditate on the holy mysteries, the goodness of God, and to pray to him for all sorts of sinners, that they may be brought to repentance and salvation, &c. They sleep but few hours: They spend most of their spare time in reading the ancient fathers of the church, and other books of devotion.

They live poorly, because whatever they have, the
poor

poor are the enjoyers of it. The time they give to the public is but very little, and not every day; and then whatever counsels they give are right, sincere, without flattery or interest. All pious, religious persons do solicit their acquaintance and conversation, but they avoid all pomp and vanity, and keep themselves, as much as they can, within the limits of solitude; and if they make some visits, it must be upon urgent necessity. Sometimes you may find them in the hospitals among the poor sick, helping and exhorting them: But they go there most commonly in the night, for what they do, they do it not out of pride, but humility.

I knew some of these exemplary men, but a very few; and I heard some of them preach with a fervent zeal about the promoting of Christ's religion, and exhorting the people to put their lives voluntarily in the defence of the Roman-catholic faith, and extirpate and destroy all the enemies of their communion. I do not pretend to judge them, for judgment belongeth to God: This I say, with St. *Paul*, that if those religious men *have a zeal of God, their zeal is not according to knowledge*.

The fifth private confession of a Nun, in the convent of S. O.

Before I begin the confession, it will not be improper to give an account of the customs of the Nuns, and places of their confessions.

BY the constitutions of their order, so many days are appointed, in which all the Nuns are obliged to confess, from the Mother Abbess to the very wheeler, i. e. the Nun that turns the wheel near the door, through which they give, and receive, every thing they want. They have a Father Confessor, and a Father Companion, who live next to the convent, and have a

small

small grate in the wall of their chamber, which answers to the upper cloister or gallery of the convent. The Confessor hath care of the souls of the convent, and he is obliged to say Mass every day, hear confessions, administer the sacraments, and visit the sick Nuns. There are several narrow closets in the church, with a small iron grate: One side answers to the cloister, and the other to the church. So the Nun being on the inside, and the Confessor on the outside, they hear one another. There is a large grate facing the great altar, and the holes of it are a quarter of a yard in square, but that grate is double, that is, one within, and another without, and the distance between both is more than half a yard. And besides these, there is another grate for relations, and benefactors of the community, which grate is single, and consists of very thin iron bars: The holes of such a grate are near a quarter and a half square. In all those grates the Nuns confess their sins; for, on a solemn day, they send for ten or twelve Confessors, otherwise they could not confess the fourth part of them, for there are in some monasteries 110 Nuns, in others 80, in others 40, but this last is a small number.

The Nuns Father Confessor hath but little trouble with the young Nuns, for they generally send for a Confessor who is a stranger to them, so that all his trouble is with the old ones, who have no business at the grate. These trouble their Confessor almost every day with many ridiculous trifles, and will keep the poor man two hours at the grate, telling him how many times they have spit in the church, how many flies they have killed, how many times they have flown into a passion with their lap-dogs, and other nonsensical, ridiculous things like these; and the reason is, because they have nothing to do, nobody goes to visit them, nor careth for them, so sometimes they chuse to be spies for the young Nuns, when they are at the grate with their gallants, and for fear of their Mother Abbess,

they

they place some of the old Nuns before the door of the parlour, to watch the Mother Abbess, and to give them timely notice of her coming; and the poor old Nuns do perform this office with a great deal of pleasure, faithfulness, and some profit too. But I shall not say any more of them, confining myself wholly to the way of living among the young Nuns.

Many gentlemen send their daughters to the nunnery when they are some five, some six, some eight years old, under the care of some Nun of their relations, or else some old Nun of their acquaintance; and there they get education till they are 15 years old. The tutress takes a great deal of care not to let them go to the grate, nor converse with men all the while, to prevent in them the knowledge and love of the world. They are caressed by all the Nuns, and thinking it will be always so, they are very well pleased with their confinement. They have only liberty to go to the grate to their parents or relations, and always accompanied with the old Mother Tutress. And when they are 15 years old, which is the age fixed by the constitutions of all the orders, they receive the habit of a Nun, and begin the year of noviciate, which is the year of trial, to see whether they can go through all the hardships, fastings, disciplines, prayers, hours of divine service, obedience, poverty, chastity, and penances practised in the monastery: But the Prioress or Abbess, and the rest of the professed Nuns, do dispense with, and excuse the Novices from all the severities, for fear that the Novices should be dissatisfied with, and leave the convent: And in this they are very much in the wrong; for, besides that they do not observe the precepts of their monastical rule, they deceive the poor, ignorant, unexperinced young Novices, who, after their profession and vows of perpetuity, do heartily repent they had been so much indulged. Thus the Novices, flattered in the year of noviciate, and thinking they will be so all their life time, when the year is expired, make profession and swear

swear to observe *chastity*, *obedience*, and *poverty*, during their lives, and *clausura*, i. e. *confinement*; obliging themselves, by it, never to go out of the monastery.

After the profession is made, they begin to feel the severity and hardships of the monastical life; for one is made a door keeper, another turner of the wheel, to receive and deliver by it all the Nun's messages, another bell Nun, that is to call the Nuns, when any one comes to visit them; another baker, another bookkeeper of all the rents and expences, and the like; and in the performance of all these employments they must expend a great deal of their own money. After this they have liberty to go to the grate, and talk with gentlemen, Priests and Fryars, who only go there as a gallant goes to see his mistress. So when the young Nuns begin to have a notion of the pleasures of the world, and how they have been deceived, they are heartily sorry, but too late, for there is no remedy. And minding nothing but to satisfy their passions as well as they can, they abandon themselves to all sorts of wickedness, and amorous intrigues.

There is another sort of Nuns, whom the people call *las forcadas*, the forced Nuns, i. e. those who have made a false step in the world, and cannot find husbands, on account of their crimes being public. Those are despised and ill used by their parents and relations, till they choose to go to the nunnery: So by this it is easily known what sort of Nuns they will make.

Now, as to the spending of their time. They get up at six in the morning and go to prayers, and to hear Mass till seven, from seven till ten, they work, or go to breakfast, either in their chambers, or in the common-hall. At ten they go to the great Mass till eleven: After it, they go to dinner, after dinner they may divert themselves till two; at two they go to prayers, for a quarter of an hour, or (if they sing vespers) for half an hour; and afterwards they are free till the next morning: So every one is waiting for her *Devoto*, that is, a

gallant,

gallant, or spiritual husband, as they call him. When it is dark evening, they send away the *Devotos*, and the doors are locked up; so they go to their own chamber to write a billet, or letter to the spiritual husband, which they send in the morning to them, and get an answer; and though they see one another almost every day, for all that, they must write to one another every morning: And these letters of love, they call the *recreation of the spirit* for the time the *Devotos* are absent from them. Every day they must give one another an account of whatever thing they have done since the last visit; and indeed there are warmer expressions of love, and jealousy between the Nun, and the *Devoto*, than between real wife and husband.

Now I come to the private Confession; and I wish I could have the style of an angel, to express myself with purity, and modesty, in this confession.

Nun. REVEREND Father, as the number of my sins are so great, and so great the variety of circumstances attending them; mistrusting my memory, I have set down in writing this confession, that you may entirely be acquainted with every thing that troubles my conscience, and so I humbly beg of you to read it.

Conf. I did approve the method of writing, but you ought to read it yourself, or else it cannot be *oris confessio*, or confession by mouth.

Nun. If it is so, I begin. I thought fit, to acquaint you with the circumstances of my life past, that you may form a right judgment of my monastical life and conversation, which, in some measure, will excuse me before the world, though not before God our righteous judge.

I am the only daughter of Counsellor *N. E.* who brought me up in the fear of God, and gave me a writing-master, which is a rare thing. I was not quite thirteen

teen years of age, when a gentleman of quality, though not very rich, began his love to me, by letters which he (gaining my writing-master) sent to me by him. There was nothing in the world so obliging, civil, modest and endearing, as his expressions seemed to me, and at last having the opportunity of meeting him at the house of one of my aunts, his person and conversation did so charm my heart, that a few days after we gave one another reciprocal promises of an eternal union: But by a letter, which unfortunately was miscarried, and fell into my father's hands, our honest designs were discovered; and without telling me any thing, he went to see the gentleman, and spoke to him in this manner: Sir, my daughter, in discharging of her duty to so good a father, has communicated to me your honorable designs, and I come to thank you for the honor you are pleased to do my family: But, being so young, we think proper to put off the performance of it, till she comes to be 15 years of age: Now she, and I also, as a father to you both (for I look upon you as upon my own son) do desire of you the favour not to give any public occasion of censure to the watchful neighbours, and if you have any regard for her, I hope you will do this and more for her, and for me: And to shew you my great affection, I offer you a Captain's commission in the regiment that the city raiseth for the King, and advise you to serve two years, and afterwards, you may accomplish your desire. The gentleman accepted it, and the next day the commission was signed and delivered to him, with an order to go to *Catalonia*. At the same time the writing-master was sent out of the town under pretence of receiving some money for my father; and I was kept close at home, so he could not get an opportunity of seeing or writing to me; for my father told him I was sick in bed. As soon as he left the town, my father told me that he was dead, and that

I must retire myself into the nunnery, for that was his will. So immediately he brought me here, and gave
severe

severe directions to the Mother-Abbess, not to let me see any body but himself. Indeed he did spare nothing to please me, till I received the habit, and made the profession and vows of a monastical life: After which he told me the whole story himself; and the gentleman was killed in *Catalonia* the first compaign.

I do confess, that ever since, I did not care what should become of me, and I have abandoned myself to all the sins I have been capable to commit. It is but ten months since I made my profession, and bound myself to perpetuity; though as I did it without intention, I am not a Nun before God, nor obliged to keep the vow of religion; and of this opinion are many other Nuns, especially ten young Nuns, my intimate friends; who, as well as I, do communicate to one another the most secret things of our hearts.

Each of this assembly has her *Devoto*, and we are every day in the afternoon at the grate: We shew one another the letters, we receive from them, and there is nothing that we do not invent for the accomplishment of our pleasures.

Conf. Pray, confess your own sins, and omit the sins of your friends.

Nun. I cannot, for my sins are so confounded with the sins of my friends, that I cannot mention the one without the other.

But coming now to my greatest sin; I must tell you that a Nun of our assembly has a Fryar her *Devoto*, the most beautiful among men, and we contrived and agreed together to bring him into the convent, as we did, and have kept him two and twenty days in our chamber: During which time we went to the grate very seldom, on pretence of being not well. We have given no scandal, for no body has suspected the least thing in the case. And this is the greatest sin I have committed with man.

Conf. Pray, tell me, how could you let him in without scandal?

Nun.

Nun. One of the assembly contrived to mat all the floor of her chamber, and sent for the mat-maker to take the measure of the length and breadth of the room, and to make it in one piece, and send it to the Sexton's chamber who is a poor ignorant fellow. When the mat was there, and the man paid for it, one day in the evening we sent the Sexton on several messages, and kept the key of his room. The Fryar had asked leave of his Prior to go into the country for a month's time, and disguising himself in a layman's habit, feeing well two porters, came, in the dusk of the evening, into the Sexton's room, and rolling up himself in the mat, the porters brought the mat to the door, where we were waiting for it; and taking it, we carried it up to one of our chambers. We were afraid that the porters would discover the thing, but by money we have secured ourselves from them; for we hired ruffians to make away with them. We put him out of the convent in a great chest which could be opened on the inside, and of which he had the key, and giving the chest to the Sexton, he, and the servant of the convent, carried it into the Sexton's room. We ordered him to leave the key at the door, for we expected some relations, which were to take a colation there; and we sent him on some errand till the Fryar had got out of the chest & of danger.

A month after, three of our friends began to perceive the condition they were in, and left the convent in one night, by which they have given great scandal to the city, and we do not know what is become of them; as for me, I design to do the same, for I am under the same apprehensions and fear; for I consider, that if I do continue in the convent, my big belly will discover me, and though one life shall be saved, I shall lose mine by the rules of our order in a miserable manner, and not only so, but a heavy reflection will fall upon the whole order, and the dishonor of my family shall be the more public: Whereas, if I quit the convent by night, I save two lives, and the world will reflect only upon me, and then I shall take care to go so far off that nobody shall hear of me; and as I am sure, in my conscience, that I am not a Nun for want of intention, when I did promise to keep *obedience, chastity, poverty,* and *perpetuity,* I shall not incur the crime of apostacy, in leaving the convent; and if I do continue in it, I am fully resolved to prevent my ruin and death by a strong operating remedy. This is all I have to say, and I do expect from you not only your advice, but your assistance too.

Conf. I do find the case so intricate, that I want experience and learning to resolve what to do in it; and I do think it proper for you to send for another Confessor of years and learning, and then you shall have the satisfaction of being well directed and advised.

Nun. Now, reverend Father, I do tell you positively, that I shall never open my heart to another Confessor, while I live; and if you do not advise me what to do, I shall call you before God for it; and now I lay upon you whatever thing may happen in my case.

Conf. Ignorance will excuse me from sin, and I tell you I am ignorant how to resolve the case.

Nun. I am resolved for all events, and if you refuse me this small comfort, I shall cry out, and say, that you have been soliciting and corrupting me in the very act of confession, and you shall suffer for it in the inquisition.

Conf. Well, have patience, means may be found out: And if you give me leave to consult the case, I shall resolve you about it in three days time.

Nun. How can you consult my case, without exposing the order, and my reputation too, perhaps, by some circumstance?

Conf. Leave it to me, and be not uneasy about it, and I do promise to come with the resolution on *Sunday* next.

Nun. Pray, Father, if it be possible, come next *Monday* morning, and I shall be free from company.

Conf.

Conf. It is very well : But, in the mean time, have before your eyes the wrath of God against those that abandon themselves, and forget that he is a living God, to punish suddenly great sinners ; and with this, farewell.

My mind never before was so much troubled as it was after this case. I was, more by the interest of others, than by my learning, appointed penitentiary Confessor in the cathedral church of St. *Salvator* ; and as the duty of such a Confessor is to be every day, in the morning, four hours in the confessionary, from eight till twelve, except he be called abroad ; every body thinks that such a Confessor must be able to resolve all cases and difficulties : But it was not so with me ; for I was young, and without experience. And as to this case, the next academical day I proposed it in the following manner :

There is a person bound by word of mouth, but at the same time without intention, nay, with a mind and heart averse to it ; bound, I say, to *obedience, chastity,* and *poverty.* If the person leaves the convent, the crime of apostacy is not committed in *foro interno* ; and if the person continues in the convent, the consequence is to be a great sin in *foro externo & interno.* The person expects the resolution, or else is fully resolved to expose the Confessor to scandal, and personal sufferings : This is the case which I humbly lay down before your learned reverences.

The President's opinion was, that in such a case, the Confessor was obliged, in the first place, to reveal it in general terms, to the holy inquisitors ; for (said he) though this case is not mentioned in our authors, there are others very like this, which ought to be revealed, viz. all those that are against either the temporal or spiritual good of our neighbour, which cases are reserved to the Bishop or to his deputy ; and this case, by the last circumstance, being injurious to the holy tribunal, the Confessor ought to prevent the scandal which might

otherwise

otherwife fall upon him, to reveal the laft circumftance. As for the firft circumftance of the cafe, in this and others, we muft judge *fecundum allegata & probata* ; and we muft fuppofe, that no penitent comes to confefs with a lie in his mouth ; therfore, if the perfon affirms that he was bound without intention, he is free before God: Befides, *in rebus dubiis minimum eft fequendum* ; fo, to prevent greater evil, I think the perfon may be advifed to quit the convent ; and this is agreeable to the Pope's difpenfations to fuch perfons ; when they fwear and produce witnefs, that (before they were bound to the vow) heard the perfons fay, they had not intention to it.

The reverend Mr. *Palomo*'s opinion was, that the Confeffor was to take the fafeft part, which was to advife the penitent to fend to *Rome* for a difpenfation, which could be obtained by money, or to the Pope's *Nuncio*, who would give leave to quit the convent for fix months, upon neceffity of preferving or recovering the bodily health ; and in that time may be the perfon would diffipate fome fumes of grief or melancholic fancies, &c.

But I did reply to this, that the perfon could not do the firft, for want of witnefs, nor the fecond, for being in perfect health, the phyfician never would grant his certificate to be produced before the Pope's *Nuncio*, which is abfolutely neceffary in fuch cafes ; and as to revealing the cafe to the holy inquifitors, it is very dangerous, both to the perfon and the Confeffor, as we could prove by feveral inftances.

To this, feveral members being of my opinion, it was refolved, that the Confeffor, firft of all, was to abfolve the penitent, having a bull of *cruzade*, and *extra confeffionem*, or out of confeffion give, as a private perfon, advice to the penitent to quit the convent, and to take a certificate. Wherein the penitent was to fpecify, that the Confeffor had given fuch advice *extra actum confeffionis*. The cafe and refolution was entered

tered in the academy's book. And accordingly, *Monday* following, I went to the Nun and performed what was resolved; and the very same week, we heard in the city, that such a Nun had made her escape out of the convent.

Two years and a half after this, I saw this very Nun one day at the court of *Lisbon*, but I did not speak with her, for as I was then dressed like an officer of the army, I thought she could not know me; but I was mistaken, for she knew me in my disguise, as well as I did her. The next day she came to my lodgings followed by a Lacquey, who, by her orders, had dogged me the night before. I was so troubled for fear to be discovered, that I thought the best way I could take was to run away and secure myself in an *English* ship: But by her first words I discovered, that her fear was greater than mine; for after giving me an account of her escape out of the convent, and safe delivery, she told me that a *Portuguese* Capt. happening to quarter in the same town where she was, took her away one night, and carried her to *Barcelona*, but that she refusing to comply with his desires, on any but honorable terms, he had married her, and brought her to *Lisbon*: That her husband knew nothing of her having been a Nun; that she took another name, and that she was very happy with her husband, who was very rich, and a man of good sense. She begged me with tears in her eyes, not to ruin her by discovering any thing of her life past.— I assured her, that nothing should happen on my account, that should disoblige her; and afterwards she asked me, why I was not dressed in a clerical habit? To which I desired her to take no notice of it, for I was there upon secret business, and of great consequence, and that as there was no body there who knew me in *Zaragoza*, it was proper to be disguised. She desired my leave to introduce me to her husband, under the title of a country gentleman, who was come thither for *Charles* the 3d's sake. I thanked her, and she
went

went home overjoyed with my promife, and I was no lefs with hers. The next day her hufband came to vifit me, and ever after, we vifited almoft every day one another, till I left that city. This I fay, fhe was a better wife, than fhe had been a Nun, and lived more religioufly in the world, than fhe had done in the cloifter of the convent.

Now I muft leave off the account of private cafes and confeffions, not to be tedious to the readers by infifting too long a time upon one fubject. But, as I promifed to the public, to difcover the moft fecret practices of the *Romifh* priefts; in this point of *auricular confeffion*, I cannot difmifs nor put an end to this firft chapter, without performing my promife.

By the account I have already given of a few private confeffions, every body may eafily know the wickednefs of the *Romifh* priefts, but more particularly their covetoufnefs and thirft of money will be detected by my following obfervations.

Firft of all, if a poor countryman goes to confefs, the Father Confeffor takes little pains with him, for, as he expects little or nothing from him, he heareth him, and with bitter words corrects the poor man, and, moft commonly, without any correction, impofing upon him a hard penance, fends him away with the fame ignorance, he went with to confefs.

2. If a foldier happens to go to make his peace with God (fo they exprefs themfelves when they go to confefs) then the Confeffor fheweth the power of a fpiritual guide. He queftions him about three fins only, *viz. thefts, drunkennefs, & uncleannefs.* Perhaps the poor foldier is free from the two firft, but if he is guilty of the laft, the Confeffor draws the confequence, that he is guilty of all the three, and terrifying him with hell, and all the devils & the fire of it, he chargeth him with reftitution, and that he is obliged to give fo much money for the relief of the fouls in purgatory, or elfe he cannot get abfolution. So the poor man, out of better confcience

conscience than his Confessor, offers a month's pay, which must be given, upon the spot, (for in the shop of Confessors there is neither trust nor credit) to appease the rough, bitter Confessor, and to get absolution; and I believe this hard way of using the poor soldiers is the reason that they do not care at all for that act of devotion; and as they are so bad customers to the Confessors shop, the Confessors use their endeavours, when they go to buy absolution, to sell it as dear as they can; so they pay at one time for two, three or more years.

I heard a soldier, damning the Confessors, say, "If I continue in the King's service 20 years, I will not go to confess, for it is easier and cheaper to lift up my finger (*) and be absolved by our chaplain, than to go to a devilish Fryar, who doth nothing but rail and grumble at me, and yet I must give him money for masses, or else he will not absolve me: I will give him leave to bury me alive, if ever he gets me near him again."

If a collegian goes to confess, he finds a mild, and sweet Confessor, and without being questioned, and with a small penance, he generally gets absolution. The reason, the Confessors have to use the collegians with so great civility and mildness, is, first, because if a collegian is ill used by his Confessor, he goes to a deaf Fryar, who absolves *ad dexteram, & ad Sinistram*, all sorts of penitents for a real of plate; and after, he inquireth and examineth into all the other Confessors actions, visits and intrigues; and when he has got matter enough, he will write a lampoon on him, which has happened very often in my time. So the Confessor dares not meddle with the collegians, for fear that his tricks

---

(*) The Custom of the *Spanish* Army in the Field, and the Day before the Battle, or before the Engagement, the Chaplain goes through all the Companies, to ask the officers whether they have a mind to confess, and if one has any thing to say, he whispers in the Chaplain's Ear, and so through all the Officers. As for the private Men: Crying out, says, he that has a Sin, let him lift up one Finger, and gives a general Absolution to all at once.

tricks should be brought to light; and another reason is because the collegians, for the generality, are like the *filles de joys in Lent, i. e.* without money, and so the Confessor cannot expect any profit by them.

I say, if absolution is denied to a collegian, he goes to a *Deaf Confessor*; for some Confessors are called *deaf*, not because they are really, but because they give small penance without correction; and never deny absolution, though the sins be reserved to the Pope. I knew two *Dominican* Fryars, who were known by the name of *Deaf Confessors*, because they never used to question the penitent.

Only one of such Confessors has more business in *Lent*, than twenty of the others, for he (like our couple-beggars, who for six-pence do marry the people) for the same sum gives absolution. And for this reason all the great and habitual sinners do go to the *Deaf Confessor*, who gives, upon the bargain, a certificate in which he says that such a one has fulfilled the commandment of the church, for every body is obliged to produce a certificate of confession to the minister of the parish before *Easter*, or else he must be exposed in the church: So as it is a hard thing for any old sinner to get absolution and a certificate from other covetous Confessors, without a great deal of money, they generally go to the *Deaf Confessors*. I had a friend in the same convent, who told me, that such Confessors were obliged to give two thirds of their profit to the community, and being only two *Deaf Confessors* in that convent, he assured me, that in one *Lent*, they gave to the Father Prior 600 pistoles a piece. I found the thing incredible, thinking that only poor and debauched people did use to go to them; but he satisfied me, saying, that rich and poor, men and women, Priests and Nuns, were customers to them, and that only the poor and loose people used to go to confess in the church; but as for the rich, Priests, and Nuns, they were sent for by them in the afternoon, and at night; and that the poor *Deafs* had scarcely time

to

to get their rest; and that when they were sent for, the common price was a pistole, and sometimes ten pistoles, according to the quality and circumstances of the person. And thus much of *deaf Confessors*.

4. If a Fryar or a priest comes to confess, every body ought to suppose, that the Father Confessor has nothing to do, but to give the penance, and pronounce the words of absolution; for both penitent and Confessor being of the same trade, and of the same corporation, or brotherhood; the fashion of this cloak of absolution is not paid among them, and they work one for another, without any interest, in expectation of the same return.

This must be understood between the Fryars only, not between a Fryar and secular priest; for these do not like one another, and the reason is, because the Fryars, for the generality, are such officious and insinuating persons in families, that by their importunities and assiduity of visits, they become at last the masters of families, and goods; so the secular priest hath nothing to busy himself with; and observe, that there are twenty Fryars to one secular priest, so the small fish is eaten by the great: Therefore if it happens sometimes, upon necessity, that a priest goes to confess to a Fryar, or a Fryar to a priest, they make use of such an opportunity, to exact as much as they can from one another.

I know a good merry priest, who had been in company with a Fryar's *devota*, i. e. in proper terms, *mistress*; and did jest a little with her: Afterwards the poor priest having something to confess, and no other Confessor in his way, but the *Devoto* of that *Devota*, he was forced to open his heart to him; but the Confessor was so hard upon him, that he made him pay on the nail two pieces of eight, to get absolution. So he did pay dear for jesting with the mistress of a Fryar; and he did protest to me, that if ever it happened, that

F that

that Fryar should come to confess to him, he should not go away at so cheap a rate.

This I can aver, that I went to a *Francifcan* convent the second day of *August*, to get the indulgences of the Jubilee of *Porciunculæ*, and my Confessor was so hard, that he begun to persuade me, he could not absolve me without a pistole in hand: I told him, that I had not confessed any reserved sin, and that he did not know I could ruin him: But the Fryar, knowing that it was a great scandal, to get up from his feet without absolution, he insisted upon it; and I was obliged, to avoid scandal, to give him his demand. After the confession was over, as I had been in a great passion at the unreasonable usage of the Fryar; I thought it was not fit for me to celebrate the Mass, without a new reconciliation, (as we call the short confession) so I went to the Father guardian or superior of the convent, and confessing that sin of passion, occasioned by the covetous usage of such a confessor, his correction to me was, to pay down another pistole for scandalizing both the Fryar and the *Francifcan* habit; I did refuse the correction, and I went home without the second absolution. I had a mind to expose both of them; but upon second thoughts, I did nothing at all, for fear that the whole order should be against me.

5. If a modest, serious, religious lady comes to confess, he useth her in another way; for he knows that such ladies never come to confess, without giving a good charity for Masses; so all the Confessor's care is, to get himself into the ladies favour, which he doth by hypocritical expressions of godliness and devotion, of humility and strictness of life. He speaks gravely and conscientiously, and if the lady has a family, he gives her excellent advices, as, to keep her children within the limits of sobriety and virtue, for the world is so deceitful, that we ought always to be upon our guard; and to watch continually over our souls, &c. And by that means and the like, (the good lady believing him

a sincere and devout man) he becomes the guide of her soul, of her house and family, and most commonly the ruin of her children, and sometimes her own ruin too. I will give the following instance to confirm this truth; and as the thing was public, I need not scruple to mention it with the real names. In the year 1706, F. *Antonio Gallardo, Augustin* Fryar, murthered *Dona Isabella Mendez*, and a child three weeks old sucking at her breast. The lady was but twenty four years of age, and had been married eight years to Don *Francisco Mendez*. The Fryar had been her spiritual guide all that while, and all the family had so great a respect and esteem for him, that he was the absolute master of the house. The lady was brought to bed, and Don *Francisco* being obliged to go into the country for four days, desired the Father to come and lie in his house, and take care of it in his absence. The father's room was always ready; so he went there the same day Don *Francisco* went into the country. At eight at night, both the Father and the lady went to supper, and after he sent all the maids and servants into the hall to sup, the lady took the child to give him suck; and the Fryar told her, in plain and short reasons, his love, and that without any reply or delay, she must comply with his request. The lady said to him, Father, if you propose such a thing to try my faithfulness and virtue, you know my conscience these eight years past; and if you have any ill design, I will call my family to prevent your further assurance. The Fryar then in a fury, taking a knife, killed the child, and wounded so deeply the mother, that she died two hours after: The Fryar made his escape; but whether he went to his convent or not, we did not hear. I myself saw the lady dead, and went to her burial in the church of the old St. *John*.

6. If a *Beata* goes to confess, which they do every day, or at least every second day, then the Confessor, with a great deal of patience, hears her, (sure of his reward.) I cannot pass by, without giving a plain description

tion of the women called *Beatas*, i. e. *blessed women*. These are most commonly tradesmen's wives (generally speaking, ugly) and of a middle age: But this rule has some exceptions, for there are some *Beatas* young and handsome. They are dress'd with modesty, and walk with a serious countenance. But since their designs, in this outward modesty, were discovered, they are less in number, and almost out of fashion, since King *Philip* came to the throne of *Spain*; for the *French* liberty and freedom being introduced amongst the ladies, they have no occasion of stratagems to go abroad when they please: So, as the design of a *Beata* was to have an excuse, on pretence of confession, to go out, *sublata causa, tollitur effectus*.

The Confessor, I said, of a *Beata*, was sure of his reward; for she, watching the living and the dead, useth to gather money for masses, from several people, to satisfy her confessor for the trouble of hearing her impertinences every day. A *Beata* sometimes makes the Confessor believe that many things were revealed to her by the Holy Spirit; sometimes she pretends to work miracles; and by such visions, fancies or dreams, the Confessors fall into horrible crimes before God and the world.

The following instance, which was published by the Inquisitors, will be a testimony of this truth. I do give the real names of the persons in this account, because the thing was made public.

IN the city of *Zaragoza*, near the college of St. *Thomas* of *Villaneuva*, did live *Mary Guerrero*, married to a taylor; she was handsome, witty, and ambitious: But as the rank of a taylor's wife could not make her shine among the quality, she undertook the life of a *Beata*, to be known by it in the city. The first step she was to make was to chuse a Confessor of good parts, and of a good reputation among the nobility; so she
pitched,

pitched upon the reverend Father *Fr. Michael Navarro*, a *Dominican* Fryar, who was D. D. and a man universally well beloved for his doctrine and good behaviour. But, *quando Venus vigilat, Minerva dormit.* She began to confess to him, and in less than a year, by her feigned modesty, and hypocritical airs; and by confessing no sins, but the religious exercises of her life; the reverend Father began to publish in the city her sanctity to the highest pitch. Many ladies and gentlemen of the first rank, desirous to see the new saint, sent for her, but she did not appear, but by her maid, gave a denial to all. This was a new addition to the fame of her sanctity, and a new incitement to the ladies to see her. So some, going to visit Father *Navarro*, desired the favour of him to go along with them, and introduce them to the blessed *Guerrero*: But the Father, (either bewitched by her, or in expectation of a bishoprick, for the making of a saint, or the better to conceal his private designs, answered, that he could not do such a thing; for, knowing her virtue, modesty, and aversion to any act of vanity, he should be very much in the wrong, to give her opportunities of cooling her fervent zeal and purity.

By that means, rich and poor, old and young, men and women, began to resort to her neighbour's house, and the *Dominican* church, only to see the blessed *Guerrero*. She shewed a great displeasure at these popular demonstrations of respect, and resolved to keep close at home; and after a long consultation with the Father *Navarro*, they agreed that she should keep her room, and that he would go to confess her, and say Mass in her room, (for the *Dominicans*, and the four *Mendicant* orders, have a privilege for their Fryars to say Mass, or, as they say, to set an altar every where.) To begin this new way of living, the Father charged her husband to quit the house, and never appear before his wife; for his sight would be a great hindrance to his wife's sanctity and purity; and the poor sot, believing every thing, went away and took a lodging for himself and apprentice.

They did continue this way of living, both she and the Father, a whole year; but the fatigue of going every day to say Mass and confess the *blessed*, being too great for the reverend, he asked leave from the reverend Father *Buenacasa*, then prior of the convent, to go and live with her as a spiritual guide. The prior, foreseeing some great advantage, gave him leave, and so he went for good and all to be her lodger and master of the house. When the Father was in the house, he began by degrees to give permission to the people now and then to see the *blessed*, through the glass of a little window, desiring them not to make a noise, for fear of disturbing the *blessed* in her exercise of devotion: She was in her own room always upon her knees, when some people were to see her through the glass, which was in the wall between her room, and that of the reverend. In a few months after, the archbishop went to see her, and conversed with her, and the Father *Navarro*, who was in great friendship with, and much honored by his Grace. This example of the prelate did put the nobility in mind to do the same. The viceroy not being permitted by his royal representation to go to her, did send his coach one night for her, and both the Father and the *blessed* had the honor to sup in private with his Excellency: This being spread abroad, she was troubled every day with coaches, and presents from all sorts and conditions of people. Many sick went there in hopes to be healed by her sight; and some that did happen to go, when nature itself was upon the crisis, or by the exercise of walking, or by some other natural operation, finding themselves better, did use to cry out, a miracle, a miracle! She did want nothing but to be carried on a pedestal upon the ignorant's shoulders: The fame of her sanctity was spread so far, that she was troubled every post-day with letters from people of quality of other provinces, so the reverend

was

was obliged to take a secretary under him, and a porter to keep the door; for they had removed to another house of better appearance, and more conveniency.—Thus they continued for the space of two years, and all this while the reverend was writing the life of the *Blessed*; and many times he was pressed to print part of her life; but the time of the discovery of their wickedness being come, they were taken by an order from the holy inquisition.

The discovery did happen thus. *Ann Moron*, a chirurgeons wife, who lived next door to the *Blessed*, had a child of ten months old, and, as a neighbour, she went to desire the reverend, to beg of the *Blessed* to take the child and kiss him, thinking that by such an holy kiss, her child would be happy forever. But the reverend desiring her to go herself and make the request to the *Blessed*, she did it accordingly. *Mary Guerrero* took the child and bid the mother leave him with her for a quarter of an hour. *Ann Moron* thought then that her child was already in heaven; but when in a quarter of an hour after she came again for the child, the *Blessed* told her, that her child was to die the night following, for so God had revealed to her in a short prayer she had made for the child. The child really died the night following, but the surgeon, as a tender father, seeing some spots and marks in his child's body, opened it, and found in it the cause of its unfortunate death, which was a dose of poison. Upon this suspicion of the child's being poisoned, and the foretelling his death by the *Blessed*, the Father went to the inquisitors, and told the nature of the thing.

Don *Pedro Guerrero* the first inquisitor was then absent, so Don *Francisco Torrejon*, second inquisitor, went himself to examine the thing, and seeing the child dead, and all the circumstances against the *Blessed*, he then ordered, that she and the reverend, and all their domestic servants, should be secured immediately, and sent to the holy inquisition. All things were done accordingly, ly, and this sudden and unexpected accident made such a noise in town, that every body did reason in his own way, but no body dared to speak of the inquisitor. At the same time every thing in the house was seized upon, with the papers of the reverend, &c. Among the papers was found the life of the *Blessed*, written by father *Navarro*'s own hand. I said in the beginning, that he was bewitched, and so many people did believe; for it seemed incredible that so learned a man, as he was in his own religion, should fall into so gross an ignorance, as to write such a piece, in the method it was found composed; for the manuscript contained about 600 sheets, which by an order of the inquisitors, were sent to the *qualificators of the holy office* to be reviewed by them, and to have their opinions thereupon. I shall speak of these qualificators, when I come to treat of the inquisitors and their practices. Now it is sufficient to say, that all the qualificators, being examinators of the crimes committed against the holy catholic faith, did examine the sheets, and their opinion was, that the book intitled *the life of the blessed Mary Guerrero*, composed by the reverend Father *Fr. Michael Navarro*, was scandalous, false, and against revealed doctrines in the scripture, and good manners, and that it deserved to be burnt in the common yard of the holy office, by the mean officer of it.

After this examination was made, the inquisitors did summon two priests out of every parish church, and two Fryars out of every convent, to come such a day to the hall of the holy tribunal to be present at the trial and examinations against *Mary Guerrero*, and *Michael Navarro*. It was my turn to go to that trial for the cathedral church of St. *Salvator*. We went the day appointed, all the summoned priests and Fryars, to the number of a hundred and fifty, besides the inquisitors, officers of the inquisition, and qualificators, these had the cross of the holy office before their breasts, which is set upon their habits in a very nice manner. The number

number of qualificators I reckoned that day in the hall were two hundred and twenty. When all the summoned were together, and the inquisitors under a canopy of black velvet (which is placed at the right corner of the altar, upon which was an image of the crucifix, and six yellow wax candles, without any other light) they made the signal to bring the prisoners to the bar, and immediately they came out of the prison, and kneeling down before the holy Fathers, the secretary began to read the articles of the examinations and convictions of their crimes.

Indeed both the Father and the *Blessed* appeared that day very much like saints, if we will believe the *Roman*'s proverb, that paleness and thin visage is a sign of sanctity. The examination, and the lecture of their crimes was so long, that we were summoned three times more upon the same trial, in which, to the best of my memory, I heard the following articles.

That by the *Blessed*'s confession to *Michael Navarro*, this in the beginning of her life says: 1st. *That blessed creature knew no sin since she was born into the world.* 2d. *She has been several times visited by the angels in her closet; and Jesus Christ himself has come down thrice to give her new heavenly instructions.* 3d. *She was advised by the divine spouse to live separately from her husband.* 4th. *She was once favoured with a visit of the holy trinity, and then she saw Jesus at the left hand of the Father.* 5th. *The holy dove came afterwards and sat upon her head many times.* 6th. *This holy comforter has foretold her, that her body after death shall be always incorruptible, and that a great king, with the news of her death, shall come to honor her sepulchre with this motto,* The soul of this *warrior* (*) is the glory of my kingdom. 7th. *Jesus Christ in a Dominican's habit appeared to her at night, and in a celestial dream she was overshadowed by the spirit.* 8th. *She had taken out of purgatory*

G

(*) *Guerro* in Spanish signifies *warrior*.

tory seven times the soul of his companion's sister. (What folly!) 9th. *The Pope and the whole church shall rejoice in her death; nay, his Holiness shall canonize her, and put her in the Litany before the apostles, &c.* After these things her private miracles were read, &c. and so many passages of her life that it would be too tedious to give an account of them. I only write these, to shew the stupidity of the reverend *Navarro*, who, if he had been in his perfect senses, could not have committed so gross an error. [This was the pious people's opinion.] The truth is, that the *Blessed* was not overshadowed by the spirit, but by her Confessor; for she being at that time with child, and delivered in the inquisition, one article against the Father was, that he had his bed near her bed, and that he was the father of the new child, or monster on earth.

Their sentences were not read in public, and what was their end we know not; only we heard, that the husband of the *Blessed* had notice given to him by an officer of the holy office, that he was at liberty to marry to any other he had a fancy for; and by this true account, the public may easily know the extravagancies of the *Romish* Confessors, who, blinded either by their own passions, or by the subtleties of the wicked *Beatas*, do commit so great and heinous crimes, &c.

There is another sort of *Beatas*, whom we call *Endemoniadas*, i. e. *Demoniacks*, and by these possessed the Confessor gets a vast deal of masses. I will tell you, reader, the nature of the thing, and by it you will see the cheat of the Confessor and the *Demoniack*. I said before, that among the *Beatas* there are two sorts, young, and of a middle age, but all married; and that the young undertake the way of confessing every day, or three times a week, to get opportunity of going abroad, and be delivered a while from their husband's jealousies: But many husbands being jealous of the flies that come near their wives, they scarcely give them leave to go to confess. Observe further, that those women

men make their husbands believe, that out of spite, a witch has given them the evil spirit, and they make such unusual gestures, both with their faces and mouths, that it is enough to make the world laugh only at the sight of them. When they are in the fit of the evil spirit, they talk blasphemously against God and his saints, they beat husbands and servants; they put themselves in such a sweat, that when the evil spirit leaves them for a while (as they say) they cannot stand upon their feet for very fatigue. The poor deceived husbands, troubled in mind and body, send for a physician; but this says, he has no remedy for such a distemper, and that physic knows no manner of devil, and so, their dealing being not with the spirit, but with the body, he sends the husband to the spiritual physician; and by that means they are, out of a good design, procurers for their own wives; for really they go to the Spiritual Father, begging his favour and assistance to come to exorcise, i. e. to read the prayer of the church, and to turn out the evil spirit out of his wife's body. Then the Father makes him understand, that the thing is very troublesome, and that if the devil is obstinate and positive, he cannot leave his wife in three or four nights; and may be, in a month or two; by which we must neglect other business of honor and profit. To this the deluded husband promises that his trouble shall be well recompensed, and puts a piece of gold in his hand, to make him easy; so he pays before hand for his future dishonor. Then the Father Exorcist goes along with him, and as soon as the wife hears the voice of the Exorcist, she flies into an unmeasurable fury, and cries out, do not let that man (meaning the Exorcist) come to torment me (as if the devil did speak in her and for her.) But he takes the hysop with holy water, and sprinkles the room. Here the *Demoniack* throweth herself on the ground, teareth her clothes and hair, as if she was perfectly a mad woman. Then the Priest tieth the blessed *Stola*, i. e.

a sort of scarf, they make use of among other ornaments to say Mass, upon her neck, and begins the prayers: Sometimes the devil is very timorous and leaves the creature immediately easy; sometimes he is obstinate, and will resist a long while before he obeys the Exorcisms of the church; but at last he retires himself into his own habitation, and frees the creature from his torments; for, they say, that the devil or evil spirit, sometimes has his place in the head, sometimes in the stomach, sometimes in the liver, &c. After the woman is easy for a while, they go all to take a refreshment, they eat and drink the best that can be found in the town.

A while after, when the husband is to mind his own business, the wife, on pretence that the evil spirit begins again to trouble her, goes into her chamber and desireth the Father to hear her confession. They lock the door after them, and what they do for an hour or two, God only knoweth. These private confessions and exercises of devotion continue for several months together, and the husband, loth to go to bed with his wife, for fear of the evil spirit, goes to another chamber, and the Father lieth in the same room with his wife on a field-bed, to be always ready, when the malignant spirit comes, to exorcise, and beat him with the holy *Stola*. So deeply ignorant are the people in that part of the world, or so great bigots, that on pretence of religious remedies to cure their wives of the devilish distemper, they contract a worse distemper on their heads and honors, which no physician, either spiritual, or corporal, can ever cure.

When in a month or two, the Father and the Demoniack have settled matters between themselves, for the time to come, he tells the husband, that the devil is in a great measure tamed, by the daily exorcisms of the holy mother the church, and that it is time for him to retire, and mind other business of his convent; and that, it being impossible for him to continue longer in
his

his house, all he can do, is to serve him and her in his convent, if she goes there every day. The husband, with a great deal of thanks, pays the Father for his trouble, who taking his leave goes to his community, and gives to the Father Prior two parts of the money (for the third part is allowed to him for his own pains.) The day following, in the morning, the *Demoniack* is worse than she was before: Then the husband, out of faith, and zeal of a good Christian, crieth out, the Father is gone, and the devil is loose: The Exorcisms of the church are not ready at hand, and the evil spirit thinks himself at liberty and begins to trouble the poor creature: Let us send her to the convent, and the bold, malignant spirit shall pay dear there for this new attempt. So the wife goes to the Father, and the Father takes her into a little room, next to the vestry, (a place to receive their acquaintance, only of the female sex) and there both in private, the Father appeases the devil, and the woman goes quiet and easy to her house, where she continues in the same easiness till the next morning. Then the devil begins to trouble her again; and the husband says, O obstinate spirit! You make all this noise because the hour of being beaten with the holy *Stola*, is near: I know that your spite and malice against the Exorcisms of the church is great; but the power of them is greater than thine: Go, go to the Father, and go through all the lashes of the *Stola*. So the woman goes again to the Father, and in this manner of life they continue for a long while.

There is of these *Beatas* in every convent church, not a few, for sometimes, one of those *Exorcists* keeps six, and sometimes ten, by whom, and their husbands, he is very well paid for the trouble of confessing them every day, and for taming the devil, but the most pleasant thing among those *Demoniacks* is, that they have different devils, that trouble them; for by a strict commandment of the Father, they are forced to tell

their

their names, so one is called *Belzebub,* another *Lucifer, &c.* And those devils are very jealous one of another. I saw several times, in the body of the church, a battle among three of those *Demoniacks,* on pretence of being in the fit of the evil spirit, threatening and beating one another, and calling one another nicknames, till the Father did come with the hysop, holy water and the *Stola,* to appease them, and bid them to be silent, and not to make such a noise in the house of the Lord. And the whole matter was (as we knew afterwards) that the Father *Exorcist* was more careful of one, than of the others; and jealousy (which is the worse devil) getting into their heads, they give it to their respective devils, who, with an infernal fury, did fight one against another, out of pet and revenge for the sake of their lodging room.

In the city *Huesca,* where (as they believe) *Pontious Pilate* was professor of law in the University, and his chair, or part of it, is kept in the bishop's palace for a show, and a piece of antiquity, (and which I saw my self) I say, I saw, and conversed both with the Father *Exorcist* and the *Beata Demoniack* about the following instance.

The thing being not publicly divulged, but among a few persons, I will give an accout of it under the names of father *John* and *Dorothea,* this *Dorothea* when 13 years old, was married, against her inclinations, to a tradesman 50 years old. The beauty of *Dorothea,* and the ugliness of her husband were very much, the one admired, and the other observed by all the inhabitants of the city. The Bishop's secretary made the match, and read the ceremony of the church, for he was the only executer of her father's will and testament: She was known by the name of *Young dancing eyes.* Her husband was jealous of her, in the highest degree; she could not go out without him, and so she suffered this torment for the space of three years. She had an aversion, and a great antipathy against him.—

Her

Her Confessor was a young, well shaped Fryar, and whether out of her own contrivance, or by the Fryar's advice, one day, unexpected by her husband, the devil was detected and manifested in her. What affliction this was to the old, amorous, jealous husband, is inexpressible. The poor man went himself to the *Jesuit*'s college, next to his house, for an *Exorcist*, but the *Jesuit* could do nothing to appease that devil, to the great surprise of the poor husband & many others too, who do believe, that a *Jesuit* can command and overcome the devil himself, and that the devils are more afraid of a *Jesuit*, than of their sovereign prince in hell.

The poor husband did send for many others, but the effect did not answer to the purpose; till at last her own Confessor came to her, and after many exorcisms, and private prayers, she was (or the devil in her) pacified for a while. This was a testimony of the Father *John*'s fervent zeal and virtue to the husband, so they settled how the case was to be managed for the future. Fryar *John* was very well recompensed upon the bargain; and both the *Demoniack* and Fryar *John* continued in daily battle with the evil spirit for two years together. The husband began to sleep quiet and easy, thinking that his wife, having the devil in her body, was not able to be unfaithful to him; for while the malignant torments the body, the woman begins to fast in public and eat in private with the *Exorcist*; and the exercises of such *Demoniacks* are all of prayers and devotions, so the deceived husband believes that it is better to have a *Demoniack* wife, than one free from the evil spirit.

The Exorcisms of Fryar *John* (being to appease not a spiritual, but a material devil) he and *Dorothea* were both discovered, and found in the fact, by a Fryar of the same convent, who, by many presents from Fryar *John* and *Dorothea*, did not reveal the thing to the Prior, but he told it to some of his friends, which were enemies to Fryar *John*, from whom I heard the story.

For

For my part, I did not believe it for a while, till at laſt, I knew, that the Fryar *John* was removed into another convent, and that *Dorothea* left her houſe and huſband, and went after him; though the huſband endeavoured to ſpread abroad, that the devil had ſtolen his wife.— Theſe are the effects of the practices of the *Demoniacks* and *Exorciſts*.

Now I come to the perſons of public authority, either in ecclesiaſtical, civil or military affairs, and to the ladies of the firſt quality or rank in the world. As to thoſe, I muſt beg leave to tell the truth, as well as of the inferior people. But, becauſe the Confeſſors of ſuch perſons are moſt commonly all Jeſuits, it ſeems very a propos to give a deſcription of thoſe Fathers, their practices and lives, and to write of them, to the beſt of my knewledge and memory, what I know to be the matter of fact.

ALMOST in all the *Roman Catholic* countries, the *Jeſuit* Fathers are the teachers of the *Latin* tongue, and to this purpoſe, they have in every college (ſo they call their convents) four large rooms, which are called the four claſſes for the grammar. There is one teacher in each of them. The city, corporation, or politic body, paying the Rector of the *Jeſuits* ſo much a year, and the young gentlemen are at no expence at all for learning the *Latin* tongue. The ſcholars lodge in town, and they go every day, from eight in the morning till eleven, to the college; and when the clock ſtrikes eleven, they go along with the four teachers to hear Maſs: They go at two in the afternoon, till half an hour after four, and ſo they do all the year long, except the holy days, and the vacations from the fifteenth of *Auguſt*, till the ninth of *September*. As the four teachers receive nothing for their trouble, becauſe the payment of the city goes to the community, they have contrived how to be recompenſed for their labour: There were in the college of *Zaragoza*,

when

when I learned *Latin*, very near six hundred scholars, noblemen, and tradesmen's sons, every one was to pay every *Saturday* a real of plate for the rule (as they call it.) There is a custom, to have a public literal act once every day, to which are invited the young gentlemen's parents, but none of the common people. The Father Rector and all the community are present, and placed in their velvet chairs. To the splendid performance of this act, the four teachers chuse twelve gentlemen, and each of them is to make, by heart, a *Latin* speech in the pulpit. They chuse besides the twelve, one Emperor, two Kings, and two Pretors, which are always the most noble of the young gentletlemen: They wear crowns on their heads that day, which is the distinguishing character of their learning. The Emperor sits under a canopy, the Pretors on each side, and the Kings a step lower, and the twelve Senators in two lines next to the throne. This act lasts three hours; and after all is over, the teachers and the Father Rector invite the nobility and the Emperor, with the Pretors, Kings and Senators, to go to the common-hall of the college, to take a refreshment of the most nice sweet-meats and best liquor. The Fathers of the Emperor, Kings, Pretors and Senators, are to pay for all the charges and expences, which are fixed to be a hundred pistoles every month. And every time there are new Emperors or Kings, &c. by moderate computation, we were sure, that out of the remainder of the hundred pistoles a month, and the real of plate every week from each of the scholars, the four Father teachers had clear, to be divided among themselves every year, sixteen hundred pistoles.

We must own, that the *Jesuits* are very fit, and the most proper persons for the education of youth, and that all these exercises and public acts (though for their interests) are great stimulations and incitements to learning in young gentlemen; for one of them will study night and day, only to get the empty title of Emperor,

H

&c. once in a month; and their parents are very glad to expend eight pistoles a year, to encourage their sons; and besides that, they believe that they are under a great obligation to the *Jesuits* college, and the *Jesuits* knowing their tempers, become, not only acquainted with them, but absolute masters of their houses: I must own likewise, that I never heard of any *Jesuit* Father, any thing against good manners or Christian conversation; for really, they behave themselves, as to outward appearance, with so great civility, modesty and policy, that no body has any thing to say against their deportment in the world, except self-interest, and ambition.

And really the *Jesuits* order is the richest of all the orders in Christendom; and because the reason of it is not well known, I will tell now the ways by which they gather together so great treasures every where. As they are universal teachers of the *Latin* tongue, and have this opportunity to know the youth, they pitch upon the most ingenious young men, and upon the richest of all, though they be not very witty: They spare neither time, nor persuasions, nor presents, to persuade them to be of the society of Jesus (so they name their order:) The poor and ingenious are very glad of it, and the noble and rich too, thinking to be great men upon the account of their quality: So their colleges are composed of witty and noble people. By the noble gentlemen, they get riches; by the witty and ingenious, they support their learning, and breed up teachers and great men to govern the consciences of Princes, people of public authority, and ladies of the first rank.

They do not receive ladies in private, in their colleges, but always in the middle of the church or chapel; they never set down to hear them. They do not receive charity for Masses, nor *Beatas*, nor *Demoniacks* in their church, (I never saw one there) their modesty and civil manners charm every one that speaks with them; though I believe, all that is to carry on their
private

private ends and interests. They are indefatigable in the procuring the good of souls, and sending missionaries to catechise the children in the country; and they have fit persons in every college for all sorts of exercises, either of devotion, of law, or policy, &c. They entertain no body within the gate of the college, so no body knows what they do among themselves. If it sometimes happens that one doth not answer their expectation, after he has taken the habit, they turn him out; for they have fourteen years trial: But as soon as they turn him out, they underhand procure a handsome setttlement for him; so he that is expelled dareth not to say any thing against them, for fear of losing his bread. And if, after he is out, he behaves himself well, and gets some riches, he is sure to die a Jesuit.

I heard of Don *Pedro Segovia*, who had been a *Jesuit*, but was turned out, but by the *Jesuits* influence, he got a prebendary in the Chathedral church, and was an eminent preacher. He was afterwards constantly visited by them, and when he came to die, he asked again the habit, & being granted to him, he died a *Jesuit*, and by his death the *Jesuits* became heirs of twenty thousand pistoles in money and lands.

Their are Confessors of kings and princes, of ministers of state, and generals, and of all the people of distinction and estates. So, it is no wonder if they are masters of the tenth part of the riches in every kingdom, and if God doth not put a stop to their covetousness, it is to be feared, that one way or other, they will become masters of all; for they do not seek dignities, being prohibited, by the constitutions of their order, to be Bishops, and Popes; it only is allowed to them to be Cardinals, to govern the Pope by that means, as well as they do rule Emperors, Kings and Princes. At this present time all the Sovereigns of Europe have *Jesuits* for their Confessors.

Now it is high time to come to say something as to their

their practices in confessions; and I will only speak of those I knew particularly well.

First, The reverend Father *Navasques*, professor of divinity in their college, was chosen Confessor of the Countess of *Fuentes*, who was left a widow at twenty-four years of age. This lady, as well as other persons of quality, kept a coach and servant for the Father Confessor. He has always a Father companion to say Mass to the lady. She alloweth so much a year to the college, and so much to her Confessor and his companion. All persons have an oratory or chapel in their houses, by dispensation from the Pope, for which they pay a great deal of money. Their way of living is thus, in the morning they send the coach and servant to the college, most commonly at eleven of the clock: The Father goes every day at that time, and the lords and ladies do not confess every day; they have Mass said at home, and after Mass, the reverend stays in the ladies company till dinner-time: Then he goes to the college till six in the evening, and at six goes again to see the lady, or lord, till eleven. What are their discourses I do not know: This I know, that nothing is done in the family without the reverend's advice and approbation: So it was with the Countess's family, and when she died, the college got four thousand pistoles a year from her.

The reverend Father *Muniessa*, Confessor of the Dutchess of *Villahermosa*, in the same manner got, at her death thirty thousand pistoles, and the reverend Father *Aranda*, Confessor to the Countess of *Aranda*, got two thousand pistoles, yearly rent from her, all for the college. Now what means they make use of to bewitch the people and to suck their substance, every body may think, but no body may guess at. An ingenious politician was asked, how the Jesuits could be rightly described and defined, and he gave this definition of them. *Amici frigid, & inimici calidi*, i. e. cold friends and warm enemies. And this is all I can write concerning their manners and practices. Be-

Before I dismiss this subject, I cannot pass by one instance more, touching the practices of Confessors in general, and that is, that since I came to these *northern* countries, I have been told by gentlemen of good sense, and serious in their conversation, that many Priests and Fryars were procurers (when they were in those parts of the world) and did shew them the way of falling into the common sin. It is no doubt they know all the lewd women by auricular confession, but I could not believe they would be so villanous and base, as to make a show of their wickedness before strangers. This I must say in vindication of a great many of them (for what I do write is only of the wicked ones) that they are many times engaged in some intrigues unknown to themselves, and they are not to be blamed, but only the persons that, with false insinuations, do make them believe a lie for a truth, and this, under a pretence of devotion. To clear this I will tell a story, which was told me by a Colonel in the *English* service, who lives at present in *London*.

He said to me, that an officer, a friend of his, was prisoner in *Spain*: His lodgings were opposite to a Counsellor's house. The Counsellor was old and jealous, the lady young, handsome and confined, and the officer well shaped and very fair. The windows and balconies of the Counsellor were covered with narrow lattices, and the officer never saw any woman of that house: But the lady, who had several times seen him at his window, could not conceal long her love, so she sent for her Father Confessor, and spoke with him in the following manner: My reverend Father, you are my spiritual guide, and you must prevent the ruin of my soul, reputation and quietness of my life. Over the way, said she, lives an *English* officer, who is constantly at the window, making signs and demonstrations of love to me, and though I endeavour not to haunt my balcony, for fear of being found out by my spouse; my waiting maid tells me that he is always there. You
know

know my spouse's temper and jealousy, and if he observes the least thing in the world, I am undone forever. So, to put a timely stop to this, I beg you would be so kind as to go over and desire him to make no more signs; and that if he is a gentleman, as he seems to be, he never will do any thing to disquiet a gentlewoman. The credulous Confessor, believing every syllable, went over to the *English* officer, and told him the message, asking his pardon for the liberty he took; but that he could not help it, being, as he was, the lady's Confessor.

The officer, who was of a fiery temper, answer'd him in a resolute manner. Hear, Fryar, said he to the Confessor, go your way, and never come to me with such false stories, for I do not know what you say, nor I never saw any lady over the way. The poor Father, full of shame and fear, took his leave, and went to deliver the answer to the lady. What, said she, doth he deny the truth? I hope God will prove my innocency before you, and that before two days. The Father did comfort her, and went to his convent. The lady seeing her design frustrated this way, did contrive another to let the officer know her inclination: So one of her servants wrote a letter to her in the officer's name, with many lovely expressions, and desiring her to be in her garden at eight in the dark evening, under a fig-tree next to the walls. And recommending to her servant the secret, sealed the letter directed to her. Two days after she sent for her Confessor again; and told him, Now my reverend Father, God has put a letter, from the officer, into my hands, to convince him and you of the truth. Pray take the letter, and go to him, and if he denies, as he did before, shew him his own letter, and I hope he will not be so bold as to trouble me any more. He did it accordingly, and the *English* gentleman answered as the first time; and as he flew into a passion, the Father told him, Sir, see this letter, and answer me; which the officer reading, soon understood

the

the meaning, and said, Now, my good Father, I must own my folly, for I cannot deny my hand-writing, and to assure you, and the lady, that I shall be a quite different man for the future, pray tell her that I will obey her commands, and that I will never do any thing against her orders. The Confessor, very glad of so unexpected good success, as he thought, gave the answer to the lady, adding to it, Now madam, you may be quiet, and without any fear, for he will obey you. Did not I tell you, said she, that he could not deny the fact of the letter? So the Confessor went home, having a very good opinion of the lady, and of the *English* officer too, who did not fail to go to the rendezvous, &c.

Every serious, religious man will rather blame the wicked lady, than the Confessor; for the poor man, tho' he was a procurer and instrument of bringing that intrigue to an effect, really he was innocent all the while; and how could he suspect any thing of wantonness in a lady so devoutly affected, and so watchful of the ruin of her soul, honor, and quietness of her life? We must excuse them in such a case as this was, and say, That many and many Confessors, if they are procurers, they do it unknown to themselves, and out of pure zeal for the good of the souls, or to prevent many disturbances in a family: But as for those that, out of wickedness, busy themselves in so base and villanous exercises, I say, heaven and earth ought to rise in judgment against them. They do deserve to be punished in this world, that, by their example, the same exercise might be prevented in others.

I have given an account of some private Confessions of both sexes, and of the most secret practices of some of the *Roman-catholic* priests, according to what I promised the public in my printed proposals. And from all that is written and said, I crave leave to draw some few inferences.

First, I say that the Pope and councils are the original causes of the aforesaid misdoings and ill practices
of

of the *Romish* priests: Marriage being forbidden to a priest, not by any commandment of God or divine scripture, but by a strict ordinance from the Pope, an indisputable canon of the council. This was not practised by them for many centuries after the death of our Saviour; and the priests were then more religious, and exemplary than they are now. I know the reasons their church hath for it, which I will not contradict, to avoid all sort of controversy: But this I may say, that if the priests, Fryars and Nuns were at lawful liberty to marry, they would be better Christians, the people richer in honor and estates, the kingdom better peopled, the King stronger, and the *Romish* religion more free from foreign attempts and calumnies.

They do make a vow of chastity, and they break it by living loose, lewd, and irregular lives. They do vow poverty, and their thirst for riches is unquenchable, and whatever they get is most commonly by unlawful means: They swear obedience, and they only obey their lusts, passions and inclination. How many sins are occasioned by binding themselves with these three vows in a monastical life? It is inexpressible, and all, or the greater number of sins committed by them, would be hinder'd, if the Pope and council were to imitate the right foundations of the primitive church, and the Apostles of Jesus Christ our Saviour.

As to particular persons, among the priests and Fryars, touching their corruptions and ill practices in *auricular* confession, I say, they do act against divine and human law in such practices, and are guilty of serveral sins especially *Sacrilege* and *Robbery*. It is true, the *Moral Summs* are defective in the instruction of Confessors, as opinions, grounded in the erroneous principles of their church: But as to the settled rules for the guiding and advising the penitent, what he ought to do, to walk uprightly, they are not defective; so the Confessors cannot plead *ignoramus* for so doing, and consequently the means they make use of in the

tribunal

tribunal of conscience, are all sinful, being only to deceive and cheat the poor, ignorant people.

Their practices, then, are against divine and humane law, contrary to holy scriptures; nay, to humanity itself: For, *Thou that teachest another, thou shalt not kill; nor commit adultery, nor steal, nor covet thy neighbour's goods, nor wife:* Dost thou all those things? And to insist only on *sacrilege* and *robbery*. What can it be but *robbery*, and *sacrilege*, to sell absolution, or which is the same thing, to refuse it to the penitent, if he doth not give so much money for masses?

This may be cleared by their own principles, and by the opinions of their casuistical authors, who do agree in this, *viz.* That there are three sorts of *sacrilege*, or a *sacrilege* which may be committed three different ways. These are the expressions they make use of. *Sacrum in sacro: Sacrem ex sacro: Sacrem pro sacro.* That is, to take a sacred thing for a sacred thing, a sacred thing in a sacred place: And a sacred thing out of a sacred place. All these three are *robbery* and *sacrilege* together, according to their opinions; and I said that the Confessors in their practices are guilty of all three; for in their opinion, the holy tribunal of conscience is a sacred thing; the absolution and consecrated church are sacred likewise. As for the money given for the relief of the souls in purgatory, *Corella* in his *moral sum* says, that that is a sacred thing too. Now it is certain among them, that no Priest can receive money for absolution directly nor indirectly: Those then that take it, do rob that money which is unlawfully taken from the penitent; and it is a *sacrilege* too, because they take a sacred thing for a sacred thing; viz. the sacred money for Masses taken for absolution. They take that sacred thing in a sacred place, viz. in the sacred tribunal of conscience: And they take a sacred thing out of a sacred place, viz. the church.

Again: Though most commonly, *Quodcumque ligaveris super terram, erit ligatum & in cœlis,* is understood

stood by them literally, and the Pope usurps the power of absolving men without contrition, provided they have attrition, or only confession by mouth, as we shall see in the following chapter of the Pope's bull: Nevertheless the Casuists when they come to treat of a perfect confession under the sacrament of penance, they unanimously say, that three things are absolutely necessary to a perfect confession, and to salvation too, viz. *Oris confessio, cordis contritio,* and *operis satisfactio.* Though at the same time they say, except in case of pontifical dispensation with faculties, privileges, indulgencies, and pardon of all sins committed by a man: But though they except this case, I am sure, they do it out of obedience, and flattery, rather than their own belief. If they then believe, that without contrition of heart, the absolution is of no effect, why do they persuade the contrary to the penitent? Why do they take money for absolution? It is, then, a cheat, robbery, and sacrilege.

Secondly. I say, that the Confessors (generally speaking) are the occasion of the ruin of many families, of many thefts, debaucheries, murthers, and divisions among several families, (for which they must answer before that dreadful tribunal of God, when, and where all the secret practices and wickedness, shall be disclosed;) add to this, that by *auricular* confession, they are acquainted with the tempers and inclinations of people, which contribute very much to heap up riches, and to make themselves commanding masters of all sorts of persons; for when a Confessor is thoroughly acquainted with a man's temper, and natural inclinations; it is the most easy thing in the world to bring him to his own opinion, and to be master over him and his substance.

That the Confessors, commonly speaking, are the occasion of all the aforesaid mischiefs, will appear by the following observations.

First. They get the best estates from the rich people,

ple, for the use and benefit of their communities, by which many and many private persons and whole families, are reduced an[d] ruined. Observe now their practices as to the sick. If a nobleman of a good estate is very ill, the Confessor must be by him night and day, and when he goes to sleep his companion supplies his place to direct, and exhort the sick to die as a good Christian, and to advise him how to make his last will and testament. If the Confessor is a downright honest man, he must betray his principles of honesty or disoblige his superior, and all the community, by getting nothing from the sick; so he chargeth upon the poor man's conscience to leave his convent thousands of Masses, for the speedy delivery of his soul out of purgatory; and besides that, to settle a yearly Mass for ever upon the convent, and to leave a voluntary gift, that the Fryars may remember him in their public and private prayers, as a benefactor of that community: And in these and other legacies, and charities, three parts of his estate goes to the church, or convents. But if the Confessor has a large conscience, then without any Christian consideration for the sick's family and poor relations, he makes use of all the means an inhuman, covetous man can invent to get the whole estate for his convent. And this is the reason why they are so rich, and so many families so poor, reduced, and ruined.

From these we may infer *thefts*, *murthers*, *debaucheries*, and *divisions* of families. I say, the Confessors are the original cause of all these ill consequences; for when they take the best of estates for themselves, no wonder if private persons and whole families are left in such want, and necessity, that they abandon themselves to all sorts of sins, and hazards of losing both lives and honours, rather than to abate something of their pride.

I might prove this by several instances, which, I do not question, are very well known by many curious people; and though some malicious persons are apt to
suspect,

suspect, that such instances are mere dreams, or forgeries of envious people, for my part I do believe, that many Confessors are the original cause of the aforesaid evils, as may be seen by the following matter of fact.

In the account of the *Jesuits* and their practices, I said, that the reverend *Navasques* was the Confessor of the Countess of *Fuentes*, who was left a widow at 24 years of age, and never married again: For the Reverend's care is to advise them to live a single life. (Purity being the first step to Heaven.) The lady Countess had no children, and had an estate of her own, of 4000 pistoles a year, besides her jewels and houshold goods, which, after her death, were valued at 15000 pistoles.— All these things, and her personal estate, were left to the *Jesuits* college, though she had many near relations, among whom I knew two young gentlemen, second cousins of her ladyship, and two young ladies kept in the house as her cousins too. She had promised to give them a settlement suitable to their quality and merits; which promise the Father Confessor did confirm to them several times: But the lady died, and both the young ladies and the two gentlemen were left under the providence of God, for the countess had forgotten them in her last will; and the Father Confessor took no notice of them afterward. The two young ladies did abandon themselves to all manner of private pleasures at first, and at last to public wickedness. As to the young gentlemen, in a few months after the lady's death, one left the city and went to serve the King, as a cadet; the other following a licentious life, was ready to finish his days with shame and dishonour on a public scaffold, had not the goodness and compassion of the Marquis of *Camarassa*, then vice-roy of *Aragon*, prevented it. Now, whether the Father Confessor shall be answerable before God, for all the sins committed by the young ladies, and one of the gentlemen, for want of what they did expect from the countess, or not?
God

God only knows: We may think and believe, that if the lady had provided for them according to their condition in the world, in all human probability, they had not committed such sins: Or if the college, or the reverend Father had been more charitable, and compassionate to the condition they were left in, they had put a timely stop to their wickedness.

Thirdly. I say, that Confessors and preachers are the occasion, that many thousands of young men and women chuse a single, retired life, in a monastery, or convent; and therefore are the cause of many families being extinguished, and their own treasures exceedingly increased.

If a gentleman has two or three sons, and as many daughters, the Confessor of the family adviseth the father to keep the eldest son at home, and send the rest, both sons and daughters, into a convent or monastery; praising the monastical life, and saying, that to be retired from the world, is the safest way to heaven. There is a proverb which runs thus in English: *It is better to be alone, than in bad company.* And the Confessors do alter it thus: *It is better to be alone, than in good company.* Which they pretend to prove with so many sophistical arguments, nay, with a passage from the scripture; and this not only in private conversion, but publicly in the pulpit. I remember I heard my celebrated Mr. F. *James Garcia* preach a sermon upon the subject of a *retired life,* and *solitude,* which sermon and others preached by him in *Lent,* in the cathedral church of St. *Salvator,* were printed afterwards. The book is in folio, and its title *Quadragesima de gracia.* He was the first preacher I heard make use of the above proverb, and to alter it in the aforesaid way; and to prove the sense of his alteration he said: *Remember the woman in the apocalypsis, that ran from heaven into the desert.* What! Was not that woman in heaven, in the company of the stars and planets, by which are represented all the heavenly spirits? Why then

quits

quits she that good company, and chuses to be alone in a desert place? Because (said he) that woman is the *holy soul*, and for a soul that desireth to be holy, 'tis better to be alone than in good company. In the desert, in the convent, in the monastery, the soul is safe, free from sundry temptations of the world; and so it belongs to a Christian soul, not only to run from bad companies, but to quit the best company in the world and retire into the desert of a convent, or monastery, if that soul desireth to be *holy* and *pure*. This was his proof; and if he had not been my master, I would have been bold to make some reflections upon it: But the respect of a disciple, beloved by him, is enough to make me silent, and leave to the reader the satisfaction of reflecting in his own way, to which I heartily submit.

These, I say, are the advices the Confessors give to the fathers of families, who, glad of lessening the expences of the house, and of seeing their children provided for, do send them into the desert place of a convent, which is really in the middle of the world. Now observe, that it is twenty to one, that their heir dieth before he marrieth and have children; so the estate and every thing else falls to the second, who is a professed Fryar, or Nun, and as they cannot use the expression of *meum*, or *tuum*, all goes that way to the community. And this is the reason, why many families are extinguished and their names quite out of memory; the convent so crowded, the kingdom so thin of people: And the Fryars, Nuns and Monasteries so rich.

Fourthly. I say, that the Confessors, Priests, and especially Fryars, make good this saying among the common people: *Fryle, o fraude es todo uno:* i. e. Fryar or fraud is the same thing; for they not only defraud whole families, but make use of barbarious, inhuman means to get the estates of many rich persons.

The Marquis of *Arino* had one only daughter, and his

his second brother was an *Augustian* Fryar, under whose care the Marquis left his daughter when he died. She was fifteen years of age, rich and handsome. Her uncle and executer was at that time doctor and professor of divinity in the university, and prior of the convent, and could not personally take care of his niece and her family; so he desired one of her aunts to go and live with her, and sent another Fryar to be like a steward and overseer of the house. The uncle was a good honest man and mighty religious. He minded more his office of a prior, his study and exercises of devotion, than the riches, pomp, magnificence, and vanity of the world; so, seeing that the discharge of his duty and that of an executer of his niece were inconsistent together, he did resolve to marry her. Which he did to the Baron *Suelves*, a young, handsome, healthy, rich gentleman: But he died seven months after his marriage, so the good uncle was again at the same trouble and care of his niece, who was left a widow but not with child. After the year of her mourning was expired, she was married to the great president of the council, who was afterwards great chancellor of the kingdom, but he died, leaving no children. The first and second husband left all their estates to her; and she was reckoned to have eighty thousand pistoles in yearly rent and goods. A year after, Don *Pedro Carillo* brigadier-general, and general governor of the kingdom married her, but has no children by her. I left both the governor and the lady alive, when I quitted the country. Now I come to the point. It was specified in all the matches between the gentlemen and the lady, that if they had no issue by her, all her estate and goods should fall to the uncle as a second brother of her father; and so *ex necessitate* the convent should be for ever the only enjoyer of it. It was found out, but too late, that the Fryar steward, before she was first married, had given her a dose to make her a barren woman; and though no body did believe that the uncle had any hand in it, (so great an opinion the world and the lady's husband had of him) every body did suspect at first the Fryar steward, and so it was confirmed at last by his own confession; for being at the point of death, he owned the fact publicly and his design in it.

Another instance. A lady of the first rank, of eighteen years of age, the only heiress of a considerable estate, was kept by her parents at a distance from all sorts of company, except only that of the Confessor of the family, who was a learned and devout man: But as these Reverends have always a Father companion to assist them at home and abroad, many times the mischief is contrived and effected unknown to the Confessor, by his wicked companion; so it happened in this instance. The fame of the wonderful beauty of this young lady was spread so far abroad, that the King and Queen being in the city for eight months together, and not seeing the celebrated beauty at their court, her Majesty asked her father one day, whether he had any children? And when he answered, that he had only one daughter, he was desired by the Queen to bring her along with him to court, the next day, for she had a great desire to see her beauty so admired at home and abroad. The father could not refuse it, and so the next day the lady did appear at court, and was so much admired that a grandee (who had then the command of the army, though not of his own passions) said, this is the first time I see the sun among the stars. The grandee began to covet that inestimable jewel, and his heart burning in the agreeable flame of her eyes, he went to see her father, but could not see the daughter. At last (all his endeavours being in vain, for he was married) he sent for the Confessor's companion, whose interest and mediation he got by money and fair promises of raising him to an ecclesiastical dignity: So by that means he sent a letter to the lady, who read it, and in very few days he got her consent to disguise himself and come to see her along with the Father companion; so one evening

evening in the dark, putting on a Fryar's habit, he went to her chamber, where he was always in company with the companion Fryar, who by crafty persuasions made the lady understand, that if she did not consent to every thing that the grandee should desire, her life and reputation were lost, &c. In the same disguise they saw one another several times to the grandee's satisfaction, and her hearty grief and vexation.

But the court being gone, the young lady began to suspect some public proof of her intrigue, till then secret, and consulting the Father companion upon it, he did what he could to prevent it, but in vain. The misfortune was suspected, and owned by her to her parents. The father died of very grief in eight days time: And the mother went into the country with her daughter, till she was free from her disease, and afterward both ladies, mother and daughter, retired into a monastery, where I knew and conversed several times with them. The gentleman had made his will long before, by which the convent was to get the estate, in case that the lady should die without children; and as she had taken the habit of a Nun, and professed the vows of religion, the prior was so ambitious, that he asked the estate, alledging, that she, being a professed Nun, could not have children; to which the lady replied, that she was obliged to obey her father's will, by which she was mistress of the estate during her life; adding that it was better for the Father prior not to insist on his demand, for she was ruined in her reputation by the wickedness of one of his Fryars, and that she, if prest, would shew her own child, who was the only heir of her Father's estate. But the prior, deaf to her threatnings, did carry on his pretension, and by an agreement (not to make the thing more public than it was, for very few knew the true story) the prior got the estate, obliging the convent to give the lady and her mother, during their lives, 400 pistoles every year, the whole estate being 5000 yearly rent.

K

I could give several more instances of this nature to convince that the Confessors, Priests and Fryars, are the fundamental, original cause of almost all the misdoings, and mischiefs that happen in the families: By the instances already given, every body may easily know the secret practices of some of the Romish Priests, which are an abomination to the Lord, especially in the holy tribunal of confession. So I may conclude and dismiss this first chapter, saying, that the confession is the *mint* of Fryars and Priests, the sins of the penitents the *metals*, the absolution the *coin* of money, and the Confessors the keepers of it.

Now, the reader may draw from these accounts as many inferences as he pleases, till, God willing, I furnish him with new arguments, and instances, of their evil practices in the second part of this work.

PART. II.

This is a true copy of the Pope's Bull out of Spanish, *in the translation of which into* English *I am tied up to the letter, almost word for word, and this is to prevent (as to this point) all calumny and objection, which may be made against it, by some critic among the Roman-Catholics.*

MDCC,XVIII.

BULL of the holy *cruzade*, granted by the holiness of our most holy Father *Clement* the XIth. to the kingdoms of *Spain*, and the isles to them pertaining, in favour to all them, that should help and serve the King Dn. *Philip* V. our lord, in the war and expences of it, which he doth make against the enemies of our Catholic faith, with great indulgences and pardons, for the year one thousand, seven hundred and eighteen.

The prophet *Joel*, sorry for the damages, which the sons of *Israel* did endure by the invasion of the *Chaldeans*

deans armies (zealous for and desirous of their defence, after having recommended to them the observance of the law) calling the soldiers to the war, saith: That he saw, for the comfort of all, a mistical spring come out from God and his house, which did water and wash away the sins of that people. Chap. 3. v. 18.

SEEING then, our most holy Father *Clement* XIth. (who at this day doth rule, and govern the holy apostolical see, for the zeal of the Catholic King of the *Spains*, Dn. *Philip* the Vth. for the defence of our holy faith, and that for that purpose gathereth together, and maintaineth his armies against all the enemies of Christianity, to help him in this holy enterprize, doth grant him this Bull, by which his holiness openeth the springs of the blood of Christ, and the treasure of his inestimable merits; and with it encourageth all the Christians to the assistance of this undertaking. For this purpose, and that they might enjoy this benefit, he orders to be published the following indulgencies, graces, and faculties, or privileges.

I. His holiness doth grant to all the true Christians of the said kingdoms and dominions, dwellers, settled, and inhabitants in them, and to all comers to them, or should be found in them; who (moved with the zeal of promoting the holy Catholic faith) should go, personally and upon their own expences, to the war in the army, and with the forces, which his Majesty sendeth, for the time of one year to fight against the *Turks*, and other *infidels*, or to do any other service, as, to help personally in the same army, continuing in it the whole year: To all these his holiness doth grant a free and full indulgence, and pardon of all their sins (if they have a perfect contrition, or, if they confess them by mouth, and if they cannot, if they have a hearty desire of it) which hath been used to be granted to them that go to the conquest of the holy land, and in the year of *Jubilee*: And declares, that all they, that should die

before

before the end of the expedition, or in the way, as they are going to the army before the expedition, should likewise enjoy and obtain the said pardon and indulgence.

He granteth also the same to them, who (though they do not go personally) should send another upon their own expences in this manner, viz. If he that sends another is a Cardinal, Primate, Patriarch, Archbishop, Bishop, son of a King, Prince, Duke, Marquis, or Earl, then he must send as many as he can possibly send, till ten; and if he cannot send ten, he must send at least four soldiers. All other persons, of whatever condition soever they be, must send one; and if they cannot send one, in such a case, two or three, or four, may join and contribute, every one according to his abilities, and send one soldier.

II. *Item.* The chapters, * all churches, monasteries of Fryars, and Nuns, without excepting *Mendicant* orders, if ten, with the consent of the chapter or community, do join to send one soldier, they do enjoy the said indulgence; and not they only, but the person too, sent by them, if he be poor.

III. *Item.* The secular priests, who, with the consent of their Diocesan and the Fryars of their superiors, should preach the word of God in the said army, or should perform any other ecclesiastical and pious office (which is declared to be lawful for them, without incurring irregularity) are empowered to serve their benefices, by meet and fit tenants, having not the cure of souls; for if they have, they cannot without his holiness's consent. And it is declared, that the soldiers employed in this war are not obliged to fast the days appointed and commanded by the church, and which they should be obliged to fast on, if they were not in the war.

IV. *Item.* His holiness grants (not only to the soldiers, but to all them too, who, (though they should not go) should encourage this holy work with the charity

rity undermentioned) all the indulgencies, graces, and privileges in this Bull contained. and this for a whole year, reckoning from the publishing of it in any place whatsoever, viz. that (yet, in time of apostolical, or ordinary *interdictum*, i. e. suspension of all ecclesiastical and divine service) they may hear Mass either in the churches and monasteries, or in the private oratories marked and visited by the Diocesan ; and if they were priests, to say Mass and other divine offices ; or if they were not, to make others to celebrate Mass before them, their familiar friends, and relations, to receive the holy sacrament of the Lord's supper and the other sacraments, except on *Easter Sunday*, provided, that they have not given occasion for the said *interdictum*, nor hindered the taking of it: Provided likewise, that every time they make use of such oratory, they should, according to their devotion, pray for union and concord among all Christian princes, the rooting out of heresies, and victory over the *infidels*.

V. *Item*. His holiness granteth, that in time of *interdictum* their corpse may be buried in sacred ground, with a moderate funeral pomp.

VI. *Item*. He grants to all, that should take this Bull, that during the year, by the counsel of both spiritual and corporal physicians, they may eat flesh in *Lent*, and several other days in which it is prohibited : And likewise that they may freely eat eggs and things with milk ; and that all these, who should eat no flesh, (keeping the form of the ecclesiastical fast) do fulfil the precept of fasting : And in this privilege of eating eggs, &c. are not comprised the * Patriarchs, Primates, Archbishops, Bishops, nor other inferior Prelates, nor any person whatsoever of the regulars, nor of the secular priests (the days only of *Lent*) notwithstanding from the mentioned persons, we except all those that are 60 years of age, and all the knights of the military orders, who freely may eat eggs, &c. and enjoy the said privilege.

VII.

VII. *Item.* The above-named, that should not go, nor send any soldier to this holy war, out of their own substance (if they should help to it, keeping a fast for devotion's sake, in some days, which are of no precept, and praying and imploring the help of God, for the victory against the *infidels*, and his grace, for the union among the Christian princes) as many times as they should do it, during the year, so many times it is granted them, and graciously forgiven fifteen years, and fifteen *quarantains* of pardon, and all the penances imposed on them, and in whatever manner due; also that they be partakers of all the prayers, alms and pilgrimages of *Jerusalem*, and of all the good works which should be done in the universal militant church, and in each of its members.

VIII. *Item.* To all those, who in the days of *Lent* and other days of the year, in which * Estations are at *Rome*, should visit five churches, or five altars, and if there is not five churches or five altars, five times should visit one church, or one altar, praying for the victory, and union above-mentioned, his holiness granteth that they should enjoy and obtain the indulgences and pardons, which all those do enjoy and obtain, that personally visit the churches of the city of *Rome*, and without the walls of it, as well as if they did visit personally the said churches.

IX. *Item.* To the intent, that the same persons with more purity, and cleanness of their consciences, might pray, his holiness grants, that they might chuse for their Confessor any secular or regular priest licensed by the Diocesan, to whom power is granted, to absolve them of all sins and censures whatsoever (though they be reserved to the apostolical see, and specified in the Bull of the Lord's supper, except of the crime of heresy) and that they should enjoy free and full indulgence and pardon of them all. But of the sins not reserved to the apostolical see, they may be absolved *toties quoties*, i. e. as many times as they do confess them, and perform salutary penance: And if to be absolved, there be need of restitution, they might make it themselves, or by their heirs, if they have an impediment to make it themselves. Likewise the said Confessor shall have power to communicate or change any vow whatsoever, though made with an oath, (excepting the vow of chastity, religion, and beyond seas) but this is, upon giving for charity what they should think fit, for the benefit of the holy *Cruzada*.

X. *Item*. That if, during the said year they should happen, by sudden death or by the absence of their Confessor, to die without confessing their sins; if they die hearty penitents; and in the time appointed by the church, had confessed and have not been negligent nor careless in confidence of this grace, it is granted, that they should obtain the said free and full indulgence and pardon of all their sins; and their corpse might be buried in ecclesiastical burying place (if they did not die excommunicated) notwithstanding the *interdictum*.

IX. Likewise his holiness hath granted by his particular brief, to all the faithful Christians, that take the Bull twice a year, that they might once more, during their lives, and once more at the point of death (besides what is said above) be absolved of all the sins, crimes, excesses of what nature soever, censures, sentences of excommunication, though comprised in the Bull of the Lord's supper, and though the absolution of them be reserved to his holiness, (except the crime and offence of heresy) and that they might twice more enjoy all the graces, indulgencies, faculties and pardons granted in this Bull.

XII. And his holiness gives power and authority to us Don *Francis Anthony Ramirez de la Piscina*, Archdeacon of *Alcarraz*, prebendary and canon of the holy church of *Toledo*, primate of the *Spain*'s, of his Majesty's council, apostolic, general commissary of the holy *cruzada*, and all other graces in all the kingdoms, and dominions of *Spain*, to suspend (during the year of the publishing

publishing of this Bull) all the graces, indulgences, and faculties, granted to the said kingdoms, dominions, isles, provinces, to whatever churches, monasteries, hospitals, brotherhoods, pious places, and to particular persons, though the granting of them did contain words contrary to this suspension.

XIII. Likewise he gives us power to reinforce and make good again the same graces and faculties, and all others whatsoever; and he gives us and our deputies power to suspend the *interdictum* in whatever place this Bull should be preached; and likewise to fix and determine the quantum of the contribution, the people is to give for this Bull, according to the abilities and quality of persons.

XIV. And we the said apostolic general commissary of the holy *cruzada* (in favour of this holy Bull, by the apostolical authority granted to us, and that so holy a work do not cease nor be hindered by any other indulgence) do suspend, during the year, all the graces, indulgences and faculties, of this or any other kind, granted by his holiness, or by other Popes his predecessors, or by the holy apostolical see, or by his authority, to all the kingdoms of his Majesty, to all churches, monasteries, hospitals and other pious places, universities, brotherhoods and secular persons; though the said graces and faculties be in favour of the building of St. *Peter*'s church at *Rome*, or of any other *Cruzada*, tho' all and every one of them should contain words contrary to this suspension: So that, during the year, no person shall obtain, or enjoy any other graces, indulgences or faculties whatsoever, nor can be published, except only the privileges granted to the superiors of the *Mendicant* orders, as to their Fryars.

XV. And in favour of this Bull, and by the said apostolical authority we declare, that all those that would take this Bull, might obtain, and enjoy all the graces, faculties and indulgences, *Jubilees* and pardons, which have been granted by our most holy Father *Paul*

the

the *5th*. and *Urbanus* the *8th*. and by other Popes of happy memory, and by the holy apostolical see, or by its authority, mentioned and comprised in the said suspension; and which, by the apostolical commission, we reinforce and make good again; and by the same authority do suspend the *interdictum* for eight days before and after the publishing this Bull, in any place whatsoever (as it is contained in his Holiness's brief:) And we command that every body, that would take this Bull, be obliged to keep by him the same which is here printed, signed and sealed with our name and seal, and that otherwise they cannot obtain, nor enjoy the benefit of the said Bull.

XVI. And, whereas you *(Peter de Zuloaga)* have given two *reales de plata*, which is the charity fixed by us, and have taken this Bull, and your name is written in it, we do declare, that you have already obtained, and are granted the said indulgences, and that you may enjoy, and make use of them in the above-mentioned form. Given at *Madrid*, the *18th* day of *March*, one thousand, seven hundred and eighteen.

Form of absolution, which by virtue of this Bull may be given to all those that take the Bull once in their lives time, and once upon the point of death.

*M*ISEREATUR *tui Omnipotens Deus, &c.*
By the authority of God and his holy apostles St. *Peter* and St. *Paul*, and of our most holy Father (*N.*) to you especially granted and to me committed, I absolve you from all censure of the greater, or lesser excommunication, suspension, *interdictum*, and from all other censures and pains, or punishments, which they have incurred and deserved, though the absolution of them be reserved to the apostolical see, (as by the same is granted to you.) And I bring you again into the union and communion of the faithful Chris-

L   tians:

tians: And also I absolve you from all the sins, crimes and excesses, which you have now here confessed, and and from those, which you would confess, if you did remember them, though they be so exceeding great, that the absolution of them be reserved to the apostolical see; and I do grant you free and full indulgence and pardon of all your sins now and whenever confessed, forgotten and out of your mind, and of all the pains and punishments, which you were obliged to endure for them in Purgatory. In the name of the Father, of the Son, and of the holy Ghost. *Amen.*

BRIEF, or sum of the estations and indulgences of Rome, *which his Holiness grants to all those that would take and fulfil the contents of this Bull.*

The first day	In St. *Sabine*, free and full indulgence	
Thursday	in St. *George*	the same
Friday	in St. *John* and St. *Paul*	the same
Saturday	in St. *Criffon*	the same
First Sunday in *Lent*,	in St. *John*, St. *Paul*	the same
Monday	in St. *Peter* ad *Vincula*	the same
Tuesday	in St. *Anastasie*	the same

* And this day every body takes a soul out of Purgatory.

Wednesday the greater	in St. *Mary* free and full indulgence	
Thursday	in St. *Laurence Panispema*	the same
Friday	in the saints apostles	the same
Saturday	in St. *Peter*	the same
Second Sunday in *Lent*	in St. *Mary* of *Navicula*, and St. *Mary* the greater	the same
Monday	in St. *Clement*	the same
Tuesday	in St. *Balbine*	the same
Wednesday	in St. *Cicile*	the same
Thursday	in St. *Mary transtiber*	the same
Friday	in St. *Vidal*	the same
Saturday	in St. *Peter* and St. *Marcelin*	the same

* And

* And this day every body takes one soul out of Purgatory.

Third Sunday in *Lent* in St. *Laurence extra Muros*   free and full indulgence.

* And this day every body takes one soul out of Purgatory.

Monday   in St. *Mark*   free and full indulgence.
Tuesday   in St. *Potenciane*   the same
Wednesday in St. *Sixte*   the same
Thursday   in St. *Cosme*, and St. *Damian*, the image of our lady of *Populi & Pacis* is shown   the same
Friday   in St. *Laurence* in *Lucina*   the same
Saturday   in St. *Susane* and St. *Mary* of the angels   the same

Fourth Sunday in *Lent* in St. *Crosse* of *Jerusalem*   the same

* This day every body takes one soul out of Purgatory.

Monday in the 4 crowned free and full indulgences.
Tuesday in St. *Laurence* in *Damascus*   the same
Wednesday in St. *Peter*   the same
Thursday in St. *Silvastre* and in St. *Mary* in the mountains   the same
Friday in St. *Eusebe*   the same
Saturday in St. *Nicholas* in prison   the same

Fifth Sunday in *Lent* in St. *Peter*   the same
Monday in St. *Crissogne*   the same
Tuesday in St. *Quirce*   the same
Wednesday in St. *Marcelle*   the same
Thursday in St. *Appollinarius*   the same
Friday in St. *Estephan*   the same

* This day every body takes one soul out of Purgatory

Saturday in St. *John ante Portam Latinam*   free and full indulgence.

* And this day every one takes a soul out of Purgatory

Sixth

Sixth Sunday in *Lent* in St. *John de Leteran*   free and full indulgence.
Monday   in St. *Praxedis*   the same
Tuesday   in St. *Priske*   the same
Wednesday   in St. *Mary* the greater   the same
Thursday   in St. *John de Leteran*   the same
Friday   in St. *Crosse* of *Jerusalem* and in St. *Mary* of the angels   the same
Saturday   in St. *John de Leteran*   the same
Easter Sunday   in St. *Mary* the greater   the same
Monday   in St. *Peter*   the same
Tuesday   in St. *Paul*   the same
Wednesday   in St. *Laurence extra muros*   the same
* This day every body takes a soul out of Purgatory.
Thursday   in the saints apostles   free and full indulgence,
Friday   in St. *Mary Rotunda*   the same
Saturday   in St. *John de Leteran*   the same
Sunday after *Easter* in St. *Pancracy*   the same

E S T A T I O N S after E A S T E R.

In the greater Litanies: St. *Mark's* day; in St. *Peter*   the same
Ascension-day   in St. *Peter*   the same
Whitsunday   in St. *John de Leteran*   the same
Monday   in St. *Peter*   the same
Tuesday   in St. *Anastasie*   the same
Wednesday   in St. *Mary* the greater   the same
Thursday   in St. *Lanrence extra muros*   the same
* This day every body takes a soul out of Purgatory
Friday   in the *saints apostles*   free and full indulgence,
Saturday   in St. *Peter*   the same

ESTATIONS in ADVENT.

First Sunday in St. *Mary* the greater	the same
And in the same church all the holy days of our *lady*	the same
Second Sunday in St. *Crosse* of *Jerusalem*	the same
The same day St. *Mary* of the angels	the same
Third Sunday in St. *Peter*	the same
Wednesday of the four *rogations*, in St. *Mary* the greater	the same
Friday in the *saints apostles*	the same
Saturday in St. *Peter*	the same
Fourth Sunday in the *saints apostles*	the same

CHRISTMAS-NIGHT.

At the first Mass in St. *Mary* the greater, in the *Manger's chapel*	the same
At the second Mass in St. *Anastasie*	the same

CHRISTMAS-DAY.

At the third Mass in St. *Mary* the greater	the same
Monday in St. *Mary* Rotunda	the same
Tuesday in St. *Mary* the greater	the same
The innocent's day, in St. *Paul*	the same
The circumcision of Christ in St. *Mary* Trunstiber	the same
The Epiphany in St. *Peter*	the same
Dominica in Septuag. in St. *Laurence extra muros*	the same
* This day every body takes a soul out of Purgatory	
Dominica in Sexag. in St. *Paul*	free and full indulgence.
Dominica in Quinquag. in St. *Peter*	the same

And because every day of the year, there is estations at *Rome*, with great indulgences, therefore it is granted to all those that take this Bull, the same indulgences

and

and pardons every day which are granted in *Rome*.

Don *Francis Anthony Ramirez*, de la *Piscina*.

❀❀❀❀❀❀❀❀❀❀❀❀

EXPLANATION OF THIS BULL, AND REMARKS UPON IT.

BULL *of* CRUZADE.

A POPE's brief, granting the sign of the cross to those that take it. All that a foreigner can learn in the dictonaries, as to this word, is the above account, therefore I ought to tell you that are foreigners, that the word *cruzada* was a grant of the cross, i. e. that when the King of *Spain* makes war against the *Turks* and *Infidels*, his coat of arms, and the motto of his colours is the cross, by which all the soldiers understand that such a war is an holy war, and that the army of the King, having in its standard the sign of the cross, hath a great advantage over the enemy, for, as they do believe, if they die in such a war, their souls go strait to heaven; and to confirm them in this opinion the Pope grants them in this *Bull*, signed with the sign of the cross, so many indulgences as you have read in it.

Again *cruz*, or cross, is the only distinguishing character of those that follow the colours of *Jesus Christ*, from whence *cruzade* is derived, that is to say, a brief of the indulgencies and privileges of the cross granted to all those that serve in the war for the defence of the Christian faith against all its enemies whatsoever.

This *Bull* is granted by the Pope every year to the King of *Spain*, and all his subjects, by which the King increases his treasure, and the Pope takes no small share of it. The excessive sums of money, which the *Bull* brings in to the King and Pope, every body may easily know by the account I am going to give of it.

It is an inviolable custom in *Spain* every year after *Christmas*, to have this *Bull* published in every city, town and borough, which is always done in the following manner.

The general commissary of the holy *cruzade* most commonly resides at *Madrid*, from whence he sends to his deputies in every kingdom or province the printed *Bulls* they want in their respective jurisdictions. This *Bull* being published at *Madrid* by the general commissary or his deputy, which is always done by a famous preacher, after the gospel is sung in the high Mass, and in a sermon which he preacheth upon this subject: After this is done at *Madrid* (I say) all the deputies of the holy *cruzada* send from the capital city, where they reside, Fryars with a petit commissary to every town and village, to preach and publish the *Bull*. Every preacher hath his own circuit and a certain number of towns and villages to publish it in, and making use of the privileges mentioned in the *Bull*, he in his sermon persuades the people, that no body can be saved that year without it, which they do and say every year again.

The petit commissary, for his trouble, hath half a real of eight, i. e. Two and four pence a day; and the preacher, according to the extent of the circuit, hath twenty or thirty crowns for the whole journey, and both are well entertained in every place.

Every soul from seven years of age and upwards is obliged to take a *Bull*, and pay two reals of plate, i. e. thirteen pence three farthings of this money; and one part out of three of the living persons take two or three, according to their families, and abilities. The regular priests are obliged to take three times every year the *Bull*, for which they pay two reals of plate: In the beginning of *Lent* another, which they call, *Bull of Lacticinios*, i. e. *Bull* to eat eggs, and things of milk, without

out which they cannot. And another in the holy week. For the *Bull* of *Lacticinios* they pay four and nine pence, and the same for the *Bull* of the holy week; the Fryars and Nuns do the same. Now if you consider the number of Ecclesiastics, and Nuns, and all the living souls from seven years of age and upwards, you may easily know what vast sums of money the King gets in his dominions by this yearly brief, of which the third part or better goes to *Rome* one way or other.

Add to this the *Bull* of the dead. This is another sort of *Bull*, for the Pope grants in it pardon of sins, and salvation to them who before they die, or after their death, their relations for them take this *Bull Defunctorum*. The custom of taking this *Bull* is become a law, and a very rigorous law in their church, for no body can be buried, either in the church, or in the churchyard without having this *Bull* upon their breasts, which (as they say) is a token and signal that they were Christians in their lives, and after their death they are in the way of salvation.

So many poor people, either beggers, or strangers, or those that die in the hospitals could not be buried without the help of the well disposed people, who bestow their charities, for the use of taking *Bulls* of the dead, that the poor destitute people might have the benefit of a consecrated burying place. The sum for this *Bull* is two reals of plate, and whatever money is gathered together in the whole year goes to the Pope, or (as they say) to the treasure of the church. Now I leave to every body's consideration, how many persons die a year, in so vast dominions as those of the King of of *Spain*, by which, in this point, the Pope's benefit, or the treasure of the church, may be nearly known.

O stupid, blind, ignorant people! Of what use or benefit is this *Bull* after death? Hear what St. *John* tells you, *Happy are they that die in the Lord*. It is certain that all those that die in the grace of the Lord, heartily penitent, and sorry for their sins, go immediately

ately to enjoy the ravishing pleasures of eternal life; and those that die in sin, go to suffer for ever in the dark place of torment. And this happens to our souls in the very instant of their separation from their bodies. Let every body make use of their natural reason, and read impartially the scripture, and he will find it to be so, or else he will believe it to be so. Then if it is so, they ought to consider, that when they take this *Bull* (which is commonly a little before they carry the corpse into the church) the judgment of God, as to the soul, is over (for in a twinkling of an eye he may lay the charges and pass the sentence) at that time the soul is either in heaven, or in hell. What then doth the *Bull* signify to them? But of this I shall speak in another place. And now I come to the explanation of the *Bull*, and remarks upon it.

This Bull I am speaking of was granted five years ago to the faithful people of *Spain*, by the late Pope, and which a gentleman of the army took accidentally from a matter of a ship out of *Biscay*, whose name is *Peter de Zoloaga*, as it is signed by himself in the same Bull, and may be seen at the publisher's. I have said already that a Bull is every year granted to the King of *Spain*, by the Pope in being, who either for the sake of money, or for fear, doth not scruple at all to grant quite contrary Bulls, to two Kings at the same time reigning in *Spain*: Now I crave leave to vindicate my present saying.

When this present King of *Spain* Philip the Vth. went there and was crowned, both the arms spiritual and temporal, representatives of the whole nation (as in these kingdoms, the house of lords and commons) gave him the oath of fidelity, acknowledging him for their lawful sovereign: And when this was done, Pope *Clement* the XIth did confirm it, nay his Holiness gave him the investiture of *Naples*, which is the sealing up all the titles and rights belonging to a lawful King, and after this he granted him the Bull of *Cruzade*, by which

which he acknowledged him King, and gave him help to defend himself and his dominions against all the enemies of christianity, and all enemies whatsoever. Every body knows that this Pope was for the interests of the house of *Bourbon*, rather than that of *Austria*; and so no wonder, if he did not lose any time in settling the crown and all the right upon *Philip* of *Bourbon*, rather than upon *Charles* the IIId. the present emperor of *Germany*.

This last, thinking that the right to the crown of *Spain* belonged to him, of which I will not talk, begun the war against *Philip*, supported by the Hereticks (as the *Spaniards* call the *English*) and being proclaimed at *Madrid*, and at *Zaragosa*, he applied to the Pope to be confirmed King, and to get both the investiture of *Naples* and the Bull of the holy *Cruzade*. As to the investiture of *Naples* I leave it to the history written upon the late war. But as to the Bull, the Pope granted it to him, giving him all the titles he gave to *Philip*. At the same time there were two Kings, and two Bulls, and one Pope, and one people. The divines met together to examine this point, viz. Whether the same people, having given their oath of fidelity to *Philip*, and taken the Bull granted to him, were obliged to acknowledge *Charles* as a King, and take the Bull granted to him.

The divines for *Philip* were of opinion that the Pope could not annul the oath, nor dispense with the oath taken by the whole nation, and that the people were obliged in conscience not to take any other Bull, than that granted to *Philip*; and their reason was that the Pope was forced by the Imperial army to do it; and that his Holiness did it out of fear; and to prevent the ruin of the church, which then was threatned.

The divines for *Charles* did alledge the Pope's infallibility, and that every Christian is obliged in conscience to follow the last declaration of the Pope, and blindly to obey it, without inquiring into the reasons that did

move

move the Pope to it. And the same dispute was about the presentation of bishops, for there was at the same time a bishoprick vacant, and *Charles* having presented one, and *Philip* another, the Pope confirmed them both, and both of them were consecrated. From this it appears that the Pope makes no scruple at all in granting two Bulls to two Kings at the same time, and to embroil with them the whole nation; which he did not out of fear, nor to prevent the ruin of the church, but out of self interest, and to secure his revenue both ways, and on both sides.

But, reader, be not surprised at this; for this Pope, I am speaking of, was so ambitious, and of so haughty a temper, that he did not care what means he made use of either to please his temper, or to quench the thirst of his ambition. I say, he was of so haughty a temper, that he never suffered his decrees to be contradicted or disputed, though they were against both human and divine laws; to clear this, I will give an account of an instance in a case which happened in his pontificate.

I was in *Lisbon* ten years ago, and a *Spanish* gentleman (whose Surname was *Gonzalez*) came to lodge in the same house where I was for a while before; and as we, after supper, were talking of the Pope's supremacy and power, he told me that he himself was a living witness of the Pope's authority on earth: And asking him, how? He gave me the following account.

I was born in *Granade* (said he) of honest and rich, though not noble parents, who gave me the best education they could in that city. I was not twenty years of age, when my father and mother died, both within the space of six months. They left me all they had in the world, recommending to me in their testament to take care of my sister *Dorothea* and to provide for her. She was the only sister I had, and at that time in the eighteenth year of her age. From our youth we had tenderly loved one another; and upon her account, quitting my studies, I gave myself up to her company,

This

This tender brotherly love produced in my heart at last another sort of love for her; and though I never shewed her my passion, I was a sufferer by it. I was ashamed within myself, to see that I could not master, nor overcome this irregular inclination; and perceiving that the persisting in it would prove the ruin of my soul, and of my sister's too, I firmly resolved to quit the country for a while, to see whether I could dissipate this passion, and banish out of my heart this burning and consuming fire of love; and after having settled my affairs, and put my sister under the care of an aunt, I took my leave of her, who being surprised at this unexpected news, she upon her knees begged me to tell the reason that had moved me to quit the country; and telling her, that I had no reason but only a mind and desire to travel two or three years, and that I begged of her not to marry any person in the world, 'till my return home, I left her, and went to *Rome*. By letters of recommendation, by money, and my careful comportment, I got myself in a little time into the favour and house of Cardinal *A. I.* Two years I spent in in his service at my own expence, and his kindness to me was so exceeding great, that I was not only his companion, but his favourite and confident. All this while, I was so raving and in so deep a melancholy, that his eminence pressed upon me to tell him the reason. I told him that my distemper had no remedy: But he still insisted the more to know my distemper. At last I told him the love I had for my sister, and that it being impossible she should be my wife, my distemper had no remedy. To this he said nothing, but the day following went to the sacred palace and meeting in the Pope's antichamber Cardinal *P. I.* he did ask him whether the Pope could dispense with the natural and divine impediment between brother and sister to be married, and as Cardinal *P. I.* said, that the Pope could not:—My protector began a loud and bitter dispute with him, alledging reasons by which the Pope could do it. The

Pope,

Pope, hearing the noise, came out of his chamber, and asking what was the matter? He was told it, and flying into an uncommon passion, said, the Pope may do every thing, I do dispense with it; and left them with these words. The protector took testimony of the Pope's declaration, and went to the datary, and drew a public instrument of the dispensation, and coming home gave it to me, and said, though I shall be deprived of your good services and company, I am very glad that I serve you in this to your heart's desire, and satisfaction. Take this dispensation, and go whenever you please to marry your sister. I left *Rome*, and came home, and after I rested from the fatigue of so long a journey, I went to present the dispensation to the bishop and to get his license: But he told me, that he could not receive the dispensation, nor give such a license: I acquainted my protector with this, and immediately an excommunication was dispatched against the bishop for having disobeyed the Pope, and commanding him to pay a thousand pistoles for the treasure of the church, and to marry me himself; so I was married by the bishop and at this present time I have five children by my wife and sister.

From these accounts, Christian reader, you may judge of that Pope's temper and ambition, and you may likewise think of the rest as you may see it in the following discourse.

The title, head or direction of this Bull is, To all the faithful Christians, in the kingdoms and dominions of *Spain*, who should help, or serve in the war, which the King makes against *Turks*, *Infidels*, and all the enemies of the holy Catholic faith; or to those that should contribute, and pray for the union among the Christian princes, and for the victory over the enemies of Christianity.

The *Roman Catholics* with the Pope say and firmly believe (I speak for the generality) that no man can be saved out of their communion; and so they reckon enemies

enemies of their faith all those that are of a different opinion: And we may be sure that the Protestants, or Hereticks (as they call them) are their irreconcileable enemies.

They pray publicly for the extirpating of Hereticks, *Turks* and *Infidels* in the Mass; and they do really believe, they are bound in conscience to make use of all sorts of means, let them be never so base, inhuman and barbarous, for the murthering of them. This is the doctrine of the church of *Rome*, which the Priests and Confessors do take care to sow in the hearts of the *Roman Catholics*, and by their advice, the hatred, malice and aversion is raised to a great height against the Hereticks, as you shall know by the following instances.

First, in the last war between *Charles* the 3d. and *Philip* the 5th. the Protestants confederate with *Charles* did suffer very much by the country people. Those encouraged by the Priests and Confessors of *Philip*'s part, thinking that if any Christian could kill an Heretick he should do God service, did murther in private many soldiers both *English* and *Dutch*. I saw, and I do speak now before God and the world, in a town called *Ficentes de Ebro*, several arms and legs out of the ground in the field, and inquiring the reason, why those corpses were buried in the field (a thing indeed not usual there) I was answered, that those were the corpses of some *English* Hereticks, murthered by the patrons, or land-lords, who had killed them to shew their zeal for their religion, and an old maxim among them: *De los Enemigos los menos*: Let us have as few enemies as we can. Fourteen *English* private men were killed the night before in their beds, and buried in the field, and I myself did reckon all of them; and I suppose many others were murthered, whom I did not see, though I heard of it.

The murtherers make no scruple of it, but out of bravery, and zeal for their religion, tell it to the Father Confessor,

Confessor, not as a sin, but as a famous action done by them in favour of their faith. So great is the hatred and aversion the Catholics have against the Protestants and all enemies of their religion. We could confirm the truth of this proposition with the cruelty of the late King of *France*, against the poor *Hugonotes*, whom we call now *Refugees*. This is well known to every body, therefore I leave *Lewis* and his counsellors, where they are in the other world, where it is to be feared, they endure more torments than the banished *Refugees* in this present one. So to conclude what I have to say upon the head or title of this Bull, I may positively affirm that the Pope's design in granting it, is, first, out of interest; secondly, to encourage the common people to make war, and to root up all the people that are not of his communion, or to increase this way, if he can, his revenues, or the treasure of the church.

I come now to the beginning of the Bull, where the Pope or his subdelegate, deputy, or general commissary, doth ground the granting of it in that passage of the prophet *Joel* chap. 3d. v. 18. expressed in these words: That *he saw for the comfort of all, a mystical fountain come out from God in his house* (or as it is in *Spanish* in the original Bull) *from God and from the Lord's house, which did water and wash the sins of that people.*

The reflections which may be made upon this text, I leave to our divines, whose learning I do equally covet and respect: I only say, that in the *Latin* bible I have found the text thus: *Et fons e domo Jehovæ prodibit, qui irrigabit vallem cedrorum Lectissimarum.* And in our *English* translation: *And a fountain shall come forth of the house of the Lord, and shall water the valley of* Shittam. Now I leave the learned man to make his reflections, and I proceed to the application.

Seeing then, our most holy Father (so goes on) *Clement* the XIth. for the zeal of the Catholic King, for the defence of our holy faith, to help him in this holy
enterprize,

enterprize, doth grant him this Bull, by which his Holiness openeth the springs of the blood of Christ, and the treasure of his inestimable merits; and with it encourageth all the Christians to the assistance of this undertaking.

I said before that the Pope grants every year such a Bull as this for the same purpose: So every year he openeth the springs of Christ's blood. O heaven! what is man that thou shouldst magnify him? Or rather, what is this man that he should magnify himself, taking upon him the title of *most holy Father*, and that of *his Holiness?* A man (really a man) for it is certain, that this man, and many others of his predecessors, had had several b———s. This man (I say) to take upon himself the power of opening the springs of Christ, and this every year. Who will not be surprised at his assurance, and at his highest provocation of the Lord and his Christ?

For my part, I really believe, that he openeth the springs of the blood of Christ, and openeth afresh those wounds of our redeemer, not only every year, but every day without ceasing: This I do believe, but not as they believe it; and if their doctrine be true among themselves, by course they must agree with me in this saying, that the Pope doth crucify afresh our Saviour Christ without ceasing.

In the treatise of vices and sins, the *Romish* divines propose a question: *Utrum*, or whether a man that takes upon himself one of God's attributes, be a blasphemous man, and whether such a man by his sins can kill God and Christ, or not? As to the first part of the question, they all do agree, that such a man is a blasphemous man. As to the second part; some are of opinion that such an expression, of *killing God*, has no room in the question: But the greater part of scholastical and moral authors do admit the expression, and say such a man cannot kill God effectively, but that he doth it affectively; that is to say, that willingly taking upon himself an attribute of God, and acting against his laws, he doth affront and offend in the highest degree that supreme Law-giver; and by taking upon himself the office of a high priest, the power of forgiving sins, which only belong to our Saviour Jesus, he affectively offends, and openeth afresh his wounds and the springs of his blood: And if it was possible for us to see him face to face, whom no man living hath seen yet; as we see him through a glass now, we should find his high indignation against such a man: But he must appear before the dreadful tribunal of our God, and be judged by him according to his deeds: He shall have the same judgment with the antichrist, for though we cannot prove by the scripture, that he is the antichrist, notwithstanding we may defy antichrist himself, whoever he be, and whenever he comes, to do worse and wickeder things than the Pope doth. O, what a fearful thing is it to fall into the hands of a living God! Now I come to the articles of the Bull, and first of all.

I. His Holiness grants a free and full indulgence and pardon of all their sins to those who, upon their own expences, go to or serve personally in the war against the enemies of the *Roman* Catholic faith: But this must be understood, if they continue in the army the whole year: So the next year, they are obliged to take this Bull, and to continue in the same service, if they will obtain the same indulgence and pardon, and so on all their life time, for if they quit the service, they cannot enjoy this benefit, therefore for the sake of this imaginary pardon, they do continue in it till they die, for otherwise there is no pardon of sins.

Let us observe another thing in this article. The same indulgence and pardon is granted to those that die in the army, or going to the army before the expedition, or before the end of the year: But this must be understood also, if they do die with perfect contrition of their sins; or if they do confess them by mouth, or if they cannot, if they have a hearty desire to confess them. As to the first condition, *if they die with perfect contrition*, no *Roman* or Protestant divine will deny that God will forgive such a man's sins, and receive him into his everlasting favour; so to such a man, a free and full indulgence and pardon is of no use; for without it, he is sure to obtain God's mercy and forgiveness.

As to the second condition, *or if they do confess them by mouth, or have a hearty desire to do it*: If a man want a hearty repentance, or is not heartily penitent and contrite, what can this condition of confessing by mouth, or having a hearty desire for it, profit such a man's soul? It being certain, that a man, by his open confession, may deceive the Confessor and his own soul, but he cannot deceive God Almighty, who is the only searcher of our hearts: And if the Catholics will say to this, that open confession is a sign of repentance, we may answer them, that among the Protestants it is so, for being not obliged to do it, nor by the laws of God, nor by those of the church, when they do it, it is, in all human probability, a sure sign of repentance: But among the *Roman-Catholics*, this is no argument of repentance, for very often their lips are near the Lord, but their hearts very far off.

How can we suppose that an habitual sinner that, to fulfil the precept of their church, confesses once a year; and after it, the very same day, falls again into the same course of life; how can we presume, I say, that the open confession of such a man is a sign of repentance? And if the *Roman-Catholics* reply to this, that the case of this first article is quite different, being only for those that die in the war with true contrition and repentance, or open confession, or hearty desire of it: I say that in this case, it is the same as in others. For whenever and wherever a man dies truly penitent and heartily sorry for his sin, such a man, without this *Bull* and its indulgences and pardons, is forgiven by God, who hath promised his holy spirit to all those that

ask

ask it; and on the other side, if a man dies without repentance, though he confesseth his sins, he cannot obtain pardon and forgiveness from God, and in such a case the Pope's indulgences and pardons cannot free that man from the punishment his impenitent heart hath deserved.

Observe likewise, that to all those warriors against the enemies of the *Romish faith*, the Pope grants the same indulgences which he grants to those, that go to the conquest of the holy land, in the year of *Jubilee*. The *Roman-Catholics* ought to consider that the greatest favour, we can expect from God Almighty, is only the pardon of our sins, for his grace and everlasting glory do follow after it. Then if the Pope grants them free, full and general pardon of their sins in this *Bull*, what need have they of the pardons and indulgences, granted to those that go to the conquest of the holy land, and in the year of *Jubilee*?

But, because few are acquainted with the nature of such indulgences and graces granted in the year of *Jubilee*, I must crave leave from the learned people, to say what I know in this matter. I will not trouble the public with the catalogue of the Pope's Bulls, but I cannot pass by one article contained in one of these Bulls, which may be found in some libraries of curious gentlemen and learned divines of our church, and especially in the Earl of *Sunderland*'s library, which is directed to the *Roman-Catholics* of *England* in these words: *Fili mei date mihi cordo vestra, et hoc sufficit vobis*: My children give me your hearts, and this is sufficient. So by this, they may swear and curse, steal and murther, and commit most heinous crimes, if they keep their hearts for the Pope; that is enough to be saved. Observe this doctrine, and I leave it to you, reader, whether such an opinion is according to God's will, nay, to natural reason, or not?

The article of the Bull for the year of *Jubilee* doth contain these words: *If any Christian and professor of our*

our Catholic faith, going to the holy land to the war against the Turks, and Infidels, or in the year of Jubilee to our city of Rome, should happen to die in the way, we declare that his soul goes straightway to heaven.

The preachers of the holy *Cruzade*, in their circuits, are careful in specifying in their sermons, all these graces and indulgences, to encourage the people, either to go to the war, or to take more Bulls than one. With this croud of litanies and pardons, the Pope blinds the common people, and increases his treasure.

In this same first article of our present Bull, it is said, that the same graces and indulgences are granted to all those, who, though they do not go personally, should send another upon their own expences; and that if he be a Cardinal, Primate, Patriarch, Archbishop, Bishop, son of a King, Prince, Duke, Marquis, or Earl, he must send ten, or at least four soldiers, and the rest of the people one, or one between ten.

Observe now, that according to the rules of their morality, no man can merit by an involuntary action; because, as they say, he is compelled and forced to it. How can, then, this noble people merit, or obtain such graces and indulgences, when they do not act voluntarily: For if we mind the Pope's expression, he compells and forceth them to send ten soldiers, or at least four: They have no liberty to the contrary, and consequently they cannot merit by it. I wish to God, they would make use of another rule of their morality and of ours too: *Vim vi repellere licet.*

The second article of this Bull.

The Pope compriseth in this command of sending one soldier, chapters, parish churches, convents of Fryars, & monasteries of Nuns, without excepting the *Mendicant* orders: But the Pope in this doth favour the ecclesiastical persons more than the laity, for as to the laity, he says, that three or four may join together and send

send one soldier: And as to the ecclesiastical persons, he enlargeth this to ten persons, that if between them, ten do send one soldier, they all, and the person sent by them, obtain the said graces. I do believe there is a great injustice done to the laity: For these have families to maintain, and the ecclesiastics have not, and the greatest part of the riches are in their hands. This I can aver, that I read in the chronicles of the *Franciscan* order, written by *Fr. Anthony Perez*, of the same order, where, extolling & praising the providence of God upon the *Franciscan* Fryars, he says, that the general of St. *Francis*'s order doth rule and govern continually 600,000 Fryars in Christendom, who having nothing to live upon, God takes care of them, and all are well clothed, and maintained. There are in the *Roman-Catholic* religion 70 different orders, governed by 70 regular generals, who, after six years of command, are made either Bishops or Cardinals. I say this by the by, to let the public know the great number of Priests and Fryars, idle and needless people in that religion; for if in one order only there is 600,000 Fayars, how many shall be found in 70 different orders; I am sure if the Pope would command the 50th part of them to go to this holy war, the laity would be relieved, the King would have a great deal more powerful army, and his dominions would not be so much embroiled with divisions, nor so full of vice and debauchery, as they are now.

The third article.

It is lawful for the Priests and Fryars to go to this war to preach the word of God in it, or serve, or help in it, without incurring irregularity. They do preach, and encourage the soldiers to kill the enemies of their religion, and to make use of whatever means they can for it, for in so doing there is no sin, but a great service done to God.

Out of this war, if a Priest strikes another and there is mutilation, or if he encourage another to revenge or murther, he incurs irregularity, and he cannot perform any ecclesiastical, or divine service, till he is absolved by the Pope, or his deputy: But in the war against the enemies of their religion, nay, out of the war, they do advise them to murther them, as I have said before, and this without incurring irregularity. O blindness of heart! He endeth this article, by excusing the soldiers from fasting when they are in the army, but not when they are out of it; a strange thing, that a man should command more than God. Our Saviour Jesus Christ commands us to fast from sin, not from meat, but of this in another article.

The fourth article.

In this article the Pope compriseth all the people, and puts them upon double charges and expences, for besides the contribution for a soldier, every body must take the Bull if he will obtain the said graces, and must give two reals of plate, i. e. thirteen pence half-penny. This is a bitter and hard thing for the people: But see how the Pope sweetens it. I grant, besides the said graces, to all those that should take this Bull and give the charity undermentioned, that even in the time of suspension of divine and ecclesiastical service, they may hear and say Mass, and other devotions, &c. Charity must be voluntary to be acceptable to God: How then can he call it charity, when the people must pay for the Bull, or some of their goods shall be sold? And not only this, but that their corpse can't be buried in sacred ground without it, as is expressed in the fifth article.

The sixth article.

The Pope doth excuse all that take this Bull not only from fasting, but he gives them license to eat flesh in *Lent* by the consent of both physicians, spiritual and temporal. This is, if a man is sick, he must consult the physician, whether he may eat flesh or not; and if the physician gives his consent, he must ask his Father Confessor's consent too, to eat flesh in *Lent* and other days of ecclesiastical prohibition. Only a stupid man will not find out the trick of this granting, for in the first place, *necessitas caret lege*; necessity knows no law: If a man is sick he is excused by the law of God, nay, by the law of nature from hurtful things, nay, he is obliged in conscience to preserve his health by using all sorts of lawful means. This is a maxim received among the *Romans*, as well as among us. What occasion is there then of the Pope's and both physicians license to do such a thing? Or if there is so great power in the Bull, why doth not the Pope grant them license absolutely, without asking consent of both physicians? We may conclude that such people must be blindly superstitious or deeply ignorant.

But this great privilege must be understood only for the laity, not for the secular, nor regular Priests, except the Cardinals who are not mentioned here, the Knights of the military order, and those that are 60 years of age and above. But the Priests, and Fryars (notwithstanding this express prohibition) if they have a mind, do evade it on pretence of many light distempers, of the assiduity of their studies, or exercise of preaching the *Lent*'s sermons; and by these and other, as they think, weighty reasons, they get a license to eat flesh in *Lent*. So we see, that they will preach to the people obedience to all the commandments of the Pope, and they do disobey them; they preach so, because they have private ends and interests in so doing; but they do not observe them themselves, because they are against their inclinations, and without any profit, and so advising the people to mind them, they do not mind them themselves.

To the same, the Pope grants fifteen years, and fifteen quarantains of pardon, and all the penances not yet performed by them, &c. Observe the ignorance of that people: The Pope grants them fifteen years and fifteen quarantains of pardon by this Bull, and they are so infatuated, that they take it every year; indeed they cannot desire more than the free and general pardon of sins; and if they do obtain it by one Bull, for 15 years and 15 quarantains, what need or occasion have they for a yearly Bull: Perhaps some are so stupid as to think to heap up pardons during this life for the next world, or to leave them to their children and relations: But observe likewise, that to obtain this, they must fast for devotion's sake some days not prohibited by the church. They do really believe, that keeping themselves within the rules of ecclesiastical fasting they merit a great deal: But God knows, for, as they say, the merit is grounded in the mortification of the body, and by this rule, I will convince them, that they cannot merit at all.

For let us know how they do fast? And what, and how they do eat? Now I will give a true account of their fasting in general; the rules which must be observed in a right fasting are these. In the morning it is allowed by all the casuistical authors, to drink whatever a body hath a mind for, and eat an ounce of bread, which they call *parva materia*, a small matter. And as for the drink, they do follow the Pope's declaration concerning chocolate: Give me leave to acquaint you with the case.

When the chocolate begun to be introduced, the *Jesuits* opinion was, that being a great nourishment, it could not be drunk without breaking fast: But the lovers of it proposing the case to the Pope, he ordered to be brought to him all the ingredients of which the chocolate is made, which being accordingly done, the

Pope drank a cup, and decided the dispute, saying, *potus non frangit jejunium:* Liquid doth not break fasting, which declaration is a maxim put into all their *moral sums:* And by it every body may lawfully drink as many cups as he pleases, and eat an ounce of bread, as a small matter in the morning: And by the same rule any body may drink a bottle of wine or two, without breaking his fasting; for liquid doth not break fasting.

At noon they may eat as much as they can of all sorts of things, except flesh: And at night, it is allowed not to sup, but to take something by way of collation: In this point of collation, the Casuists do not agree together; for some say that nobody can lawfully eat but eight ounces of dry and cold things, as bread, walnuts, raisins, cold, fry'd fishes, and the like: Other authors say, that the quantity of this collation must be measured with the constitution of the person who fasts: For if the person is of a strong constitution, tall, and of a good appetite, eight ounces are not enough, and twelve must be allowed to such a man, and 10 of the rest. This is the form of their fasting in general: Though some few religious and devout persons do eat but one meal a day: Nay, some used to fast 24 hours without eating any thing; but this is once in a year, which they call *a fast with the bells,* that is, in the holy week; among other ceremonies, the Roman-catholics do put the consecrated host or wafer in a rich *urna* or box, on *Thursday,* at twelve of the clock in the morning; and they take it out on *Friday* at the same time: These 24 hours every body is in mourning, nay, the altars are vailed, and the monument where they do place the image of J. C. upon the cross, is all covered with black: The bells are not heard all this while; and, as I said, many use to fast with the bells; and they do make use of this expression to signify that they fast 24 hours without eating any thing at all.

From these we may easily know whether their bodies are

are mortified with fasting or not? For how can a man of sense say, that he mortifies his body with fasting, when he drinketh two or three cups of chocolate, with a small toast in the morning, eats as much as he can at dinner, and eight ounces at night: Add to this, that he may sit in company & eat a crust of bread, & drink as many bottles of wine as he will, this is not accounted collation, because liquid doth not break fasting. This is the form of their fasting, and the rules they must observe in it, and this is reckoned a meritorious work, and therefore doing this, they obtain the said indulgences and pardons of this Bull.

Observe likewise, that the Roman-catholics of *Spain* are allowed to eat, in some days, prohibited by the church, and especially *Saturdays*, the following things: The head and pluck of a sheep, a cheevelet of a fowl, and the like; nay, they may boil a leg of mutton, and drink the broth of it. This toleration of eating such things was granted by the Pope to King *Ferdinand*, who being in a warm war against the *Moors*, the soldiers did suffer very much in the days of fasting for want of fish, and other things eatable for such days; and for this reason the Pope did grant him and his army license to eat the above-mentioned things on *Saturdays*, and other days of fasting commanded by the church; and this was in the year 1479. But this toleration only to the army was introduced among the country people, especially in both Old & New *Castilla*, and this custom is become a law among them. But this is not so in other provinces of *Spain*, where the common people have not the liberty of eating such things; among the quality, only those that have a particular dispensation from the Pope for them and their families.

There is an order of Fryars, called *La orden de la victoria*, the order of the victory; whose first founder was St. *Francis de Paula*, and the Fryars are prohibited by the rules, statutes and constitution of the order, to eat flesh; nay, this prohibition stands in force during their lives, as it is among the *Carthusians*, who, though in great sickness, cannot eat any thing of flesh; but this must be understood within the convent's gate; for when they go abroad they may eat any thing without transgressing the statute of the order.

But the pleasantness of their practices will shew the tricks of that religion. As to the *Victorian* Fryars, I knew in *Zaragoza* one Father *Conchillos*, professor of divinity in his convent, learned in their way, but a pleasant companion: He was, by his daily exercise of the public lecture, confined in his convent every day in the afternoon; but as soon as the lecture was over, his thought and care was to divert himself with music, gaming, &c. One evening, having given me an invitation to his room, I went accordingly, and there was nothing wanting of all sorts of recreation, music, cards, comedy, and very good, merry commany: We went to supper, which was composed of nice, delicate, eatable things, both of flesh and fish, and for the desert the best sweetmeats. But observing, at supper, that my good *Conchillos* did use to take a leg of partridge and go to the window, and come again and take a wing of a fowl, and do the same; I asked him whether he had some beggar in the street to whom he threw the leg and wing? No, said he to me: What then do you go with them out of the window? What, said he, I cannot eat flesh within the walls, but the statute of my order doth not forbid me to eat it without the walls; and so, whenever we have a fancy for it, we may eat flesh, putting our heads out of the window. Thus they give a turn to the law, but a turn agreeable to them: And so they do in all their fastings and abstinences from flesh.

As to the *Carthusians*, and their abstinence and fasting, I could say a great deal, but am afraid I should swell this treatise beyond its designed bigness, if I should amuse you with an account of all their ridiculous ways,

ways. This I cannot pass by, for it conduceth very much to the clearing this point of abstinence and fasting. This order's constitution is, first, a continual abstinence from flesh; and this is observed so severely and strictly, that I knew a Fryar, who, being dangerously ill, the physicians did order to apply, upon his head, a young pigeon, opened alive at the breast, which being proposed by the Prior to the whole community, they were of opinion that such a remedy was against the constitution, and therefore not fit to be used any way: That those poor Fryars must die rather than touch any fleshly thing, though it be for the preserving their health.

Secondly. Perpetual silence and confinement is the next precept of St. *Brune*, their founder: That is, That the Fryars cannot go abroad out of the convent, or garden walls, only the Prior and Procurator may go upon business of the community. The rest of the Fryars lives are thus: Each of them have an apartment with a room, bed-chamber, kitchen, cellar, closet to keep fruit in, a garden, with a well, and a place in it for firing. Next to the apartment's door there is a wheel in the wall, which serves to put the victuals in at noon, and at night, and the Fryar turns the wheel, and takes his dinner and supper, and in the morning he puts in the wheel the plates, by which the servant, that carries the victuals, knows they are in good health; and if he finds the victuals again, he acquaints the Father Prior with it, who strait goes to visit them. The Prior hath a Master-Key of all the rooms, for the Fryars are obliged to lock the door on the inside, and to keep the room always shut, except when they go to say Mass in the morning, and to say the canonical hours in the day time; then, if they meet one another, they can say no other words but these: One says, *Brother, we must die*, and the other answers, *We know it*. Only on *Thursday*, between three and four in the afternoon, they meet together for an hour's time, and if it be fair weather,

weather, they go to walk in the garden of the convent, and if not, in the common hall, where they cannot talk of other things, but of the lives of such or such a saint; and when the hour is over, every one goes into his own chamber. So they do observe fasting and silence continually, but, except flesh, they do eat the most exquisite and delicate things in the world; for commonly in one convent there are but twenty Fryars, and there is not one convent of *Carthusians*, which hath not five, six, and many, twenty thousand pistoles of yearly rent.

Such is their fasting from flesh and conversation; but let us know their fasting from sins.

Dr. *Peter Bernes*, secular Priest, belonging to the parish church of the blessed *Mary Magdalene* (as they do call her) being 32 years of age, and dangerously ill, made a vow to the glorious Saint, that if he should recover from that sickness, he would retire into a *Carthusian* convent. He did recover, and accordingly, renouncing his benefice and the world, he took the *Carthusian* habit, in the convent of the *Conception*, three miles from *Zarogoza*. For the space of three years he gave proofs of virtue and singular conformity with the statutes of the order. His strict life was so crouded with disciplines and mortifications, that the Prior gave out, in the city, that he was a saint on earth. I went to see him, with the Father Prior's consent, and indeed I thought there was something extraordinary in his countenance, and in his words; and I had taken him myself for a man ready to work miracles. Many people went to see him, and among the croud a young woman, acquainted with him before he took the habit, who, unknown to the strict Fryars, got into his chamber, and there she was kept by the pious Father eighteen months. In that time the Prior used to visit him in his chamber, but the *Senora* was kept in the bed-chamber, till at last the Prior went one night to consult him upon some business, and hearing a child cry, did afk him what was the matter; and though my friend *Bernes* did endeavour to conceal the cafe, the Prior found it out, and fhe, owning the thing, was turned out with the child, and the Father was confined for ever; and this was his virtue, fafting and abftinence from flefh, &c.

To thofe that either do faft, in the abovefaid manner, or keep fafting for devotion's fake, his Holinefs grants (taking this Bull of *Cruzade*) all the faid graces, pardons and indulgences; and really, if fuch graces were of fome ufe or benefit, the people thus doing, do want them very much; or may be, the Pope knowing thefe practices, doth this out of pity and compaffion for their fouls, without thinking that this Bull is a great encouragement and incitement to fin.

The ninth article.

This article contains, firft, that to pray with more purity, every body taking this Bull may chufe a Confeffor to his own fancy, who is empowered to abfolve all fins, except the crime of *Herefy*, referved to the Pope or apoftolical fee. You muft know, what they do mean by the crime of *Herefy*: *Salazar Irribarren* and *Corella*, treating of the referved fins, do fay, that the crime of herefy is, viz. If I am all alone in my room, and the door being locked up, talking by myfelf; I fay, I do not believe in God, or in the Pope of *Rome*, this is *herefy*. They do diftinguifh two forts of herefies; one *interna*, and another *externa*, that is public and fecret. The public herefy, fuch as that I have now told you of, nobody can abfolve but the Pope himfelf. The fecond being only in thought, every body can abfolve, being licenfed by the Bifhop, by the benefit of this Bull. So, whoever pronounces the Pope is not infallible: The *Englifh* or Proteftants may be faved: The Virgin *Mary* is not to be prayed to: The Prieft hath not power to bring down from heaven

ven J. C. with five words: Such an one is a public heretic, and he muſt go to *Rome*, if he deſireth to get abſolution.

Secondly, This article contains, that by the benefit of this Bull, every body may be free from reſtitution, during his own life; and that he may make it by his heirs after his death. O what an unnatural thing is this! What if I take away from my neighbour three hundred pounds, which is all he hath in the world to mantain his family, muſt I be free from this reſtitution, and leave it to my heir's will to make it after my death? Muſt I ſee my neighbour's family ſuffer by it; and can I be free before God of a thing that God, nature and humanity, require of me to do? Indeed this is a diabolical doctrine. Add to this, what I have ſaid of the Bull of compoſition, that is, if you take ſo many Bulls to compound the matter with your Confeſſor, you will be free forever from making reſtitution: But really you ſhall not be free from the eternal puniſhment.

Likewiſe, by the power of this Bull, any Confeſſor may commute any vow, except thoſe of chaſtity, religion and beyond ſeas: But this is upon condition that they ſhould give ſomething for the *Cruzade*. O God, what expreſſion is this! To commute any vow, except thoſe of chaſtity, &c. So, if I make a vow to kill a man, if I promiſe upon oath to rob my neighbour, the Confeſſor may commute me theſe vows, for ſixpence: But if I vow to keep chaſtity, I muſt go to *Rome* to the Pope himſelf? What expreſſion is this! I ſay again, how many millions have vowed chaſtity? If I ſay two millions, I ſhall not lie: And how many of theſe two millions do obſerve it? If I ſay 500, I ſhall not lie: And for all this, we ſee no body go to *Rome* for abſolution.

The Roman-catholics will ſay, that by theſe words, *vow of chaſtity*, muſt be only underſtood abſtaining from marriage; but I will leave it to any man of reaſon, ion, whether the nature of chastity compriseth only that? Or let me ask the Roman-catholics, whether a Priest, who hath made a vow of chastity, that is, never to marry, if he commits the sins of the flesh, will be accounted chaste or not? They will and must say, not. Then, if so many thousands of Priests do live lewdly, breaking the vow of chastity, why do they not go to the Pope for absolution? To this they never can answer me, therefore the Pope, in this Bull, doth blind them, and the Priests do what they please, and only the common people are imposed upon, and suffer by it. God Almighty, by his infinite power, enlighten them all, that so the Priests may be more sincere and the people less darkened.

The tenth article.

The Pope grants the same indulgences to those that should die suddenly, if they die heartily sorry for their sins. Of this I have spoken already, and said, that if a man dies truly penitent he hath no occasion for the Pope's pardon, for his true penitence hath more interest (if I may thus express myself) with God Almighty, than the Pope with all his infallibility. So I proceed to the next, which is

The eleventh article.

In this article the Pope grants, besides the said indulgences, to those that take this Bull, that they may twice more in the same year, be absolved of all their sins, of what nature soever, once more during their lives, and once more at the point of death. This is a bold saying, and full of assurance. O poor, blind people! Where have you your eyes or understanding? Mind, I pray you, for the light of your consciences, this impudent way of deceiving you, and go along with me. The Pope has granted you, in the aforesaid articles,

cles, all you can wish for, and now again, he grants you a nonsensical privilege, viz. that you may twice at the point of death, be absolved of all your sins. Observe, passing by that a simple Priest, who hath not been licensed by the ordinary to hear confessions, upon urgent necessity, i. e. upon the point of death, is allowed by all the Casuistical authors, nay, by the councils, to absolve all sins whatsoever, if there be not present another licensed priest. Again, nobody can get such absolution, as is expressed in this Bull, but at the point of his soul's departing from the body, i. e. when there is no hopes of recovery; and the Confessors are so careful in this point, that sometimes they begin to pronounce the absolution, when a man is alive, and he is dead before they finish the words.

Now, pray tell me, how can a man be twice in such a point? And if he got once as much, as he can't get the second time, what occasion hath he for the second full, free, and plenary indulgence, and absolution of all his sins? I must stop here, for if I was to tell freely my opinion upon this point, some will think I do it out of some private ends; which I never do upon delivering of matters of fact.

The twelfth article.

Here the most holy Father gives his power and authority to the general apostolical Commissary of the *Cruzade*, and all other graces and faculties, to revoke and suspend all the graces and indulgencies granted in this Bull, by his Holiness, during the year of publishing it; and not only to suspend them, upon any restriction or limitation, but absolutely, tho' this, or any other Bull, or brief of indulgences, granted by this or other Popes, did contain words contrary to it, viz. Suppose if *Clement*, or another Pope, should say, I grant to such an one such faculties, and I anathematize all those that should attempt to suspend the said faculties. This last

last expression would be of no force at all, because this Bull specifies the contrary.

So it is a thing very remarkable, that the Pope dispossesseth himself, by this Bull, of all his power and authority, and giveth it to the general apostolical Commissary, insomuch that the apostolical Commissary hath more power than the Pope himself, during the year: And this power and authority is renewed & confirmed to him by his Holiness. And not only he has this power over the Pope, but over all the Popes, and their briefs, in whatsoever time granted to any place, or person whatsoever. For it is in the apostolical Commissary's power to suspend all graces and privileges whatsoever, granted since the first Pope began to grant indulgences, which things are all inconsistent with the independency and supremacy of the holy Father, nay, according to the principles and sentiments of their own authors, but we see, they are consistent with their blindness and ignorance.

The thirteenth article.

This article sheweth us plainly the reason, why the Pope acts thus in the granting of his power to the general apostolical Commissary of the *Cruzade*, for he grants him authority to revoke and suspend all the indulgences here granted by himself and other Popes, but he grants him the same authority to call again the very same indulgences, and to make them good again. And next to this power (observe this) he grants him and his deputies power to fix and settle the price or charity, the people ought to give for the Bull. This is the whole matter, and we may use the *English* saying, *No cure, no pay*, quite reverse, *No pay, no cure*, no indulgence nor pardon of sins. The treasure of the church (being a spiritual gift) cannot be sold for money, without Simony. And if the *Romans* say that the Pope has that power derived from Christ, or given *gratis*

'tis to him, let them mind the words: *Quod gratis accepistes, gratis date.* If the Pope payeth nothing for having such power, if he has it *gratis*, why does he sell it to the faithful? Can a private man, or his deputy put a price on a spiritual thing? O blindness of heart!

The fourteenth article.

In this article the general apostolical Commissary makes use of his power and authority, he says, *In favour of this holy Bull, we do suspend, during the year, all the graces, indulgences, and faculties of this, or any other kind, &c. Though they be in favour of the building of St. Peter's church at Rome. Except only from this suspension the privileges granted to the superiors of the Mendicant orders.* He excepts only from this suspension the privileges of the four *Mendicant* orders, because, the Fryars of those orders, being *Mendicants* or *beggars*, they can be no great hindrance of this project. I ask my countrymen this question: If Dn. *Francis Anthony Ramirez* has such a power, to do and undo, in despite of the Pope, whatever he pleases for a whole year; and this power is renewed to him every year, by a fresh Bull: Of what use is the Pope in *Spain*? And if he has resigned his authority to Don *Ramirez*: Why do they send every year to *Rome* for privileges, dispensations, faculties, Bulls, &c. and throw their money away? If *Ramirez* has power to stop, and make void any concession by the Pope, what need have they for so great trouble and expence? Is not this a great stupidity, and infatuity? Observe the next article.

The fifteenth article.

All these prohibitions and suspensions, aforementioned, are only to oblige the people to take the Bull; for the general apostolical Commissary says: *We declare that*

that all those that take this Bull, do obtain, and enjoy all the graces, and faculties, &c. which have been granted by the Popes Paul *the* 5th. *and* Urbanus *the* 8th. &c. So if a poor man takes no Bull, though he be heartily penitent, there is no pardon for him. I say, there is no pardon for him from the Pope and his Commissary, but there is surely pardon for him from God; and he is in a better way, than all the bigots that take the Bull, thinking to be free by it from all their sins.

Observe also the last words of this article: *We command that every body that takes this Bull, be obliged to keep by him the same, which is here printed, signed and sealed with our name and seal; and that otherwise they cannot obtain, nor enjoy the benefit of the said Bull.* This is a cheat, robbery and roguery; for the design of the general apostolical Commissary is, to oblige them to take another Bull. The custom is, that when they take every year a new Bull, they ought to show the old one, or else they must take two that year. Now let us suppose that all the contents of the Bull are as efficacious as the bigots do believe them to be. A man takes the Bull, pays for it, and performs and fulfilleth the contents of it. Is not this enough to enjoy all the graces, &c? What is the meaning then of commanding to keep the same Bull by them, but a cheat, robbery and roguery? I do not desire better proof of this, than what the Commissary affords me in his following words, by which he contradicts himself. He says, and *whereas you* (speaking with *Peter de Zuloaga,* who was the man that took the Bull which is left at the publishers shop) *have given two reals of plate, and have taken this Bull, and your name is written in it, we declare that you have already obtained and are granted the said indulgences, &c. And that you may enjoy and make use of them, &c.*

If he has already obtained all, of what use may it be to keep the Bull by him? How can the Commissary make these expressions agree together? 1st. *If he doth*

doth not keep the Bull by him, he cannot enjoy the benefit of the Bull. 2d. *As soon as he takes it, he has already obtained all the graces, &c. and enjoys the benefit of the Bull.* These are two quite contrary things. Then the design in the first, is robbery and roguery, and in the second, cheat, fraud and deceit.

Reflect again: *Whereas you have taken the Bull, and payed for it, you have already obtained all the indulgences and pardon of sins.* By this declaration, infallible to the *Romans*, let a man come from committing murther, adultery, sacrilege, &c. if he takes and payeth for the Bull, his sins are already pardoned. Is not this a scandalous presumption? If a man is in a state of sin, and has no repentance in his heart, how can such a man be pardoned at so cheap a rate as two reals of plate? If this was sure and certain, the whole world would embrace their religion, for they then would be sure of their salvation. Again, if they believe this Bull to be true, how can they doubt of their going to heaven immediately after death? For a man whose sins are pardoned, goes straightway to heaven; so if the sins of all men and women (for every body takes the Bull) are pardoned by it, and consequently go to heaven, why do they set up a purgatory? Or why are they afraid of hell?

Let us say, that we may suspect, that this Bull sends more people into hell, than it can save from it; for it is the greatest encouragement to sin in the world. A man says, I may satisfy my lusts and passions, I may commit all wickedness, and yet I am sure to be pardoned of all, by the taking of this Bull for two reals of plate. By the same rule, their consciences cannot be under any remorse nor trouble; for if a man commits a great sin, he goes to confess, he gets absolution, he has by him this Bull, or permission to sin, and his conscience is at perfect ease, insomuch that after he gets absolution, he may go and commit new sins, and go again for absolution.

If we press with these reflections and arguments the *Roman-catholic* Priests, especially those of good sense, they will answer, that they do not believe any such thing; for if a man (say they) doth not repent truly of his sins, he is not pardoned by God, though he be absolved by the Confessor. Well, if it is so, why does the Pope, by his general apostolical Commissary, say, *Whereas you have taken and paid for this Bull, you have already obtained pardon of your sins, &c*? We must come then to say, that the cheat, fraud and deceit is in the Pope, and that Don *Ramirez* is the Pope's instrument to impose so grosly upon the poor *Spaniards*. Let the *Romans* call him *Holy and most Holy Father*, the truth is, that he, affronting God and our Saviour in so high a degree, is in this particular a devilish and most hellish Father.

The form of absolution followeth after the articles, in which you may make as many remarks as you please. For my part, I was full of confusion to remember the ignorance I was in, when I was of that communion. The Confessor grants free and full indulgence and pardon of all sins, and of all the pains and punishments which the penitent was obliged to endure for them in purgatory. By virtue of this absolution then, we may say, no soul goes to purgatory, especially out of the dominions of the King of *Spain*, for as I said, in the beginning of the explanation of the Bull, every living soul, from seven years of age and upwards, is obliged to take the Bull, and consequently, if every soul obtains the grant of being pardoned of all the pains which they were to endure and suffer in purgatory, all go to heaven. Why do the Priests ask Masses, and say them for the relief of the souls in purgatory?

Let us from these proceed to the sum of the estations and indulgences granted to the city of *Rome*, which the Pope grants likewise to all those that take the Bull and fulfil the contents of it.

Estations, in this place, signify the going from one
church

church to another, in remembrance of Christ's being, or remaining so long on Mount *Calvary*, so long in the garden, so long on the cross, so long in the sepulchre.

We call also *estations*, or to walk the estations, to go from the first cross to the Mount *Calvary*, &c. This is a new thing to many of this kingdom, therefore a plain account of that custom among the *Romans* will not be amiss in this place.

There is, in every city, town and village, a Mount *Calvary* out of the gates, in remembrance of the *Calvary* where our Saviour was crucified. There are fourteen crosses placed at a distance one from another. The first cross is out of the gates, and from the first to the second, the *Romans* reckon so many steps or paces, more or less from the second to the third, and so on from one to another of the remaining, till they come to the twelfth cross, which is in the middle of two crosses, which represent two crosses where the two malefactors were crucified on each side of Christ. They walk these twelve estations in remembrance of all the steps and paces our Saviour walked from the gate of the city of *Jerusalem* to Mount *Calvary*, where he was crucified. In the first estation, you will see the image of Jesus, with the cross on his shoulders, in the second, falling down, &c. In the last cross, or last estation of the three crosses, Jesus is represented crucified between two malefactors.

Every *Friday* in the year the devout people walk the estations, and kneel down before every cross, and say so many *pater nosters*, &c. and a prayer for the meditation of what did happen to our Jesus at that distance. When the weather hinders the people to go to the great *Calvary*, they have another in every church, and in the cloisters of the convents, and monasteries, and they walk the estations there. And especially in *Lent*, there is such a crowd of people every *Friday* in the afternoon, that there is scarcely room enough in the high-way for all to kneel down.

On

On good *Friday* in the evening is the great procession, at which almost all the people assist with lanthorns in their hands. The people, both men and women, old and young, go to church in the afternoon: The parish minister drest in a surplice, and a sacerdotal cloak on, and a square black cap on his head, and the rest of the clergy in their surplices, and the reverend Father preacher in his habit. This last begins a short exhortation to the people, recommending to them devotion, humility, and meditation of our Saviour's sufferings; after he has done, the Prior of the fraternity of the blood of Christ ordereth the procession in this manner: First of all, at the head of it, a man in a surplice carrieth the cross of the parish, and two boys on each side with two high lanthorns, immediately after begins the first estation of our Saviour, painted in a standard, which one of the fraternity carrieth, and the brethren of that estation follow him in two lines: And the twelve estations, ordered in the same manner, follow one another. After the estations, there is a man representing J. C. drest in a *Tunica*, or *Nazarene*'s gown, with a crown of thorns on his head, that carrieth on his shoulders a long, heavy cross, and another man representing *Simon* of *Cirene*, behind helps the *Nazarene* to carry the cross. After him the preacher, clergy, and parish minister, and after them all the people, without keeping any form or order. Thus the procession goes out of the church, singing a proper song of the passion of Jesus; and when they come to the first cross of the estations of *Calvary*, the procession stops there, and the preacher makes an exhortation, and tells what our Saviour did suffer till that first step, and making the same exhortations in each of the eleven crosses; when they come at the twelfth, the preacher, on the foot of the cross, which is placed between the two crosses of the malefactors, begins the sermon of the passion and sufferings of Christ, and when he has done, the procession comes back again to the

the church, and there the preacher difmiffes the people with an act of contrition, which the people repeat after him.

These are the eftations of the holy *Calvary:* But befides thefe, there are the eftations of the holy fepulchre; that is, to vifit feven churches, or feven times one church, on holy *Thurfday,* when Jefus is in the monument :— But of thefe things I fhall treat in another place.

Now, by thefe foregoing indulgences, and full pardon of fins, the Pope doth grant to all thofe that take the Bull, and fulfil the contents of it (which are only to pay for it) any body may eafily know a lift of the days in which any one, that vifits the churches, mentioned in it, enjoys at *Rome* all the aforefaid faculties, pardon of fins, and indulgences, and as you may obferve, at the end of the *fummario,* that every day of the year there are, at *Rome,* many indulgences & pardons granted in fome church or other, to all thofe that go to vifit them. So, by the grant of the Pope, in the Bull of *Cruzade,* the fame indulgences and pardons are given, and in the fame day (that is every day of the year) to all thofe that take the Bull. From this any body may draw the fame confequence as before, that a man cannot be afraid, in the *Romifh* church, to go to hell; he may commit every day all villanies in the world, and yet every day, having the Bull, is fure of getting free and full pardon of his fins, and this without the trouble of going to confefs: For if they will take the pains to read the contents of the Bull, with a ferious mind, they will find the truth of what I fay: That without the trouble of confeffing fins, any body obtains full pardon of all the crimes he has committed.

For the general apoftolical Commiffary (who has the Pope's power and authority) fays, that he that takes the Bull, payeth for it, and writes his name in it, *ipfo facto,* i. e. already obtains all the indulgences and pardon of fins, &c. mentioned in the Bull; and he doth not fay, *If he confeffeth,* or *if he is a hearty penitent,* but already, without any limitation, or refervation, *already he enjoyeth all*, and *may make ufe of all the graces*, &c. So, by thefe expreffions, it appears that a man, taking the Bull, paying for it, and writing his name in it, may commit murther and robbery, &c. and yet obtain every day free and full pardon of his fins, without the trouble of confeffing them to a Prieft, who, if covetous, will afk money for abfolution, or money for Maffes, for the relief of the fouls in purgatory.

This I muft own of my country people, that they are kept in fo great ignorance by the Priefts, that I might dare to fay, that not one of a thoufand that takes the Bull, readeth it, but blindly fubmits to what the minifter of the parifh tells him, without further inquiry. This is a furprifing thing to all the Proteftants, and it is now to me, but I cannot give other reafons for their ignorance in point of religion, as for the generality, but their bigotry, and blind faith in what the preachers & Priefts tell them; and, next to this, that it is not allowed to them to read the fcripture, nor books of controverfy about religion.

I come now to the days in which every body takes a foul out of purgatory. Obferve thofe marked with a ftar, and befides them, there is in every convent and parifh church, at leaft, one privileged altar, i. e. any body that fays five times *Pater Nofter*, &c. and five times *Ave Maria*, with *Gloria Patria*, &c. takes a foul out of purgatory, and this at any time, and in any day of the year, not only in *Spain*, by the virtue of the Bull, but in *France, Germany, Italy*, and in all the Roman-catholic countries where they have no Bull of *Cruzade*. From this, I fay, that if there is a purgatory, it muft be an empty place, or that it is impoffible to find there any foul at all, and that the Roman-catholics take every year more fouls out of it, than can go into it:— Which I fhall endeavour to prove by evident arguments, grounded on their principles and belief.

For, firft of all, there is in the Bull nine days in the year

year in which every living person takes a soul out of purgatory, and by this undeniable truth among themselves, it doth appear, that every living person, man, woman or child, from seven years of age and upwards, takes every year nine souls out of purgatory.

Secondly. Every body knoweth the Roman-catholics opinion, that no body can be saved out of their communion; and by this infallible (as they believe) principle, they do not allow any place in purgatory to the souls of Protestants, and other people of other professions; and so only Roman-catholic souls are the proprietors of that place of torment.

Thirdly. It is undeniable, by the *Romans*, that ever since that place of purgatory was built up by the Popes and councils, the Roman-catholics have enjoyed the granting of a privileged altar in every church, that, by their prayers, the souls of their parents or friends may be relieved and delivered out of that place.

Fourthly. That to this granting, the Popes have been so generous, that they have granted, in such days, special privileges to some churches, for all those that should visit them, to take souls out of purgatory.

Fifthly. That all the prayers said before such altars for such a soul in purgatory, if the soul is out of it, when the person says the prayers, those prayers go to the treasure of the church; and by this opinion, undeniable by them, the treasure of the church is well stocked with prayers, and when the Pope has a mind to grant, at once, a million of prayers, he may take a million of souls out of purgatory.

These five principles and observations are uncontestable by any of the Roman-catholics. Now let us compute the number of Roman-catholics that are alive, and the number of the dead every year. I say, compute, that is, suppose a certain number of the living and of the dead every year. And I begin with the kingdom of *Spain*, and its dominions, as the only partakers of the privileges granted in the Bull of *Cruzade*.

First

First. Let us suppose, that in the whole dominions of *Spain*, there are but six millions of living persons; I speak of the Roman-catholics: And that three millions of those catholics die every year; and that all their souls go to purgatory; for though the supposition is disadvantagious to my purpose, I will allow them more than they can expect. In the first place, by reasonable computation, half of the living persons do not die every year: But I suppose this, to make my argument so much the stronger. Secondly. In their opinion, very many of the souls of those that die go to Heaven, and some to Hell, which is contrary to the Bull. By this computation the three millions of people that remain alive, by the Bull, take out of purgatory, seven and twenty millions of souls that very year. For there are nine days, in the Bull fixed, on which every living person takes one soul out of purgatory; if then, only three millions of people die every year, how can the three remaining alive take out twenty-seven millions, it being impossible that there should be more than three millions in purgatory that year. And besides this plain demonstration, and besides the nine days appointed in the Bull, according to their belief, and every day of the year, and, *toties quoties*, they pray at a privileged altar, they take out of purgatory that soul for which they pray, or if that soul is not in purgatory, any other which they have a mind for, or else the prayer goes to the treasure of the church: And so, by this addition, we may say that if, out of three millions of living persons, only half a million of people pray every day, this half million takes out of purgatory, every year, 182 millions and a half of souls. If they scruple this number, let them fix any other living persons, and then multiply nine times more the number of souls delivered out of purgatory every year, by virtue of the nine days mentioned in the Bull; or by the privileged altars, multiply one to 365 souls delivered out of the flames every year, by every living person, as I shall demonstrate more plainly by and by.   As

As for *France, Germany, Italy, Portugal*, and other Roman-catholic countries, as I said before, they have their privileged altars to take a soul out of purgatory, *toties quoties*, a *Roman* says so many *Pater Nosters* and *Ave Marias* before them. And so use the same multiplication to convince them, that there cannot be so many souls in purgatory as they deliver out of it every year, or that purgatory by course, must be an empty place, &c.

If they answer to this strong reason, that we must suppose for certain, that the souls of many millions of people, for many years past, are in purgatory, and that there is stock enough taken out of it every year, if there were ten times more living persons than there are now in the Roman-catholic countries: I say, that the supposition has no room at all, and that it is impossible; for let us begin at the time when purgatory was first found out by the Pope, and let us suppose, **gratis**, that there is such a place, which we deny.

The first year, that that imaginary place was settled among the *Romans*, the very same year the privileged altars were in fashion: The people that were left alive that year, took out all the souls of the persons dead the same year, and more too, for as the new privilege was granted then, every body was more charitable in taking the souls of his relations and friends out of sufferings at so cheap a rate as five *Pater Nosters*, &c. The next year the same, and so on, year by year, till this present time, so that it is impossible to believe that there are a greater number of souls than of persons dead.

I say again, that by these principles, sure among the *Romans*, the *Catholics* only of *Spain*, and all the dominions belonging to it, are enough to deliver out of purgatory all the souls of all the *Catholics* dead from the beginning of the world in Christendom; and if what they believe was certain, it should be certain too, that since the Bull is granted to the *Catholic* Kings and their dominions, which is since the reign of King *Ferdinand*,

the

the *Catholic*, only the *Spaniards* have delivered out of purgatory more souls than persons are dead since the universal flood; for every living person, from that time till this present day, has taken out of purgatory, every year, 365 souls by the privileged altars, and 9 more by virtue of the Bull: Now I leave to the curious reader to make use of the rule of multiplication, and he will find clear demonstrations of my saying. I do not talk now of those innumerable souls that are freed from this place every day of the year by the Masses, leaving this for another place.

Indeed I have searched among the sophistries of the Roman catholics, to see whether I could find some reason or answer to this, & I protest, I could not find any, for as I am sure, they will endeavour to cloud this work with groundless subterfuges and sophistries, I was willing to prevent all sorts of objections, which may be made by them; only one answer, which I may believe they will give me, comes now into my head, and it is this, that as the *Romans* cannot answer any thing contrary to my demonstration, it is to be feared that they will say, that I reason & argue as an ignorant, because I do not know that the souls in purgatory are fruitful beings, that one produces a great many little ones every year, I say, it is to be feared, that being prest, they must come at last to such nonsensical, fantastical, dreaming reasons to answer to this urgent argument. So we may safely conclude, & with a Christian confidence say, that if there is such a place as purgatory, it must be an empty place, or that it is impossible to find there any souls, or that the Roman-catholics take every year more souls out of it, than can go into it; all which, being against the evidence of natural reason, and computation made, it is a dream, fiction, or to say the truth, roguery, robbery and a cheat of the Pope and Priests. As for the Pope (if the report in the public news is true) I must beg leave to except for a while this present Pope, who in his behaviour makes himself the

exception

exception of the rule. I say, for *a while*, for by several instances (as I shall speak to in the second part) many Popes have had a good beginning, and a very bad end. God enlighten him with his holy spirit, that he may bring in all Papist countries to our reformation. And I pray God Almighty, from the bottom of my heart, to give to all the *Romans* such a light as his infinite goodness has been pleased to grant me, and that all my country people, and all those that call themselves Roman catholics, would make the same use of that light that I have endeavoured to make use of myself, to know the corruptions of their church, and to renounce them with as firm and hearty resolution, as I have done myself; and I pray God, who must be my judge, to continue in me the same light, and his grace, that I may live and die in the religion I have embraced, and to give me the desired comfort of my heart, which is to see many of my beloved country people come and enjoy the quietness of mind and conscience I do enjoy, as to this point of religion and way of salvation; and I wish I could prevail with them to read the Bull, which, they believe, is the *sancto sanctorum*, the passport to heaven, and I am sure they would find the contrary, and see that it is only a dream, a dose of opium to lull them asleep, and keep them always ignorant: That God Almighty may grant to them and me too all these things, is my constant prayer to him.

PART.

PART. III.

A practical account of their Masses, privileged Altars, Transubstantiation and Purgatory.

I do comprise all the four heads in one chapter, because there is a near relation between them all, though I shall speak of them separately, and as distinct articles.

ARTICLE I.

Of their Masses.

THE Mass for Priests and Fryars is better, and has greater power and virtue than the loadstone, for this only draws iron, but that allures and gets to them silver, gold, precious stones, and all sorts of fruits of the earth; therefore it is proper to give a description of every thing the Priests do make use of to render the Mass the most magnificent and respectful thing in the world, in the eyes of the people.

The Priest every morning, after he has examined his conscience, and confess'd his sins (which they call *reconciliation*) goes to the vestry and washes his hands, afterwards, he kneels down before an image of a crucifix, which is placed on the draws, where the ornaments are kept, and says several prayers and psalms, written in a book, called *preparatorium*. When the Priest has done, he gets up, and goes to dress himself, all the ornaments being ready upon the draws, which are

are like the table of an altar; then he takes the *Ambito*, which is like an holland handkerchief, and kissing the middle of it, puts it round about his neck, and says a short prayer. After he takes the *Alva*, which is a long surplice with narrow sleeves, laced round about with fine lace, and says another prayer while he puts it on. The clerk is always behind to help him. Then he takes the *Cingulum*, i. e. the *girdle*, & says a prayer; after he takes the *Stola*, which is a long list of silk, with a cross in the middle, and two crosses at the ends of it, and says another prayer while he puts it on his neck, & crosses it before his breast, and tieth it with the ends of the girdle. After he takes the *Manipulum*, i. e. a short list of the same silk, with as many crosses in it, and tieth it on the left arm, saying a prayer. Then he takes the *Casulla*, i. e. a sort of a dress made of three yards of a silk stuff, a yard wide behind, and something narrower before, with an hole in the middle to put his head through it. After he is thus drest, he goes to the corner of the table, and taking the *chalice*, cleans it with a little holland towel, with which the *chalice*'s mouth is covered, after he puts a large Host on the *patena*, i. e. a small silver plate gilt, which serves to cover the *chalice*, and puts on the host a neat piece of fine holland laced all over. Then he covers all with a piece of silk, three quarters of a yard in square. After he examines the *corporales*, i. e. two pieces of fine, well starched holland, with lace round about; the first is three quarters of a yard square, and the second half a yard, and folding them both, puts them in a flat cover, which he puts on the *chalice*, and taking a squared cap, if he is a secular Priest, puts it on his head, and having the *chalice* in his hands, makes a great bow to the crucifix, says a prayer, and goes out of the vestry to the altar, where he designs to say Mass. This is, as to the private Mass. Now before I proceed to the great Mass, which is always sung, it is fit to talk of the riches of their ornaments.

As in the <u>Romish</u> church are <u>several festivals, viz.</u>

those of our Saviour Christ, Christmas, Circumcision, Epiphany, Easter, Ascension, Pentecostes, and Transfiguration: Those of the Holy Cross; those of the blessed Virgin *Mary*; those of the Angels, Apostles, Martyrs, Confessors, Virgins, &c. So there are several sorts of ornaments and of divers colours, white for all the festivals of Jesus Christ, except Pentecostes, in which the ornaments are red; white also, for the festivals of the Virgin *Mary*, Confessors, and Virgins; red for Martyrs; violet colour for Advent and Lent; and black for the Masses of the dead.

The same rule is observed in the fronts of the Altar's table, or *ara altaris*, which are always adorned with hangings of the colour of the day's festivals. In every parish church and convent there are many ornaments of each of the said colours, all of the richest silks, with silver, gold and embroidery. There are many long cloaks or *palia* of all sorts of colours, several dozens of *alvas*, or surplices of the finest holland, with the finest laces round about them, *chalice* of silver, the inside of the cup gilt, many of gold, and many of gold set with diamonds and precious stones. There is one in the cathedral of St. *Salvator*, in the city of *Zaragosa*, which weighs five pounds of gold, set all over with diamonds, and is valued at 15000 crowns, and this is not accounted an extraordinary one.

A possenet of silver gilt all over, to keep the holy water and hysop, with a silver handle, to be used in holy days at church, is an indispensable thing almost in every church; as also two big candlesticks four feet high, for the two *accolits* or *assistants* to the great Mass. In several churches there are two *cirialss*, i. e. big candlesticks five feet high all of silver, which weigh 200 pounds in some churches, and another bigger than these for the blessed candle on Candlemas day. Six other middle silver candlesticks, which serve on the *ara* or altar's table, silver (and in many churches,) gold bottles and plate to keep the water and wine that is used

in

in the Mass, a small silver bell for the same use, an incensary, and stand for the *Missal*, or Mass-book, and another stand of silver two feet high, for the *deacon* and *subdeacon* to read on it the epistle and gospel.

There is also in the great altar the *custodia*, i. e. a figure of a sun and beams made of gold, and many of them set with precious stones to keep in the center of it the great consecrated Host, in the middle of two chrystals: The foot of the *custodia* is made of the same metal; it is kept in a gilt tabernacle, and shewn to the people upon several occasions, as I will mention in another place.

Besides this rich *custodia*, there is a big silver or gold cup kept in the same, or another tabernacle on another altar, which is to keep the small consecrated wafers for the communicants. Before those tabernacles a silver lamp is burning night and day. The altars are adorn'd on several festivals with the silver bodies of several saints, some as big as a man, some half bodies with crowns or mitres set with precious stones.

I could name several churches and convents, where I saw many rarities and abundance of rich ornaments, but this being a thing generally known by the private accounts of many travellers, I shall only give a description of the rarities and riches of the church of the lady *del Pilar*, and that of St. *Salvator*, in the city of *Zaragosa*; because I never met with any book which did mention them, and the reason (as I believe) is, because foreigners do not travel much in *Spain*, for want of good conveniencies on the roads, and for the dismal journey in which they cannot see an house, sometimes in twenty miles, and sometimes in thirty.

In the cathedral church of St. *Salvator* there is forty-five Prebendaries, besides the Dean, Archdeacon, Chanter, and sixty-six Beneficiates, six Priests and a Master, and twelve boys for the music, and sixty clerks and under clerks, and sextons. The church contains thirty chapels, big and small, and the great altar thirty feet high

high & ten broad, all of marble stone, with many bodies of saints of the same, and in the middle of it the transfiguration of our Saviour in the Mount *Tabor*, with the apostles all represented in marble figures. The front of the altar's table is made of solid silver, the frame gilt and adorned with precious stones. In the treasure of the church they keep sixteen bodies of saints of pure silver, among which that of St. *Peter Argues*, (who was a prebendary in the same church, and was murthered by the *Sarracens*) is adorned with rich stones of a great value. Besides these they keep twelve half silver bodies of other saints, and many relicks set with gold and diamonds. Forty-eight silver candlesticks for the altar's table, two big ones, and the third for the blessed candle, three hundred pound weight each: Thirty six small silver candlesticks; and six made of solid gold, for the great festivals. Four possenets of silver, two of solid gold, with the handles of hysops, of the same. Two big crosses, one of silver, the other of gold, ten feet high, to carry before the processions. Ten thousand ounces of silver in plate, part of it gilt, to adorn the two corners of the altar on great festivals, and when the Archbishop officiates, and says the great Mass. Three and thirty silver lamps, of which the smallest is an hundred and fifty pounds weight, and the biggest, which is before the great altar, gilt all over, is six hundred and thirty pounds weight. Abundance of rich ornaments for Priests, of inexpressible value. Eighty-four chalices, twenty of pure gold, and sixty-four of silver, gilt on the inside of the cup; and the rich chalice which only the Archbishop makes use of in his pontifical dress.

All these things are but trifles in comparison with the great *custodia* they make use of to carry the great Host through the streets on the festival of *Corpus Christi*: This was a present made to the cathedral by the Archbishop of *Sevil*, who had been Prebendary of that church before. The circumference of the sun and

beams

beams is as big as the wheel of a coach: At the end of each beam there is a ſtar. The center of the ſun, where the great Hoſt is placed between two cryſtals, ſet with big diamonds; the beams are all of ſolid gold ſet with ſeveral precious ſtones, and in the middle of each ſtar, a rich emerald ſet in gold. The cryſtal with the great Hoſt is fixed in the mouth of the rich chalice, and the chalice on a pedeſtal of ſilver, all gilt over, which is three feet high. The whole *cuſtodia* is five hundred pound weight: And this is placed on a gilt baſe which is carried by twelve Prieſts, as I ſhall tell you in another article. Several goldſmiths have endeavoured to value this piece, but no body could ſet a certain ſum on it. One ſaid that a million of piſtoles was too little. And how the Archbiſhop could gather together ſo many precious ſtones, every body was ſurpriſed at, till we heard that a brother of his Grace died in *Peru*, and left him great ſums of money, and a vaſt quantity of diamonds and precious ſtones.

I come now to ſpeak of the treaſure and rarities of the Lady *del Pilar*. In the church of this lady is the ſame number of prebendaries and beneficiates, muſicians, clerks and ſextons, as in the cathedral church of St. *Salvator*, and as to the ornaments and ſilver plate they are very much the ſame, except only that of the great *cuſtodia*, which is not ſo rich. But as to the chapel of the bleſſed Virgin, there is without compariſon more in it than in the cathedral. I ſhall treat of the image in another chapter. Now, as to her riches, I will give you an account as far as I remember, for it is impoſſible for every thing to be kept in the memory of man.

In the little chapel, where the image is on a pillar, are four angels as big and tall as a man, with a big candleſtick, each of them all made of ſilver gilt. The front of two altars is ſolid ſilver, with gilt frames, ſet with rich ſtones. Before the image there is a lamp (or as they call it) a ſpider of cryſtal, in which twelve

wax

wax candles burn night and day: The several parts of the spider are set with gold and diamonds, which was a present made to the Virgin by Don *John* of *Austria*, who also left her in his last will his own heart, which accordingly was brought to her, and is kept in a gold box set with large diamonds, and which hangs before the image. There is a thick grate round about the little chapel of solid silver: Next to this is another chapel to say Mass in before the image; and the altar-piece of it is all made of silver from the top to the altar's table, which is of jasper stone, and the front of silver, with the frame gilt, set with precious stones. The rich crown of the Virgin is twenty-five pounds weight, set all over with large diamonds, so that no body can see any gold in it, and every body thinks it is all made of diamonds. Besides this rich one, she has six crowns more of pure gold, set with rich diamonds and emeralds, the smallest of which is worth half a million.

The roses of diamonds and other precious stones she has to adorn her mantle are innumerable; for tho' she is drest every day in the colour of the church's festival, and never useth twice the same mantle, which is of the best stuff imbroidered with gold, she has new roses of precious stones every day for three years together, she has three hundred and sixty-five necklaces of pearls and diamonds, and six chains of gold set with diamonds, which are put on her mantle on the great festivals of Christ.

In the room of her treasure are innumerable heads, arms, legs, eyes and hands made of gold and silver, presented to her by the people, which have been cured (as they believe) by miracle through the Virgin's divine power and intercessions. In this second chapel are one hundred and ninety-five silver lamps in three lines one over the other: The lamps of the lowest rank are bigger than those of the second, and these bigger than those of the third. The five lamps facing the image are

are about five hundred pound weight each, the sixty of the same line four hundred pound weight. Those of the second line are two hundred pound weight, and those of the third line, one hundred pound weight. There is the image of the Virgin in the treasure made in the shape of a woman five feet high, all of pure silver, set with precious stones, and a crown of gold set with diamonds, and this image is to be carried in a public procession the days appointed. I will speak of the miraculous image in the following chapter.

I remember that when the Right Honorable Lord *Stanhope*, then General of the *English* forces, was in *Zaragosa*, after the battle, he went to see the treasure of the Lady of *Pilar*, which was shewn to him, and I heard him say these words: *If all the Kings of Europe should gather together all their treasures & precious stones, they could not buy half of the riches of this treasury.* And by this expression of so wise and experienced a man, every body may judge of their value.

After this short account of the ornaments to be used at Mass, and the incomparable treasures of the *Romish* church, I proceed to a description of the great or high Masses, their ceremonies, and of all the motions and gestures the Priests make in the celebration of a Mass.

Besides the Priest, there must be a deacon, subdeacon, two *acoliti*, i. e. two to carry the big candlesticks before the Priest, and one to carry the incensary. The *incenser* helps the Priest when he dresseth himself in the vestry, and the two *acoliti* do help the deacon and subdeacon. When all three are drest, the *incenser* and two *acoliti* in their surplices, and large collars round about their necks, made of the same stuff as that of the Priest's *casulla*, and the deacon and subdeacon's *aalmaticas*, i. e. a sort of *casulla*, with open sleeves, I say, the *incenser* puts fire in the incensary, and the *acoliti* takes the candlesticks with the wax candles lighted, and the subdeacon takes the chalice and corporals, and making a bow to the crucifix in the vestry, they go

out

out into the church to the great altar. There is commonly three steps to go up to the altar, and the Priest and five assistants do kneel down at the first step, then leaving the *incense* and *acoliti* to stay there, the Priest, deacon and subdeacon go up to the altar's table and all kneel down there again. The subdeacon leaveth the chalice on a little table next to the altar's table at the right hand, and then they turn back again to the highest step, and kneeling down again, the Priest, deacon and subdeacon get up, leaving the *incenser* and *acoliti* on their knees, and begin the Mass by a psalm, and after it the Priest says the general confession of sins, to which the deacon and subdeacon answer: *Mesereator tui*, &c. Then they say the general confession themselves, and after it, the Priest absolveth them, and saying another psalm, they go up again to the altar's table, which the Priest kisseth, and he and the two assistants kneel down, and rise again. Then the *incenser* brings the incensary and incense, and the Priest puts in three spoonfuls of it, and taking the incensary from the deacon's hands, he incenses three times the tabernacle of the *Eucharistia*, and goes twice to each side of it, he kneels down then, and the deacon takes up the hem of the Priest's *casulla*, and so goes from the middle of the altar to the right corner, incensing the table and returning from the corner to the middle, then kneels down and gets up, and goes to the left corner, and from the left goes again to the right corner, and giving the incensary to the deacon, he incenses three times the Priest, and gives the incensary to the *incenser*, and this incenses twice the deacon. The assistants always follow the Priest, making the same motions that he doth.

The *incenser* has the *Missal* or Mass-book ready on the altar's table at the right corner, and so the Priest begins the psalm of the Mass: All this while the musicians are singing the beginning of the Mass till *kyrie eicison*; and when they have finished, the Priest sings these three words: *Gloria in elcelsis deo*. And the musicians

musicians sing the rest. While they are singing, the Priest, deacon and subdeacon, making a bow to the tabernacle, go to sit on three rich chairs at the right hand of the *ara* or altar's table; and as soon as the music has ended the *gloria*, they go to the middle of the table, kneel down, and get up, and the Priest kissing the table turns to the people, opening his arms, and says, in *Latin*, *The Lord be with you*, to which and all other expressions the music and the people answer; then turns again his face to the altar, kneels down, gets up, and the assistants doing the same, the Priest goes to the right corner, and says the *collect* for the day, and two or sometimes five or six prayers in commemoration of the saints; and last of all, a prayer for the Pope, King and Bishop of the diocess, against *Hereticks*, *Infidels* and enemies of their religion, or the holy Catholic faith.

Then the subdeacon, taking the book of the epistles, and gospels, goes down to the lowest step, and sings the epistle, which ended, he goes up to the Priest, kisseth his hand, leaves the book of the gospels on the little table, takes the *Missal* or Mass-book, and carrieth it to the left corner. Then the priest goes to the middle, kneels down, kisseth the altar, says a prayer, and goes to say the gospel, while the musick is singing a plasm, which they call *Tractus gradualis*. The gospel ended, the Priest goes again to the middle, kneels down, riseth and kisseth the table, and turns half to the altar and half to the people, and the deacon, giving him the incense-box, he puts in three spoonfuls of it, and blesses the incense: The *incenser* takes it from the deacon, who taking the book of the gospel, kneels down before the Priest and asketh his blessing: The Priest giveth the blessing and the deacon kisses his hand, and then he goes to the left corner and sings the gospel, viz. the left corner, as to the people of the church, but as to the altar, it is the right. While the deacon sings the gospel, the Priest goes to the opposite corner and there

there stands till the gospel is ended: Then the deacon carrieth to him the book open, and the Priest kissing it, goes to the middle of the table and kneeling, rising, kissing the table, the assistants, doing the same, he turns his face to the people, openeth his arms, and says again, *The Lord be with you.* Then he turns again before the altar, and says, *Let us pray.* The music begins the *offertory*, when there is no creed to be sung, for there is no creed in all their festivals.

While the musicians sing the *offertory*, the deacon prepares the chalice, that is, puts the wine in it, and after him, the subdeacon pours in three drops of water and cleaning nicely the mouth of the cup, the deacon gives it to the Priest, who takes it in his hands, and offering it to the eternal, sets it on the clean *corporales*, and covers it with a small piece of fine holland: Then he says a prayer, and putting incense in the incensary, as before, kneels, and then rising, incenses the table, as is said, which done, the subdeacon poureth water on the Priest's fore-fingers, which he washeth and wipeth with a clean towel, and after returns to the middle of the table, and after some prayers, he begins to sing the preface, which ended, he says some other prayers. Before the consecration, he joineth his two hands, and puts them before his face, shuts his eyes, and examines his conscience for two or three minutes; then opening his eyes and arms, says a prayer, and begins the consecration. At this time every body is silent, to hear the words, and when the Priest comes to pronounce them, he says, with a loud voice, in *Latin, Hoc est enim corpus meum.* Then he leaves the consecrated Host on the *ara*, kneels down, and getting up, takes again the Host with his two thumbs and two foremost fingers, and lifts it up, as high as he can, that every body may see it, and leaving it again on the same *ara*, kneels down, and then rising up, takes the chalice, and after he has consecrated the wine, leaves it on the *ara,* and making the same motions and bows, he he lifts it up as he did the Host, and placing it on the *ara*, covereth it, and with the same gestures, he says a prayer in remembrance of all the saints, all parents, relations, friends, and of all the souls in purgatory, but especially of that soul for whom the sacrifice of that Mass is offered to God by Jesus Christ himself. I say, by Jesus Christ himself, for as *Chrysostom* and *Amb.* * say, the Priest, not only representing Christ, but in the act of celebrating and consecrating is the very same Christ himself. Thus it is in the catechism published by decree of the council of *Trent* †

Between this and the sumption, or the taking of the Host, and drinking of the cup, the Priest says some prayers, and sings *Our Father*, in *Latin*, kneeling down several times. When he comes to the communion, he breaks the Host by the middle, leaves one part on the table, and breaketh off the other half, a little piece, and puts it into the cup; this done, he eateth the two half Hosts, and drinketh the wine, and for fear that any small fragments should remain in the cup, the deacon puts in more wine, and the Priest drinks it up, and going to the corner with the chalice, the subdeacon poureth water upon the Priest's two thumbs and foremost fingers, and being well washed, goes to the middle of the table and drinks up the water. Then the deacon takes the cup and wipes it, and putting on every thing, as when they came to the altar, gives it to the subdeacon, who leaves it on the little table near the altar.—— After this is done, the Priest, kneeling and getting up, turning to the people and opening his arms, says, *The Lord*

---

* Hom. 2. in 2d. *Timoth.* and Hom. de prod. *Judæ Amb.* lib. 4 de sacram. C. 4.

† Sed unus etiam, atque idem **Sacerdos** est Christus Dominus: Nam **Ministri** qui Sacrificium faciunt, non suam sed Christi personam accipiunt, cum ejus Corpus and Sanguinem conficiunt, id quod and ipsius Consecrationis Verbis ostenditur, Sacerdos inquit: Hoc est Corpus **meum**, personem videlicet Christi Domini gerens, panis and vidi **Substantiam** in veram ejus Corporis and Sanguinis Substantiam convertit.

Lord be with you, and two or more prayers; and last of all, the gospel of St. *John*, with which he endeth the Mass; so in the same order they went out of the vestry, they return into it again, saying a prayer for the souls in Purgatory. After the Priest is undrest, the *incenser* and *acoliti* kneel down before him, and kiss his right hand: Then they undress themselves, and the Priest goes to the humiliatory to give God thanks for all his benefits.

The same ceremonies, motions and gestures the Priest makes in a private Mass, but not so many in a Mass for the dead. They have proper Masses for the holy Trinity, for Christ, the Virgin *Mary*, Angels, apostles martyrs, confessors, virgins, and for the dead, the ornaments for this last are always black. This is a true description of the ceremonies of the Mass: Now let us give an account of the means the Priests make use of for the promoting of this sacrifice, and increasing their profit.

The custom, or rule for public Masses, which are always sung, is this; the person that goes to the clerk and asks a Mass to be sung, carrieth at least, six wax candles which burn on the altar's table, while the Mass lasts, and a good offering for the Priest, and besides that, must give the charity, which is a crown, and the same for a Mass sung for the dead; but if a person has a mind to have a Mass sung, such or such a day for ever, he must give, or settle upon the chapter or community, a pistole every year, and these are called *settled Masses*, and there are of these Masses in every parish, church and convent, more than the Priests and Fryars can say in a year; for ever since the comedy of the Mass began to be acted on the stage of the church, the bigots of it successively have settled Masses every year; the Priests and Fryars then cannot discharge their conscience, while they do keep the people ignorant of the truth of the matter.

Thus they blind the people: Suppose to be in a
convent

convent 100 Fryars, Priefts, and that in that convent are 200 private and public Maffes fettled every day, the charity of 100 is a manifeft fraud and robbery, for they do receive it, and cannot fay the Maffes. And neverthelefs they accept every day new foundations and fettlements of Maffes; for if the people afk the Dean, or Prior, whether there is vacancy for a Mafs, they will never anfwer no; and this way they increafe the yearly rents continually.

This is to be underftood of the chapter, or community, and I muft fay that the chapters, and parifh churches are not fo hard upon the people, as the convents of Fryars are, though they are not fo rich, as the communities: The reafon is, becaufe a parifh Prieft hath, during his life, his tithes and book-money. But a Prior of a convent commands that community only three years, therefore, while the office lafts, they endeavour to make money of every thing. I knew feveral Priors very rich after their Priorfhip, and how did they get riches, but by blinding and cheating the people, exacting money for Maffes which never were faid, nor fung, nor never will be?

As to the private Priefts and Fryars, and their cheating ways, there is fo much to be faid on them that I cannot, in fo fmall a book as this is, give a full account of all; fo I fhall only tell the moft ufual methods they have to heap up riches by gathering thoufands of Maffes every year.

Obferve firft of all, that if a Prieft is parifh minifter, or Vicar, he has every day of the year certain families, for whofe fouls, or for the fouls of their anceftors, he is to celebrate and offer the facrifice of the Mafs. And if he is a Fryar, he has but one Mafs every week left to him, for fix days he is obliged to fay Mafs for the community: So by this certain rule, a parifh minifter cannot in confcience receive any money for Maffes, when he knoweth that he cannot fay more Maffes, than thofe fettled for every day of the year; and by the fame rule,

rule, a Fryar cannot in conscience receive more money than for 52 Masses every year, and consequently those that receive more are deceivers of the poor ignorant people, robbers of their money, and commit sacrilege in so doing.

And that they take more, than they in justice can, shall appear in several instances. First. I never saw either secular or regular Priest refuse the charity for a Mass, when a Christian soul did ask them to say it; and I knew hundreds of Priests mighty officious in asking Masses from all sorts of people. Secondly, in all families whatsoever, if any one is dangerously sick, there are continually Fryars and Priests waiting till the person dieth, and troubling the chief of the family with petitions for Masses for the soul of the dead; and if he is rich, the custom is, to distribute among all the convents, and parishes 1000, or more Masses to be said the day of the burial: When the Marquiss of St. *Martin* died, his lady distributed 100000 Masses, for which she paid the very same day 5000 pounds sterling, besides 1000 Masses, which she settled upon all the convents and parish churches, to be said every year for ever, which amounts to a 1000 pistoles a year for ever.

Thirdly, The Fryars, most commonly, are rich, and have nothing of their own; (as they say) some are assisted by their parents, but these are very few: They give two thirds of whatever they get to the community; and in some strict orders the Fryars ought to give all to the convent; nevertheless, they are never without money in their pockets, for all sorts of diversions; and it is a general observation, that a Fryar at cards is a resolute man; for as he doth not work to get money, or is sure of getting more if he loseth, he doth not care to put all on one card; therefore gentlemen do not venture to play with them, so they are obliged to play with one another.

I saw several Fryars, who had nothing in the world,
but

but the allowance of their community, and the charity of 52 Masses a year, to venture on one card 50 pistoles: Another to lose 200 pistoles in half an hour's time, and the next day have money enough to play. And this is a thing so well known, that many of our officers that have been in *Spain*, can certify the truth of it, as eye-witnesses.

Now, as to the method they have to pick up money for so many Masses, they do not tell it; but as I never was bound not to discover it, and the discovery of it, I hope, will be very useful to the Roman catholics, though disadvantageous to Priests, and Fryars, I think myself obliged in conscience, to reveal this never revealed secret, for it is for the public good, not only of Protestants, who by this shall know thoroughly the cheats of the *Romish* Priests, but of the Roman-catholics too, who bestow their money for nothing to a people that make use of it to ruin their souls and bodies.

The thing is this, that the Fryars are said to have a privilege from the Pope (I never saw such a privilege myself, though I did all my endeavours to search and find it out) of a *centenaria missa*, i. e. a brief where the Pope grants them the privilege of saying one Mass for an hundred; which privilege is divulged among Priests and Fryars, who keep it in secret among themselves; so that, as they say, one Mass is equivalent to an hundred Masses. I did not question when I was in that communion, that the Pope could do that and more, but I was suspicious of the truth of such a grant. Now observe, that by this brief, every Fryar, having for himself 52 Masses free every year, and one Mass being as good as an hundred, he may get the charity of 5200 Masses, and the least charity for every Mass being two reals of plate: i. e. Fourteen-pence of our money, he may get near 300 pounds a year.

The secular Priests, by this brief of *centenaria missa*, have more Masses, than the private Fryars; for though they have 365 settled Masses to say in a year, they have,

and

and may get the charity of 99 Masses every day, which comes to three millions, six thousand, one hundred, and thirty-five Masses every year. In the convents that have 120 Fryars, and some 400, the Prior having 6 Masses every week from each of his Fryars, by the same rule, the Prior may have millions of millions of Masses.

Hear now, how they do amuse the credulous people. If a gentleman or gentlewoman, or any other person goes to church, and desires one Mass to be said for such or such a soul, and to be present at it, there is always a Fryar ready, from six in the morning, till one, to say Mass. He takes the charity for it, and he goes to say it; which he says for that soul, as I say it now: For till such time, as he gets the charity of an hundred Masses, which is above 5 pound sterling, he will not say his own Mass, or the Mass for him. And so the rest of the Fryars do, and many Priests too: The person that has given the charity and has heard the Mass, goes home fully satisfied that the Mass has been said for him, or to his intention.

As to the communities: If some body dieth, and the executors of the testament go to a Father Prior, and beg of him to say 1000 Masses, he gives them a receipt, whereby the Masses are said already; for he makes them believe, that he has more Masses said already by his Fryars to his own intention, and that out of the number, he applies 1000 for the soul of the dead person; so the executors upon his word, take the receipt of the Masses which they want to shew to the Vicar-General, who is to visit the testament, and see every spiritual thing ordered in it, accomplished accordingly.

This custom of asking money for Masses, is not only among the Fryers, but among the *beatas*, Nuns, and whores too, for a *beata* with an affected air of sanctity, goes up and down to visit the sick, and asks before-hand many Masses from the heads of families,

alledging

alledging that by her prayers & so many Masses, the sick may be recovered, & restored to his former health; but these, if they get money for Masses, they give it to their spiritual Confessors, who say them as the *Beata* ordereth. And according to their custom and belief, there is no harm at all in so doing. The evil is in the Nuns, who get every where abundance of Masses, on pretence they have Priests and Friars of their relations, who want the charity of Masses. And what do they with the money? Every Nun, having a *Devoto* or gallant to serve her, desireth him to say so many Masses for her, and to give her a receipt; he promiseth to do it, but he never doth say the Masses, though he giveth a receipt: So the Nun keeps the money, the Friar is paid by her in an unlawful way, the people are cheated, and the souls in purgatory (if there was such a place) shall remain there forever, for want of relief.

But the worst of all is, that a public, scandalous woman will gather together a number of Masses, on pretence that she has a cousin in such a convent, who wants Masses, i. e. the charity for them. And what use do they make of them? This is an abomination to the Lord. They have many Friars who visit them unlawfully, and pay for it in Masses; so the woman keeps the money in payment of her own and their sins, gets a receipt from the Friars, and these never say the Masses; for how can we believe that such men can offer the holy sacrifice (as they call the Mass) for such an use? And if they do it, which is, in all human probability, impossible, who would not be surprised at these proceedings? Every body indeed.

There is another custom in the church of *Rome*, which brings a great deal of profit to the Priests and Friars, *viz.* the great Masses of brotherhoods, or Fraternities. In every parish church, and especially in every convent of Friars and Nuns, there is a number of these fraternities, i. e. corporations of tradesmen: And every corporation has a saint for their advocate or *patron*,

tron, *viz.* the corporation of shoe-makers has for an advocate St. *Crispin* and *Crispinia*; the butchers St. *Bartholomew*, &c. and so of the rest. There is a Prior of the corporation, who celebrates the day of their advocate with a solemn Mass, music, candles, and, after all, an entertainment for the members of the fraternity, and all the Friars of the community. To this the corporation gives eight dozen of white wax candles to illuminate the altar of their patron, when the solemn Mass is sung, and whatever remains of the candles goes to the convent. The Prior payeth to the community 20 crowns for the solemn Mass, and 10 crowns to the musicians. The day following the corporation gives 3 dozen of yellow candles, and celebrates an anniversary, and have many Masses sung for the relief of their brethren's souls in purgatory; for every Mass they pay a crown: And besides all these, the corporation has a Mass settled every Friday, which is to be sung for the relief of the brethren's souls, for which, and candles, the convent receiveth 6 crowns every Friday. There is not one church nor convent without two or three of these corporations every week; for there are saints enough in their church for it; and by these advocates of the Friars, rather than of the members of the corporation, every body may form a right judgment of the riches the Priests and Friars get by these means.

One thing I cannot pass by, though it has no relation with the main subject of the Mass; and this is, that after the solemn Mass is finished, the Prior of the corporation, with his brethren, and the Prior of the convent, with his Friars, go all together to the *Refectory*, or common-hall, to dinner. There they make rare demonstrations of joy, in honor of the advocate of that corporation. The Prior of the convent makes a short speech before dinner, recommending to them to eat and drink heartily, for after they have paid all the honor and reverence to their advocate that is due, they ought to eat and drink and be merry: So they drink till they are happy, though not drunk.

I heard a pleasant story, reported in town, from a faithful person, who assured me he saw, himself, a Friar come out of the *Refectory* at 8 at night, and as he came out of the convent's gate, the moon shining that night, & the shadow of the house being in the middle of the street, the merry Friar thinking that the light of the moon, in the other half part of the street was water, he took off his shoes and stockings, and so did walk till he reached the shadow; and being asked, by my friend, the meaning of such extravagant folly, the Friar cried out, *A miracle! A miracle!* The gentleman thought that the Friar was mad; but he cried the more, *A miracle, A miracle. Where is the miracle?* (the people that came to the windows asked him); *I came this minute through this river* (said he) *and I did not wet the soles of my feet*; and then he desired the neighbours to come and be witnesses of the miracle. In such a condition the honor of the advocate of that day did put the reverend Friars; and this and the like effects such festivals occasion, both in the members of the convents and corporation.

Now I come to the means and persuasions, the Friars make use of for the extolling, and praising this inestimable sacrifice of the Mass, and the great ignorance of the people in believing them. First of all, as the people know the debaucheries and lewd lives of many Friars and Priests, sometimes they are loth to desire a sinful Friar to say Mass for them, thinking that his Mass cannot be so acceptable to God Almighty, as that which is said by a Priest of good morals: So far the people are illuminated by nature; but to this, Priests and Friars make them believe, that though a Priest be the greatest sinner in the world, the sacrifice is of the same efficacy with God, since it is the sacrifice made by Christ on the Cross for all sinners; and that it was so declared by the Pope, and the council of Trent.

Put it together with what the same council declares, that the Priest doth not only represent Christ when he offereth

offereth the sacrifice, but that he is the very person of Christ at that time, and that therefore *David* calls them Christs, by these words ; *Nolite tangere Christos meos.* O execrable thing ! If the Priest is the very Christ in the celebration of the Mass, how can he at the same time be a sinner ? It being certain that Christ knew no sin : And if that Christ-Priest, offering the sacrifice, is in any actual mortal sin, how can the sacrifice of the Mass, which is (as to them) the same sacrifice Christ did offer to his eternal Father on the Cross, be efficacious to the expiation of the sins of all people ? For, in the first place, that sacrifice offered by a Priest-Christ, in an actual mortal sin, cannot be an expiation of the sin, by which the Priest is spiritually dead. Secondly, if the Christ Priest is spiritually dead by that mortal sin, how can such a Priest offer a lively spiritual sacrifice ? We must conclude then, that the Priests, by such blasphemous expressions, not only deceive the people, but rob them of their money, and commit a high crime, but that the sacrifice he offers is really of no effect, or efficacy to the relief of the souls in the pretended purgatory.

From what has been said it appears, that the Priests and Friars make use of whatever means they can to cheat the people, to gratifie their passions and increase their treasure. For what cheat, fraud and roguery can be greater than this of the *centenaria missa* with which they suck up the money of poor and rich, without performing what they do promise ?

If the Pope's privilege for that *hundred-Mass* was really true, natural reason shews, it was against the public good, & therefore ought not to be made use of : For by it, Friars and Priests will never quench their thirst of money and ambition, till they draw to them the riches of Christendom, and by these means, they will wrong the supposed souls in purgatory, and ruin their own too. Decency in the sacerdotal ornaments is agreeable to God our Lord, but vanity and profaneness is an abomination

abomination before him. Of what use can all the riches of their churches and ornaments be? To make the sacrifice of the Mass more efficacious, it cannot be for; the efficacy of it proceeds from Christ himself, who made use of different ornaments, than those the Priests make use of. Nor is it to satisfy their own ambition; for they could get more by saving of them; it is only to make Mistress Mass the more admired, and gain the whole people to be her followers and couriers.

O that the *Roman* laity would consider the weight of these Christian observations, and if they will not believe them because they are mine, I heartily beg of them all, to make pious and serious reflections upon them themselves, to examine the designs of the Priests and Friars, to mind their lives and conversations, to observe their works, to cast up accounts every year, and see how much of their substance goes to the clergy and church for Masses: Sure I am, they will find out the ill and ambitious designs of their spiritual guides: They will experience their lives not at all (most commonly) answerable to their characters, and sacerdotal functions; and more, their own substances and estates diminished every year: Many of their families corrupted by the wantonness, their understandings blinded by the craft, their souls in the way to hell by the wicked doctrines, and their bodies under sufferings by the needless impositions of Priests and Friars.

They will find also, that the pomp and brightness of a solemn Mass, is only vanity to amuse the eyes, and a cheat to rob the purse. That the *centenaria missa* never known to them before, is a trick and invention of Priests and Friars to delude and deceive them, and by that means impoverish and weaken them, and make themselves masters of all.

They will come at last to consider and believe, that the Roman Catholic congregations, ruled and governed by Priests and Friars, do sin against the Lord:

i. e.

i. e. The spiritual heads do commit abomination before the Lord, and that they cannot prosper here nor hereafter, if they do not leave off their wicked ways. Pray read the fifth chapter, the seventeenth verse, and the following, of *Judith*; and you shall find the case and the truth of my last proposition. *While* (saith he) *these people sinned not before their God, they prospered, because the God that hateth iniquity was with them. But when they departed from the way, that he appointed them, they were destroyed.* This was spoken of the *Jews*, but we may understand it of all nations, and especially of the *Romans*, who are very much of a piece with the *Jews* of old, or no better. We see the Priests departed from the way, that he appointed them. What can they expect but destruction, if they do not leave off their wickedness, and turn unto the Lord? And the worst is, that the innocent laity will suffer along with them, for God punisheth, as we see in the Old Testament, a whole nation for the sins of their rulers. And it is to be feared the same will happen to the *Roman* church, for the sins of their Priests. God enlighten them. Amen.

ARTICLE II.

Of the privileged altar.

A PRIVILEGED altar is the altar to which (or to some image on it) the Pope has granted a privilege of such a nature, that whosoever says before it, or before the image, so many *pater nosters*, &c. and so many *ave Maria*'s, with *gloria patri*, &c. obtains remission of his sins, or relieveth a soul out of purgatory: Or whoever ordereth a Mass to be said on the *ara* of such an altar, and before the image, has the privilege (as they believe) to take out of purgatory that soul for which the sacrifice of the Mass is offered.

The Cardinals, Patriarchs, Primates, Archbishops and

and Bishops, can grant to any image forty days of full and free indulgence, and 15 *quarantains* of pardon, for those that visit the said image, and say such a prayer before it, as they have appointed at the granting of such graces: So not only the images of the altars in the church, but several images in the corners of the streets, and on the highway, have those graces granted to them by the Bishop of the diocess: Nay, the beads or rosary of the Virgin *Mary*, of some considerable persons, have the same grants: And what is yet more surprising, the picture of St. *Anthony*'s pig, which is placed at the saint's feet, has the granting of fifteen quarantains of pardon of sins for those that visit and pray before him. What the people do on St. *Martin*'s day, I shall tell in another chapter.

I will not dispute now, whether the Pope and Bishops have authority to grant such privileges; but I only say, that I do not believe such a dream: For the Pope has usurped the supremacy and infallability, and his ambition being so great, he never will dispossess himself of a thing by which he makes himself more supreme, infallible, and rich; by keeping all those graces in his own hands, he would oblige all the bigots to seek after him, pay him for them, and have him in more veneration than otherwise he would be in.

These privileges are a great furtherance to carry on the ecclesiastical interests, and to bring the people to offer their prayers and money, and to be blinded and deceived by those papal inventions. But because I have already treated of these privileges, I proceed to the third article.

ARTICLE

Of Transubstantiation, or the Eucharist.

I SHALL say nothing touching the scholastical opinions of the *Romish* church about the sacrament of the Eucharist, or the real presence of Jesus Christ in it; for these are well known by our learned and well instructed laity: So I will confine myself wholly to their practices in the administration of this sacrament, and the worship paid to it by the Priests and Laity; and what strange notions the preachers do put in the people's heads about it.

First, as to the administration of this sacrament, actual or habitual intention being necessary in a Priest, to the validity and efficacy of the sacrament, open confession and repentance of his sins: He goes to consecrate the bread and wine, and (as they say, believe, and make the people believe) with five words they oblige Jesu Christ to descend from Heaven to the Host with his body, soul and divinity, and that so, he remains there as high and almighty as he is in Heaven; which they endeavour to confirm with pretended miracles; saying, that many Priests of pure lives have seen a little boy, instead of a wafer, in the consecrated Host, &c.

In winter, twice every month, and in summer, every week, the Priest is to consecrate one great Host, and a quantity of small ones: Which they do in the following manner. After the Priest has consecrated the great & small, besides the Host which he is to receive himself, the Priests of the parish, or Friars of the convent, come in two lines, with wax candles lighted in their hands, and kneel down before the altar, and begin to sing an hymn and anthem to the sacrament of the altar (so it is called by them); then the Priest openeth the tabernacle where the old great Host is kept between two christals, and takes out of the tabernacle the *custodia*, and a cup of small consecrated wafers, and

puts

puts them on the table of the altar; then he takes the great old Host, eats it, and so he does the small ones; then he puts the new, great, consecrated Host between the two crystals of the *custodia*, and the new small ones into the communion cup; because the small ones serve the common people. Then he incenses the great Host on his knees, and having a white, neat towel round his neck, with the ends of it he takes the *custodia*, and turns to the people and makes the figure of a cross before the people, and turning to the altar, puts the *custodia* and the cup of the small wafers in the tabernacle and locketh the door, and the Priests go away.

The reason why the great Host and the small ones are renewed twice a month in winter, and every week in summer (as they say) is (mind this reason, for the same is against them) because in summer, by the excessive heat, the Host may be corrupted and putrified, and produce worms, which many times has happened to the great Host, as I myself have seen. So to prevent this, they consecrate every week in summer-time; but in winter, which is a more favourable time to preserve the Host from corruption, only once in a fortnight.

If Christ is then in the Host with his body, soul and divinity, and *David* says, that the *holy One*, i. e. (Christ who is God blessed for evermore) *Never shall see corruption*. How comes it, that that Host, that holy one, that Christ, is sometimes corrupted and putrified? The substance of bread being only subject to corruption, being vanished, and the body of Jesus Christ substituted in its place, this body by a just inference is corrupted; which is against the scripture, and against the divinity of Jesus Christ.

Again, I ask, whether the worms, engendered in that Host, come out of the real body of Christ, or out of the material substance of the Host? If out of the body of Christ: Every body may infer from this the consequences his own fancy suggests. And if they say, that the worms are engendered in the material substance of

U   bread

bread; then the substance of the bread remains after the consecration, and not, as they say, the real substance of the body of Christ.

Again, It is a rule given by all the Casuists, that that Host must be eaten by the Priest. I do ask the Priest that eats the Host with the worms, whether he believeth that Host and worms to be the real body of Christ, or not? If he says, no: Why doth he eat it to the prejudice of his own health? And if he believeth it to be the real body of Christ, I do ask again, whether the worms are Christ, with body, soul and divinity, or not? If they are not, I give the said instance: And if they answer in the affirmative; then I say, that a Priest did not eat the Host and worms, (as I saw myself) on pretence of the loathing of his stomach, and after the Mass was ended, he carried the Host, (two Priests accompanying him with two candles) and threw it into a place, which they call *Piscina*, a place where they throw the dirty water after they wash their hands, which runs out of the church into the street. What can we say now? If the worms and corrupted Host is the real body of Christ, see what a value they have for him, when they throw it away like dirty water; and if that Host comes out of the running *piscina* into the street, the first dog, or pig passing by (which is very common in *Spain*) may eat it. And if they are not, besides the said instance of eating it to the prejudice of their health, we may add this: Namely, Why do the Priest and two more carry the Host in form of procession and with so great veneration, with lights and psalms, as if it was the real body of Christ?

Now, as to the way of administring the sacrament to the people, they do it in the following manner, which is also against their fantastical transubstantiation. I said that the Priest, or Friar consecrates small Hosts once a week, to give them to the people when they go to receive. The Priest in his surplice and with the *stola* on, goes to the altar, says the prayer of the sacrament,

openeth

openeth the tabernacle, and taking out of it the cup, opens it, and turning to the communicants, takes one of the wafers with his thumb, and the foremost finger of his right hand, lifts it up, and says: *See the Lamb of God that taketh away the sins of the world*, which he repeats three times; and after goes straightway to the communicants, and puts a wafer into each of their mouths. When all have received, he puts the cup again into the tabernacle, and goes to the vestry. This is when the people receive before or after Mass, but when they do receive at Mass, the Priest consecrates for himself a great Host, and after he has eaten it, he takes the cup out of the tabernacle, and gives the small wafers, consecrated before by another Priest, to the communicants, and putting again the cup into the tabernacle, or *sacrarium* (as they call it) drinks the consecrated wine himself.

I will not spend my time in proving, that the denying of the chalice to the laity is a manifest error, and that it is only to extol and raise the ecclesiastical dignity to the highest pitch: But I come to their ridiculous, nonsensical practices in several accidental cases, viz. First, I myself gave the sacrament to a lady, who had on that day a new suit of clothes; but she did not open her mouth wide enough to let the wafer on her tongue, and by my carelessness it fell upon one of her sleeves, and from thence to the ground; I did order her not to quit the place, till I had done; so, after the communion was over, I went to her again, and cutting a piece of the sleeve, where the water had touched, and scratching the ground, I took both the piece and dust, and carried them to the *piscina*, but I was suspended *ab officio* and *beneficio* for eight days, as a punishment for my distraction, or for not minding well my business. By this rule and custom of throwing into the *piscina*, among the dirty water, every thing that the Host has touched, they ought to throw the fingers of the Priest, or at least the tongues of men and women,

into

into the same place, and thus, their tricks and superstitious ceremonies, never would be discovered nor spread abroad. How inconsistent this custom is with right sense and reason, every body may see.

Secondly. In the *Dominicans* convent it happened, that a lady who had a lap-dog, which she always used to carry along with her, went to receive the sacrament with the dog under her arm, and the dog looking up and beginning to bark when the Friar went to put the wafer in the lady's mouth, he let the wafer fall, which happened to drop into the dog's mouth. Both the Friar and the lady were in a deep amazement and confusion, and knew not what to do; so they sent for the reverend Father Prior, who did resolve this nice point upon the spot, and ordered to call two Friars and the clerk, and to bring the Cross, and two candlesticks with candles lighted, and to carry the dog in form of procession into the vestry, and keep the poor little creature there with illuminations, as if he was the Host itself, till the digestion of the wafer was over, and then to kill the dog and throw it into the *piscina*. Another Friar said, it was better to open the dog immediately, and take out the fragments of the Host; and a third was of opinion, that the dog should be burnt upon the spot. The lady who loved dearly her *Cupid* (this was the dog's name) entreated the Father Prior to save the dog's life, if possible, and that she would give any thing to make amends for it. Then the Prior and Friars retired to consult what to do in this case, and it was resolved, that the dog should be called for the future, *El perillo del sacramento*, i. e. The sacrament's dog. 2. That if the dog should happen to die, the lady was to give him a burying in consecrated ground. 3. That the lady should take care not to let the dog play with other dogs. 4. That she was to give a silver dog, which was to be placed upon the tabernacle where the Hosts are kept. And, 5. That she should give twenty pistoles to the convent. Every article was performed

formed accordingly, and the dog was kept with a great deal of care and veneration. The case was printed, and so came to the ears of the Inquisitors, and Don *Pedro Guerrero* first Inquisitor, thinking the thing very scandalous, sent for the poor dog, and kept him in the inquisition to the great grief of the lady: What became of the dog nobody can tell. This case is worthy to be reflected on by serious, learned men, who may draw consequences to convince the *Romans* of the follies, covetousness, and superstitions of the Priests.

This I do aver, that after this case was published, it was disputed on in all the moral acadamies ; but as I cannot tell all the sentiments and resolutions of them, I will confine myself to those of the academy of the holy trinity, wherein I was present, when the case was proposed by the president, in the following terms :

Most reverend and learned brethren, the case of the dog (blasphemously called the sacrament's dog) deserves your application and searching, which ought to be carried on with a wise, Christian and solid way of arguing, both in this case, or any other like it. For my part, I am surprised when I think of the irregular, unchristian method, the Priors and Friars did take in the case, and both the case and their resolution call for our mature consideration. Thanks be to God, that our people give full obedience to our mother the church, and that they inquire no further into the matter, after some of our teachers have advised them ; otherwise the honor and reputation of our brethren would be quite ruined. For my part (*salva fide*) I think, that upon the same case, the Priest ought to let the thing drop there, and to take no further notice, rather than to give occasion to some criticks to scandalize, and to laugh at the whole clergy. Besides, that it is to abate the incomparable value of the *Eucharistia*, and to make it ridiculous before good, sensible men. Thus the president spoke ; and 15 members of the academy were of his opinion. One of the members said, that being certain

tain that the dog had eaten the real body and blood of Jesus Christ, the Priest, after the communion was over, was obliged to call the lady in private, and give a vomit to the dog, and to cast into the *piscina*, what he should throw up. Another said, that the sacrament being a spiritual nourishment to the soul, he was obliged to ask a question, and it was, whether the sensitive soul of the dog was nourished by the sacrament or not? All did agree in the affirmative, upon which the questionist formed by the following argument. The soul nourished by the sacrament of the body and blood of Christ, who is eternal life, is immortal; but the sensitive soul of the dog was nourished by Christ, according to your opinions: *Ergo*, the soul of the dog is immortal; then, if immortal, where is the soul to go after death; to heaven, to hell, or to go to purgatory? We must answer, to neither of these places: So we disown that the dog did eat the body of Christ; and there is more in the sacrament, than we can comprehend; and (*salva fide*, and in the way in argument) I say, that the dog did eat what we see in the Host, and not what we believe: Thus the member ended his discourse.

After all these disputes, the case was thus resolved, that the Priest should ask the Inquisitors advice, who being the judges in matters of faith, may safely determine what is to be done in such a case, and the like.

3*dly*. I have said already in another place, that the Reverend Father Friar *James Garcia* was reputed among the learned, the only man for divinity in this present age; and that he was my master, and by his repeated kindness to me, I may say, that I was his well beloved disciple. I was to defend a public thesis of divinity in the university, and he was to be president, or moderator. The thesis contained the following treatises. *De Essentia & Attributis Dei : De Visione beatifica ; De Gratia Justificante & auxiliante : De Providentia : De Actu Libero : De Trinitate : & de Sacramentis in genere.* All which I had learned from him.

him. The shortest treatise, of all he taught publicly in the university, was the *Eucharistia*. The proofs of his opinion were short, and the objections against them very succinct and dark. I must confess, that I was full of confusion, and uneasy, for fear that some doctor of divinity would make an argument against our opinion touching the sacrament of *Eucharistia*. And I did endeavour to ask my master to instruct me, and furnish me with answers suitable to the most difficult objections that could be proposed; but though he desired me to be easy about it, and that, upon necessity, he would answer for me; I replied with the following objection: God never will punish any man for not believing what is against the evidence of our senses, but the real presence in *Eucharistia* is so: *Ergo (Salva fide)* God will not punish any man for not believing the real presence of Christ there. To this he told me, that none of the doctors would propose such an argument to me, and he advised me not to make such an objection in public, but to keep it in my heart. But Father (said I) I do ask your answer; my answer is (said he) *aliud Lingua doceo, aliud Corde credo. i. e.* I teach one thing, and I believe another. By these instances, I have given now, every body may easily know the corruptions of the Romish church, and the nonsensical opinions of their Priests and Friars, as also, that the learned do not believe in their hearts, that there is such a monster as *transubstantiation*, though for some worldly ends, they do not discover their true sentiments about it.

Now I proceed to the worship, and adoration, both the clergy and laity pay to the holy Host or sacrament.

And I shall not say any thing of what the people do, when the Priest in a procession under a canopy carrieth the sacrament to the sick, for this custom and the pomp of it, and the idolatrous worship and adoration offered to it, is well known by our travellers & officers of the army.

Philip the 4*th*. King of *Spain*, as he was a hunting, met in the way a croud of people following a Priest,

and

and asking the reason, he was told, that the Priest did carry the consecrated wafer in his bosom to a sick person; the Priest did walk, and the King leaving his horse, desired the Priest to mount and ride on it, and holding the stirrup, bareheaded, he followed the Priest all the way to the house, and gave him the horse for a present. From the King to the shepherd, all people pay the same adoration to the holy Host; which shall be better known by the pomp and magnificence they carry the great Host with, in the solemn festival of *corpus Christi*, or of *Christ's body*. I shall describe only the general procession made on that day in *Zaragosa*, of which I was an eye-witness.

Though the festival of *corpus Christi* be a moveable Feast, it always falls on a *Thursday*. That day is made the great general procession of *corpus Christi*; and the *Sunday* following, every congregation, through the streets of the parish, and every convent of Friars and Nuns through the cloisters of the convent do go with great pomp to the private procession of Christ's body. As to the general great one, the festival is ordered in the following manner.

The Dean of the cathedral church of St. *Salvator* sends an officer to summon all the communities of Friars, all the clergy of the parish churches, the Viceroy, Governor and Magistrates, the judges of the civil and criminal council, with the Lord chancellor of the kingdom and all the fraternities, brotherhoods, or corporations of the city, to meet together on the *Thursday* following, in the Metropolitan cathedral church of St. *Salvator*, with all the standards, trumpets, giants, * both of the greater and lesser size in their respective habits of office or dignity; and all the clergy of the parish

---

* Three big giant men, and three giant women; and six little ones, drest in men and women's clothes, made of thin wood, and carried by a man hid under the clothes. The big ones are 15 feet high, which are kept in the hall of the city, for the magnificence and splendor of that day.

parish churches, and Friars of convents, to bring along with them in a procession, with due reverence, all the silver bodies of saints on a base or pedestal, which are in their churches and convents: *Item*, orders are published in every street, that the inhabitants, or housekeepers are to clean the streets, which the sacrament is to go through, and cover the ground with greens, and flowers, and to put the best hangings in the fronts of the balconies, and windows: All which is done accordingly; or else he that doth not obey and perform such orders, is to pay 20 pistoles without any excuse whatsoever.

At three in the afternoon, the Vice-roy goes in state with the Governor, Judges, Magistrates, and officers, to meet the Archbishop in his palace, and to accompany his Grace to church, where all the communities of Friars, Clergy, and Corporations, are waiting for them. The Dean and Chapter receive them at the great porch, and after the Archbishop has made a prayer before the great altar, the musick begins to sing, *Pange lingua gloriosa*, while the Archbishop takes out of the tabernacle the Host upon the rich chalice, and placeth it on the great *custodia*, on the altar's table. Then the Quire begins the evening songs, in which the Archbishop in his pontifical habit officiateth, and when all is over, his Grace giveth the blessing to the people with the sacrament in his hands. Then the Archbishop, with the help of the Dean, Archdeacon, and Chanter, placeth the *custodia* on a gilt pedestal, which is adorned with flowers and the jewels of several ladies of quality, and which is carried on the shoulders of 12 Priests, drest in the same ornaments they say Mass in. This being done, the procession begins to go out of the church in the following order.

First of all the bagpipe, and the great and small giants, dancing all along the streets. 2. The big silver Cross of the cathedral, carried by a Clerk-Priest, and two young assistants, with silver candlesticks and lighted candles.

candles. 3. From the Cross to the piper, a man with a high hook goes and comes back again while the procession lasts. The hook is called St. *Paul's hook*, because it belongs to St. *Paul's* church. That hook is very sharp, and they make use of it in that procession, to cut down the signs of taverns and shops, for fear that the holy *custodia* should be spoiled. 4. The standard and sign of the youngest corporation, and all the members of it, with a wax candle in their hands, forming two lines, whom all the corporations follow one after another in the same order. There are 30 corporations, and the smallest is composed of 30 members. 5. The boys and girls of the blue hospital with their master, mistress, and the chaplain in his *alva, stola,* and long sacerdotal cloak. 6. The youngest religion (the order of St. *Francis*, is called St. *Francis's religion*, and so are all orders, which they reckon 70, and which we may really, in the phrase of a satirical gentleman, call 70 *religions without religion*) with their Reverend and two Friars more at the end of each order, drest in the ornaments they use at the altar: And so all the orders go one after another in the same manner. There are 20 convents of Friars, and on this solemn festival, every one being obliged to go to the procession, we reckon there may be about 2000 present on this occasion; and 16 convents of Nuns, the number of them by regular computation is 1500. 7. The clergy of the youngest parish, with the parish Cross before, and the minister of it behind them in sacred ornaments. And so the clergy of the other parishes follow one another in the same order, every Friar and Priest having a white wax candle lighted in his hand.

The number of secular Priests constantly residing in *Zaragosa* is 1200 in that one town: So by the said account, we find all the ecclesiastical persons to amount to 4700, when the whole of the inhabitants come to 15000 families.

8. The clergy of the cathedrals of St. *Salvator*, and
the

the lady of *Pilar*, with all their sacerdotal ornaments, as also the musicians of both the cathedrals which go before the *custodia* or sacrament, singing all the way. Then the 12 Priests more, that carry the canopy, under which the sacrament goes, and under the end of it the Dean, and two Prebends, as Deacon and Subdeacon. The Archbishop in his pontifical habit goes at the Subdeacon's right hand, the Vice-roy at the Archbishop's, and the Deacon and Subdeacon one at the right, and the other at the left, all under the canopy. Six Priests, with incense and incensaries on both sides of the *custodia*, go incensing the sacrament without intermission; for while one kneels down before the great Host, & incenses it three times, the other puts incense in his incensary, and goes to relieve the other, and thus they do, from the coming out of the church, till they return back again to it.

9. The great Chancellor, Presidents, and councils follow after, and after all, the nobility, men and women, with lighted candles. This procession lasts 4 hours from the time it goes out, till it comes into the church again. All the bells of the convents, and parishes ring all this time; and if there were not so many idolatrous ceremonies in that procession, it would be a great pleasure to see the streets so richly adorned with the best hangings, and the variety of persons in the procession.

The riches of that procession are incredible to a foreigner; but matters of fact (the truth of which may be inquired into) must be received by all serious people. I have spoken already of the rich *custodia*, which the Archbishop of *Sevil* gave to the cathedral, and of the rich chalice set in diamonds. Now besides these two things, we reckon 33 silver Crosses belonging to convents, and parish churches, 10 feet high, and about the thickness of a pole of a coach; 33 small Crosses which the priests and Friars, who officiate that day, carry in their hands; these Crosses though small, are

richer

richer than the big one; because in the middle of the Cross there is a relick, which is a piece of wood (as they say) of the Cross, on which our Saviour was crucified, and which they call *holy wood*. This relick is set in precious stones, and many of them set in diamonds. Thirty-three sacerdotal cloaks to officiate in, made of *Tufy d'or*, edged with pearls, emeralds, rubies, and other rich stones. Sixty-six silver candlesticks, four feet high. A large gold possenet, and a gold handle for the hysop, six incensaries, four of them silver, and two of gold; four silver incense boxes, and two gold ones. Three hundred and eighty silver bodies of saints on their rich gilt pedestals, of which two hundred are whole bodies, and the rest half, but many are gilt, and several wear mitres on their heads, embroidered with precious stones. The image of St. *Michael* with the devil under his feet, and the image with wings, are of solid silver gilt all over.

With this magnificence they carry the sacrament through the principal streets of the city, and all the people that are in the balconies and lattice windows throw roses and other flowers upon the canopy of the sacrament as it goes by. When the procession is over, and the sacrament placed in the tabernacle: There is a stage before the altar to act a sacramental or divine comedy, which lasts about an hour, and this custom is practised also on *Christmas* eve. By these, every body may know their bigotries, superstitions and idolatries.

Now I come to say something of the strange notions, the priests and Friars, Confessors and preachers put in the people's heads, concerning the Host. First, they preach and charge the people to adore the sacrament, but never to touch the consecrated Host or wafer, this being a crime against the Catholic faith, and that all such as dare to touch it, must be burned in the inquisition. Secondly, to believe that the real flesh and blood of Jesus Christ is in the *Eucharist*; and that, though

they

they cannot see it, they ought to submit their understanding to the Catholic faith. Thirdly, that if any body could lawfully touch the Host, or wafer, and prick it with a pin, blood shall come out immediately, which they pretend to prove with many miracles, as that of the *corporales* of *Daroca*, which, as it comes *a propos*, I cannot pass by without giving an account of it.

Daroca is an ancient city of the kingdom of *Aragon*, which bordereth on *Castilla*. It is famous among the *Spaniards* for its situation and strength, and for the mine that is in a neighbouring mountain to it. For the floods coming with impetuosity against the walls, and putting the city in great danger, the inhabitants dug three hundred yards from one end of the mount to the other, and made a subterranean passage, and the floods going that way, the city is ever since free from danger. But it is yet more famous for what they call *corporales*. The story is this: When the *Moors* invaded *Spain*, a curate near *Daroca* took all imaginable care to save the consecrated wafers, that were in the tabernacle, and not to see them profaned by the *Infidels*, and open enemies of their faith. There were but five small Hosts in all, which he put within the fine holland on which the Priest puts the great Host when he says Mass: And this piece of holland is called *corporales*. The *Moors* were at that time near, and no body could make an escape, and the Priest ready to lose his own life, rather than to see the Hosts profaned, tied the *corporales* with the five wafers in it, on a blind mule, and whipping the beast out of town, said, speed you well, for I am sure that the sacrament on your back will guide you to some place free from the enemies of our religion. The Mule journeyed on, and the next day arrived at *Daroca*, and some people observing the *corporales* tied with the holy *stola* to the mule's belly, were surprised at so rare and unexpected a thing, and calling a Priest of the great parish church, he came to the mule, and

and examining the thing, found the five wafers converted into blood, and stamped on the holland cloth; which spots of blood (or painting) of the bigness of a ten-penny piece, are preserved till this present time. Then the Priest crying out, *a miracle.* the clergy in great devotion and procession came with candles and a canopy, and taking the mule under it, went to the great church; and when the minister of the parish had taken the *stola* and *corporales* from off the mule, he went to place the *corporales* on the *ara altaris,* or the altar's table, but the mule not well pleased with it, left the company, and went up to the steeple or belfry: Then the parish minister (though not so wise as the mule) followed the mule up stairs, and seeing the beast mark a place there with its mouth, he soon understood, that the mule being blind, could neither go up, nor mark that place without being inspired from above; and having persuaded the people of the same, all agreed that there should be a little chapel built to keep the holy *corporales.* When this resolution was approved by the clergy and laity, the mule died on the steeple. At the same time the curate having made his escape, and by divine inspiration following the mule's steps, came to *Daroca,* and telling the whole case of his putting the sacrament on the mule to save it from profanation, both clergy and laity began to cry out, *a miracle from Heaven:* And immediately further agreed, that the mule should be embalmed and kept before the holy *corporales* in the steeple, *ad perpetuam Rei Memoriam: Item,* to make a mule of the best stone could be found, in honor of the mule, and that for the future his name should be the *holy mule.* All things being done accordingly, and the city having never been mastered by the *Moors* (as the inhabitants say) they instituted a solemn festival, to which ever since the neighbours, even fourteen leagues distant, come every year. Those that go up to the steeple to see the holy miracle of the wafers converted into blood, and the holy mule, must pay four reals

reals of plate. The people of *Daroca* call it sometimes, *the holy mystery*, another time, *the holy miracle*; *the sacrament of the mule* by some ignorants: *The holy sacrament on a mule* by the wise, &c. I myself took a journey to see this wonder of *Daroca*, and paying the fees, went up to have a full view of every thing: And really I saw a mule of stone, and a coffin wherein the embalmed mule was kept (as the clerk told me) but he did not open it, for the key is kept always at the Bishop's palace: I saw likewise the linen with five red spots in a little box of gilt silver, two candles always burning before it, and a glass lamp before the mule's coffin. At that time I did believe every part of the story. All sorts of people do believe as an infallible truth, that every body's sight is preserved during life, in the same degree of strength and clearness it is in at the time they see these bloody spots, which is proved by many instances of old women, who by that means have excellent eyes to the last. *Item*, They give out that no blind person ever came before the *corporales*, without his sight being restored to him; which I firmly believe; for no blind person ever was up in the steeple. I cannot swear this, but I have very good reason to affirm it; for in the first place, there is a small book printed, called *directions for the faithful people*, teaching them how to prepare themselves before they go up to see the holy mystery of the *corporales* of *Daroca*. One of the advices to the blind is, that they must confess and receive the sacrament, and have the soul as clean as crystal, and to endeavour to go up to the steeple from the altar's table without any guide; and that if some cannot go as far as the chapel of the belfrey, it is a sign that that man is not well prepared. The distance between the altar and the steeple's door is about forty yards, and there are nine strong pillars in the body of the church: So the poor blind people before they can reach the belfrey's door, commonly break their noses, some their heads, &c. And some more cautious

tious and careful, and happy in finding out the door, when they are in the middle of the stairs, find a snare or stock, and break their legs; for I do remember very well, when I went up myself, I saw a sort of a window in the middle of one of the steps, and asking the use of it, the clerk told me, it was to let down through it the rope of the great bell. Then I did not inquire further; but now, being sure, that there was but that small window shut up in the whole pair of winding stairs, I conclude, that it could not be there for the said use, and in all probability that window was the snare to catch the poor blind people in. Therefore the clerk being not sure of the miracle, by this prevents the discovery of the want of virtue in the holy *corporales*, to cure all diseases, and at the same time gives out a miracle, and the miracle is, that the blind man has broke his leg, and that it is a just punishment, for daring to go up either unprepared or with little faith: So no blind man has recovered sight by the virtue of the *corporales*.

By means of this same direction, no sick person dareth to go up; but if they recover, it must be a miracle of the holy mystery. And if a mule happen to be sick, the master of it goes and makes the beast give three turns round the steeple, thinking that its brother mule has power to cure it.

Many will be apt to suspect the truth of this story; nay, some will think it a mere forgery; but I do appeal to several officers of the army that went through *Daroca*, to be witnesses for me. It may be they were not told all the circumstances of it, because the people there have strange notions of an Heretick; but the mule and *corporales* being the most remarkable thing in the city, I am sure many did hear of it, though nobody of the Hereticks could see the holy mystery, being a thing forbidden by their church.

With this, and the like pretended miracles, Priests and Friars, Confessors and preachers, make the people
believe

believe the real presence of Christ's body in the Host, and the ineffable virtue of this sacrament to cure all bodily distempers: Nay, what is more than all these, they perswade, and make the people believe, that if a man or a woman has the consecrated wafer by them, they cannot die suddenly; nay, nor be killed by violent hands: So great is the power of the Host (they say) that if you shew it to the enraged sea, the storm immediately ceaseth; if you carry it with you, you cannot die, especially a sudden death. And really they may venture to give out this doctrine as an infallible point; for they are sure no body will dare touch the Host, and much less to carry it with him, it being so high a crime, that if any body was found out with the consecrated wafer on his body, the sentence is already past by the Inquisitors, that such a person is to be burnt alive.

A parish Priest carrying the consecrated Host to a sick person, out of the town, was killed by a flash of lightening, which accident being clearly against this pretended infallible power of the Host, the people took the liberty to talk about it; but the clergy did order a funeral sermon, to which the nobility and common people were invited by the common cryer. Every body did expect a funeral sermon; but the preacher, taking for his text *Judicium sibi manducat*, did prove, That that Priest, killed by a flash of lightening, was certainly damned, and that his sudden death, while he had the consecrated Host in his hands, was the reward of his wickedness; and that this death was to be looked upon as a miracle of the holy Host, rather than an instance against the infinite power of it; for, said he, we have carefully searched and examined every thing, and have found that he was not a Priest, and therefore had no authority to touch the Host, nor administer the sacrament of the *Eucharist*. And with this the murmur of the people ceased, and every body afterwards thought, that the sudden death of the Priest was a manifest

nifest miracle wrought by the Host, and a visible punishment from heaven for his sacrilegious crimes.

The truth is, that the Priest was ordained by the Bishop of *Tarasona*, in *Aragon*. The thing did happen in the city *Calatayed*, in the same kingdom; his name was *Mossen Pedro Aquilar*, he was buried in the church, called *the sepulchre of our Lord*. The reverend Father *Fombuena* was the preacher, and I was one of the hearers, and one that did believe the thing as the preacher told us, till after a while, some members of the academy having examined the case, and found that he was really a Priest, did propose it to the assembly, that every body might give his opinion about it. The President said that such a case was not to be brought into question, but the doctrine of the church touching *Eucharistia* to be believed without any scruples.

Again, That the Host has no virtue nor power to calm the raging sea, I know myself by experience; and as the relation of the thing may prove effectual to convince other Roman Catholics of their erroneous belief, as well as the passage itself did me, it seems fit in this place to give an account of it, and I pray God Almighty, that it may please him to give all the Roman-Catholics the same conviction, some way or other, his infinite goodness was pleased to give me, that they may take as firm a resolution as I have taken, to espouse the safest way to salvation; for if we take our measures concerning the truths of religion from the rules of the holy scriptures, and the platform of the primitive churches; nay, if the religion of Jesus Christ, as it is delivered in the New Testament, be the true religion (as I am certain it is) and the best and safest way to salvation; then certainly the Protestant religion is the purest, that is, at this day, in the world; the most orthodox in faith, and the freest on the one hand, from idolatry and superstition, and on the other, from whimsical novelties and enthusiasms of any now extant; and not only a safe way to salvation, but the safest of any

any I know in the world. Now I come to my story.

After I left my country, making use of several stratagems & disguises, I went to *France*, dressed in officer's clothes, and so I was known by some at *Paris*, under the name of the *Spanish officer*. My design was to come to *England*, but the treaty of *Utrecht* being not concluded, I could not attempt to come from *Calais* to *Dover*, without a pass. I was perfectly a stranger in *Paris*, and without any acquaintance, only one *French* Priest, who had studied in *Spain*, and could speak *Spanish* perfectly well, which was a great satisfaction to me, for at that time I could not speak *French*. The Priest (to whom I made some presents) was interpreter of the *Spanish* letters to the King's Confessor, Father *le Telier*, to whom he introduced me; I spoke to him in *Latin*, and told him, I had got a great fortune by the death of an uncle in *London*, and that I should be very much obliged to his Reverence, if by his influence I could obtain a pass. The Priest had told him that I was a Captain, which the Father did believe; and my brother having been a Captain, (though at that time he was dead) it was an easy thing to pass for him: The first visit was favourable to me, for the Father Confessor did promise me to get me a pass, and bid me call for it two or three days after, which I did; but I found the Reverend very inquisitive, asking me several questions in divinity: I answered to all, that I had studied only a little *Latin*: He then told me, there was no possibility of obtaining a pass for *England*, and that if I had committed any irregular thing in the army, he would give me a letter for the King of *Spain*, to obtain my pardon, and make my peace with him again. I confess this speech made me very uneasy, and I began to suspect some danger; so I thanked him for his kind offer to me, and told him I had committed nothing against my King or country, which I would convince him of, by refusing his favour, and by returning back into *Spain*, that very week: So I

took

took my leave of him, and the day following I left *Paris*, and went back to St. *Sebastian*, where I kept my lodgings, till I got the opportunity of a ship for *Lisbon*. The merchants of *Zaragosa* do trade to St. *Sebastian*, and I was afraid of being known, and discovered by some of them, and for this reason, I kept close in my room, giving out that I was not well. How to get a ship was the only difficulty; but I was freed from this, by sending for the Father Rector of the Jesuits, on pretence that I was very ill, and was willing to confess my sins: Accordingly, he came to me that very day, and I began my confession, in which I only told him, that as I was an officer in the army, and had killed another officer, for which the King had ordered me to be taken up, so that my life being in danger, and my conscience in trouble, on account of the murder, I did put both life and soul into his hands. He asked me all the usual questions; but I confessing no other sin, the Father thought I was a good Christian, and something great in the world; so he bad me be easy, and mind nothing but to keep myself in a readiness for my voyage, and that he would send a Captain of a ship to me that very night, who should take me along with him into the ship, and sail out the next morning: And so all was performed accordingly, and I went that night to embark. What directions the Father Rector gave the Captain, I knew not; this I know, that I was treated as if I was the son of a grandee, and served by the Captain himself. This was the first time of my life being at sea, so I was very sick the two first days; the third day, a great storm began, which put me in fear of losing my life. But then calling to my memory, that the divine power was said to be in a consecrated Host to calm the raging sea, and knowing that a Priest had power to consecrate at any time, and every where, upon urgent necessity, I went into the Captain's cabin, and took one of the white wafers he made use of for sealing letters, and being alone, I made this promise

before

before God Almighty, from the bottom of my heart, that if he would graciously condescend to remove my scruples at once, by manifesting the real presence of his body in the Host, and its infinite power, by calming the raging tempest at the sight of the one I was now going to consecrate, then I would straight turn back again into my church and country, and live and die in the *Romish* communion; but if the effect did not answer to the doctrine preached of the Host, then I would live and die in the church that knoweth no such errors, nor obeyeth the Pope. After this promise, I said my prayers of preparation to consecrate; and after I had consecrated one wafer (which I was sure in my conscience was duly consecrated, for the want of ornaments and a decent place, is no hindrance to the validity of the Priest's consecration) I went up, and hiding the wafer from the Captain and crew of the ship, I shewed it to the sea, and trembling all over, stood in that condition for half an hour: But the storm at that time increased so violently, that we lost the mast of the ship, and the Captain desired me to go down. I was willing to wait a little longer for the efficacy of the Host, but finding none at all, I went down, and kneeling, I began to pray to God, and thinking I was obliged to eat the consecrated Host for reverence sake, I did eat it, but without any faith of the efficacy and power of it. Then I vowed before God, never to believe any doctrine of the *Romish* church, but those that were taught by *Jesus Christ* and his apostles, and to live and die in that only. After this vow, though the storm did continue for a day and a night, my heart was calmed, all my tears vanished, and, though with manifest danger of our lives, we got into *Vigo*'s harbour, and safe from storm.

I left the ship there, and by land I went to *Portugal*, having an inward joy and easiness in my heart; but having stopped at *Porto-Porto*, to take a little rest, I fell sick of an intermitting fever, which brought me to the very point of death, three times, in three months and

and nine days. The minister of the parish being told by my landlord, the condition I was in, past hopes of recovery, came to visit me, and desired me to confess and receive as a good Christian ought to do; but I thanking him for his good advice, told him, that I was not so sick as he did believe, and that I would send for him if I had any occasion, and really I never believed that I was to die of that distemper, and by this thought, I was freed from Priests and Confessors.

When I was out of danger, and well recovered, I went to *Lisbon*, where I had the opportunity of talking with some *English* merchants, who did explain to me some points of the protestant religion, and my heart was in such a disposition, that their words did affect me more than all the sermons and moral sums of the *Romish* church had ever done before.

I knew a Captain in the *Spanish* army, Don *Alonso Corsega* by name, who was killed at the siege of *Lerida*, in whose bosom was found (in a little purse) the consecrated wafer, for which his body was burnt to ashes. It is very likely, that the poor man thinking to escape from death by that means, he took it out of his mouth when he went to receive, and kept it as an amulet against the martial instruments, which paid no respect to its fancied divinity.

Now by these instances I have given you already, it appears, that the practices of the *Romish* Priests in the administration of the *Eucharist*, either to healthy or sick people, are only observed for interest's sake, as the worship and adoration given to the consecrated wafer tends only to the increase of their treasure. And lastly, the doctrine of transubstantiation and real presence of Christ, which they do endeavour to make the people believe by supposed miracles, is only to cheat and blind the poor laity, and raise in them a great reverence and admiration of their persons and office.

O Lord God, who receiveth into thy favour those that fear thee, and do work righteousness, suffer not so many

many thousands of innocent people to be led in the way of error, but enlighten them with thy spirit, put the light of thy gospel upon the candlestick, that all those who are in darkness may by that means come to the safe way of salvation, and live and die in the profession of thy truth, and the purity of that perfect religion taught by thine only son, our Saviour Jesus Christ our Lord. *Amen.*

ARTICLE IV.

Of Purgatory.

I CANNOT give a real account of Purgatory, but I will tell all I know of the practices and doctrines of the *Romish* Priests and Friars, in relation to that imaginary place, which indeed must be of a vast extent, and almost infinite capacity, if, as the Priests give out, there are as many apartments in it, as conditions and ranks of people in the world among Roman-Catholics.

The intenseness of the fire in Purgatory is calculated by them, which they say is eight degrees, and that of Hell only four degrees. But there is a great difference between these two fires; in this, viz. That of Purgatory (though more intense, active, consuming and devouring) is but for a time, of which the souls may be freed by the suffrages of Masses; but that of Hell is for ever: In both places, they say, the souls are tormented, and deprived of the glorious sight of God; but the souls in Purgatory (though they endure a great deal more than those in Hell) have certain hopes of seeing God sometime or other, and that hope is enough to make them to be called *the blessed souls.*

Pope *Adrian* the third did confess, that there was no mention of Purgatory in scripture, or in the writings of the holy Fathers; but notwithstanding this, the council of *Trent* has settled the doctrine of Purgatory without alledging any one passage of the holy scripture,

ture, and gave so much liberty to Priests and Friars by it, that they build in that fiery palace, apartments for Kings, Princes, Grandees, Noblemen, merchants and tradesmen, for ladies of quality, for gentlemen and tradesmen's wives, and for poor common people. These are the eight apartments, which answer to the eight degrees of *intensus ignus*, i. e. Intense fire; and they make the people believe, that the poor people only endure the least degree; the second being greater, is for gentlewomen and tradesmen's wives, and so on to the eighth degree, which being the greatest of all, is reserved for Kings. By this wicked doctrine they get gradually Masses from all sorts and conditions of people, in proportion to their greatness. But as the poor cannot give so many Masses as the great, the lowest chamber of purgatory is always crowded with the reduced souls of those unfortunately fortunate people, for they say to them, that the providence of God has ordered every thing to the ease of his creatures. and that foreseeing that the poor people could not afford the same number of Masses that the rich could, his infinite goodness had placed them in the place of less sufferings in Purgatory.

But it is a remarkable thing, that many poor, silly tradesmen's wives, desirous of honor in the next world, do ask the Friars, whether the souls of their fathers, mothers, or sisters, can be removed from the second apartment (reckoning from the lowest) to the third, thinking by it, that though the third degree of fire is greater than the second, yet the soul would be better pleased in the company of ladies of quality: But the worst is, that the Friar makes such women believe, that he may do it very easily, if they give the same price for a Mass, the ladies of quality do give. I knew a shoemaker's wife, very ignorant, proud, and full of punctilioes of honor, who went to a *Franciscan* Friar, and told him, that she desired to know, whether her own father's soul was in Purgatory or not, and in what apartment

apartment. The Friar asked her how many Masses she could spare for it, she said two; and the Friar answered, your father's soul is among the beggars.—Upon hearing this, the poor woman began to cry, and desired the Friar to put him, if possible, in the fourth apartment, and she would pay him for it; and the *Quantum* being settled, the Friar did promise to place him there the next day: So the poor woman ever since gives out that her father was a rich merchant, for it was revealed to her, that his soul is among the merchants in Purgatory.

Now what can we say, but that the Pope is the chief Governor of that vast place, and Priests and Friars the Quarter-masters that billet the souls according to their own fancies, and have the power, and give for money the King's apartments to the soul of a shoemaker, and that of a lady of quality to her washer-woman.

But mind reader, how chaste the Friars are in procuring a separate place for ladies in Purgatory: They suit this doctrine to the temper of a people whom they believe to be extremely jealous, and really not without ground of them, and so no soul of a woman can be placed among men. Many serious people are well pleased with this Christian caution; but those that are given to pleasure, do not like it at all; and I knew a pleasant young collegian, who went to a Friar, and told him: Father, I own, I love the fair sex; and I believe, that my soul will always retain that inclination: I am told, that no man's soul can be in company with ladies, and it is a dismal thing for me to think, that I must go there (but as for Hell, I am in no danger of it, thanks to the Pope) where I shall never see any more women, which will prove the greatest of torments for my soul; so I have resolved to agree with your Reverence beforehand, upon this point. I have a bill of 10 pistoles upon *Peter la Vinna Banquer*, and if you can assure me, either to send me straight to Heaven, when I die, or to the ladies apartment in Purgatory, you shall have the bill;

bill; and if you cannot, I must submit to the will of God, like a good Christian. The Friar seeing the bill which he thought ready money) told him, that he could do either of the two, and that he himself might choose (which of the two places he pleased. But Father (said the collegian) the case is, that I love *Donna Teresa Spinola*, and she doth not love me, and I do not believe I can expect any favour from her in this world, so I would know whether she is to go before me to Purgatory, or not? O! That is very certain (said the Friar.) I choose then (said the collegian) the lady's apartment, and here is the bill, if you give me a certificate under your hand, that the thing shall be so: But the Friar refusing to give him any authentic certificate, the collegian laught at him, and made satirical verses upon him, which were printed, and which I myself read. I knew the Friar too, who being mocked publicly, was obliged to remove from his convent to another in the country.

Notwithstanding all these railleries, of which the Inquisitors cannot take notice, being not against the Catholic faith, Priests and Friars do daily endeavour to prove that Purgatory is a real existent place, and that by Masses, the souls detained in it are daily delivered out of it. And this they prove by many revelations made to devout, pious people; and by many apparitions.

They not only preach of them publicly, but books are printed of such revelations and apparations. I remember many of them, but I shall not trouble the reader with them; only I will tell some of the most remarkable ones of my time.

In the latter end of King *Charles* the second's reign, a Nun of *Guadalajara* wrote a letter to his Majesty, acquainting him, that it was revealed to her, by an angel, that the soul of his Father, *Philip* the IV. was still in Purgatory (all alone in the royal apartments) and likewise in the lowest chamber, the said King *Philip's* shoemaker, and that upon saying so many Masses, both

should

should be delivered out of it, and should go to enjoy the ravishing pleasures of an eternal life. The Nun was reputed a saint upon earth, and the simple King gave orders to his Confessor to say, or order so many Masses to be said, for that purpose; after which, the said Nun wrote again to his Majesty, congratulating and wishing him joy for the arrival of his Father to Heaven; but that the shoemaker, who was seven degrees lower than *Philip* in Purgatory, was then seven degrees higher than his Majesty in Heaven, because of his better life on earth, who never had committed any sin with women, as *Philip* had done all his life-time, but that all was forgiven to him on the account of the Masses.

Again, They give out in the pulpit, that the Pope has an absolute power to make the Mass efficacious to deliver the soul, for which it is said, out of that place; and that his Holiness can take at once all the souls out of it; as *Pius* the Vth. did (as they report) who, when he was Cardinal, was mighty devout, and a great procurer of the relief of souls, and who had promised them with a solemn oath, that, if by their prayers in Purgatory he should be chosen Pope, then he would empty Purgatory of all the souls at once. At last by the intercession of the souls with God Almighty, he was elected Pope, and immediately he delivered all the souls out of that place; but that Jesus Christ was so angry with the new Pope, that he appeared to him, and bad him not to do any such thing again, for it was prejudicial to the whole clergy and Friarship. That Pope delivered all the souls out of Purgatory, by opening the treasure of the church, in which were kept millions of Masses, which the Pope's makes use of for the augmenting the riches of the holy See: But he took care not to do it again; for though, *quodcunque solveritis in Terra, erit, solutum & in Cælis*, there is not specified the same power in Purgatory, therefore ever since, the Popes take no authority, nor liberty to

sweep

sweep Purgatory at once, for it would prove their ruin, and reduce the clergy to poverty.

When some ignorant people pay for a Mass, and are willing to know whether the soul, for which the Mass is said, is, after the Mass, delivered out of Purgatory; the Friar makes them believe, that the soul will appear in the figure of a mouse within the tabernacle of the altar, if it is not out of it, and then it is a sign that that soul wants more Masses; and if the mouse doth not appear, the soul is in Heaven. So when the Mass is over, he goes to the tabernacle backwards, where is a little door with a crystal, and lets the people look through it: But, O pitiful thing! They see a mouse which the Friars keep, (perhaps for this purpose) and so the poor sots give more money for more Masses, till they see the mouse no more. They have a revelation ready at hand, to say, that such a devout person was told by an angel, that the soul for which the Mass is said, was to appear in the figure of a mouse in the *Sacrario*, or tabernacle.

Many other Priests and Friars do positively affirm, and we see many instances of it forged by them in printed books, that when they consecrate the Host, the little boy Jesus doth appear to them in the Host, and that that is a sign that the soul is out of Purgatory. There is a fine picture of St. *Anthony de Paula*, with the Host in his hand, and the little Jesus is in the Host, because that divine boy frequently appeared to him when he said Mass, as the history of his life gives an account. But at the same time, they say, that no layman can see the boy Jesus, because it is not permitted to any man but to Priests to see so heavenly a sight: And by that means they give out what sort of stories they please, without any fear of ever being found out in a lie.

As to the second day of *November*, which is the day of the souls of Purgatory, in which every Priest and Friar sayeth three Masses for the delivery of so many souls out of the pains of it (they generally say) that

from

from three of the clock of the first day of *November* (all saint's day) till three in the afternoon, the next day, all the souls are out of Purgatory, and entirely free from the pains of it; (those four and twenty hours being granted by his Holiness for a refreshment to them) and that all that while they are in the air diverting themselves, and expecting the relief of so many Masses, to get by them the desired end, *viz.* The celestial habitations. On these twenty-four hours, they ring the bells of all the churches and convents, which (as they say) is a great suffrage and help to the souls, and on that day only, Priests and Friars get more money than they get in two months time beside; for every family, and private persons too, give yellow wax candles to the church, and money for Masses and *Responsa*, i. e. a prayer for the dead, and all these twenty-four hours the churches are crowded with people, and the Priests and Friars continually singing prayers for the dead, and this they call *the Priests and Friars fair-day*. Which they solemnize with the continual ringing of the bells, though they give out, that it is a suffrage for the souls of Purgatory.

And on the same pretence, there is a man in every parish that goes in the dark of the evening through all the streets with a bell, praying for the souls, and asking charity for them in every house, always ringing the bell as a suffrage. The Duke of *Ossuna* made a witty repartee to Pope *Innocent* the XIth, on this subject. The Duke was Ambassador for the King of *Spain* at *Rome*, and he had a large bell on the top of his house, to gather his domesticks when he was a going out. Many Cardinals lived by his palace, and complained to the Pope, that the Ambassador's bell disturbed them; (for the Duke used to order to ring the bell when he knew the Cardinals were at home) and the Pope spoke immediately to the Duke, and asked his Excellency the reason of keeping so big a bell? To which the Duke answered, that he was a

very

very good Christian, and a good friend to the souls of Purgatory, to whom the ringing of the bell was a suffrage. The Pope took in good part this raillery, and desired him to make use of some other signal to call his servants; for that of the bell was very noisy, and a great disturbance to the Cardinals, his neighbours; and that if he was so good a friend to the souls of Purgatory, he would do them more service by selling the bell, and giving the money for Masses.

To tell the truth, the Duke did not care for the souls, but all his design was to vex the Cardinals: So the next day he ordered to bring down the bell, and to put in the same place a cannon, or great piece of ordnance, and to give twelve shots every morning, and twelve at midnight, which was the time the Cardinals were at home. So they made a second complaint to the Pope; upon this, he spoke to the Duke again, and he answered to his Holiness, that the bell was to be sold, and the money to be delivered to the Priests for Masses; but that he had ordered the cannon as a suffrage for the souls of the poor soldiers that had died in the defence of the holy See. The Pope was very much affronted by this answer, and as he was caressing a little lap-dog he had in his arms, got up, and said,— Duke, I take more care of the souls of the poor soldiers than you of your own soul; at which, the Duke taking out of the Pope's arms the lap-dog, and throwing him through the window, said, and I take care to shew the Pope how he ought to speak with the King of *Spain*, to whom more respect is due. Then the Pope (knowing the resoluteness of the Duke, and that his Holiness could get nothing by an angry method, chose to let the thing drop there, rather than to make more noise: So the Duke kept his cannon piece, and the Cardinals were obliged to remove their families into a more quiet place.

A *Mendicant* Friar one day asked some charity from the same Duke, for the souls of Purgatory, and said,
my

my Lord, if you put a piſtole in this plate, you ſhall take out of Purgatory that ſoul for which you deſign it. The Duke gave the piſtole, and aſked the Friar, whether the ſoul of his brother was already out of it? And when the Friar ſaid, yea; the Duke took again his piſtole, and told the Friar, Now you cannot put his ſoul into Purgatory again. And it is to be wiſhed that every one was like that Duke, and had the ſame reſolution to ſpeak the truth to the Pope himſelf and all his quarter-maſters.

I have told in the firſt article of this chapter, that every *Friday* is appointed to ſay Maſſes for the ſouls in Purgatory, which did belong to corporations of fraternities, and what great profit Prieſts, and eſpecially Friars, get by it: Now, by this infallible cuſtom and practice, we may ſay, that Purgatory contains as many corporations of ſouls, as there are corporations of tradeſmen here below, which fraternities are more profitable to all ſorts of communities of Friars, than the living members of them upon earth. But ſome of theſe people, either out of pleaſantry, or out of curioſity, aſk ſometimes in what part of the world, or of the air, is that place of Purgatory? To which the Friars anſwer, that it is between the center of the earth and this earthly ſuperficies; which they pretend to prove, and make them believe by revelations, and eſpecially by a ſtory from a *Jeſuit* Father, who in his travels ſaw the earth open by an earthquake, and in the deep a great many people of a flaming red colour, from which nonſenſical account they conclude, to blind the poor people, that thoſe were the ſouls of Purgatory red as the very flame of fire. But obſerve, that no Prieſt or Friar would dare tell ſuch frivolous ſtories to people of good ſenſe, but to the ignorants, of which there are great numbers in thoſe parts of the world.

When they preach a ſermon of the ſouls, they make uſe of brimſtone, and burn it in the pulpit, ſaying, that ſuch flames are like thoſe of the fire in Purgatory.— They make uſe of many pictures of ſouls that are in

the

the middle of devouring fire, lifting up their hands to Heaven, as if they were crying for help and assistance. They prove their propositions with revelations and apparitions, for they cannot find in the scripture any passage to ground their audacious thoughts on, and such sermons are to the people of sense better diversion than a comedy; for besides the wretchedness of style and method, they tell so many sottish stories, that they have enough to laugh at afterwards for a long while.

I went once to hear an old Friar, who had the name of an excellent preacher, upon the subject of the souls in Purgatory, and he took his text out of the twenty-first chapter of the *Apoc.* 27th verse. *And there shall in no wise enter into it any thing that defileth, neither whatsoever worketh abomination*; by which he settled the belief of a Purgatory, proving by some romantick authority, that such a passage ought to be understood of Purgatory, and his chief authority was, because a famous interpreter, or expositor, renders the text thus: *There shall not enter into it* (meaning Heaven) *any thing which is not proved by the fire, as silver is purified by it.* When he had proved his text, he came to divide it, which he did in these three heads: *First*, that the souls suffer in Purgatory three sorts of torments, of which the first was fire, and that greater than the fire of Hell. *Secondly*, to be deprived of the face of God: And *Thirdly*, which was the greatest of all the torments, to see their relations and friends here on earth diverting themselves, and taking so little care to relieve them out of those terrible pains. The preacher spoke very little of the two first points, but he insisted upon the third a long hour, taxing the people of ingratitude and inhumanity; and that if it was possible for any of the living to experience, only for a moment, that devouring flame of Purgatory, certainly he would come again, and sell whatever he had in the world, and give it for Masses: And what pity it is (said he) to know that there are the souls of many of my hearers relations there, and none

of

of them endeavour to relieve them out of that place: He went on, and said: I have a catalogue of the souls, which, by revelation and apparition, we are sure are in Purgatory; for in the first place, the soul of such a one (naming the soul of a rich merchant's father) did appear the other night to a godly person, in the figure of a pig, and the devout person, knowing that the door of his chamber was locked up, began to sprinkle the pig with holy water, and conjuring him, bad him speak, and tell him what he wanted? And the pig said, I am the soul of such an one, and I have been in Purgatory these ten years for want of help. When I left the world, I forgot to tell my Confessor where I left 1000 pistoles, which I had reserved for Masses: My son found them out, and he is such an unnatural child, that he doth not remember my pitiful condition; and now by the permission of Heaven I come to you, and command you to discover this case to the first preacher you meet; that he may publish it, and tell my son, that if he doth not give that money for Masses for my relief, I shall be forever in Purgatory, and his soul shall certainly go to Hell.

The sottish merchant, terrified with this story, believing every tittle of it, got up before all the people & went into the vestry, and when the Friar had finished, he begged of him to go along with him to his house, where he should receive the money, which he did accordingly, for fear of a second thought; and the merchant gave freely the 1000 pistoles, for fear that his father's soul should be kept in Purgatory, and he himself go to Hell.

And besides these cheats and tricks, they make use of themselves to exact money, they have their solicitors and agents, that go from one house to another, telling stories of apparitions and revelations, and these are they which we call *Beatas* and *Devotas*; for as their modesty in apparel, their hypocritical air, and daily exercises of confessing and receiving is well known in the world, the common people have so good an opinion of them, that they believe, as an article of faith, whatever stories they tell, without further inquiry into the matter: So those cunning disguised devils (or worse) instructed by the Friar their Confessor, go and spread abroad many of these apparitions, by which they get a great deal of money for Masses, which they give to the Father Confessor.

Nay, of late, the old Nuns, those that, to their grief, the world despises, have undertaken the trade of publishing revelations and apparitions of souls in Purgatory, and give out that such a soul is, and shall be in it, 'till the father, mother, or sister, go to such a Friar, and give him so many Masses, which he is to say himself and no other. And the case is, that by agreement between the old skeleton, and the covetous Father, he is to give her one third of all the Masses that he receives by her means and application. So you see the nature of this place of Purgatory, the apartments in it, the degrees of the fire of it, the means the Priests and Friars make use of to keep in repair that profitable palace; and above all, the stupidity, sottishness and blindness of the people to believe such dreams as matters of fact. What now can the Roman Catholics say for themselves? I am very much afraid that they will say that I am a deceiver and impostor. The *Jews* said of our Saviour (*John* vii. v. 12.) some, *that he was a good man*; others said, *nay, but he deceiveth the people*, when he was telling the truth. So I shall not be surprised at any calumny nor injury dispersed by them; for I am sure in my conscience, before God and the world, that I write the truth. And let no body mind the method in this account, for now I look upon the practices and cheats of the Priests and Friars in this point of Purgatory, as the most ridiculous, nonsensical, and roguish of all their tricks; so how can a man that has been among them, and now is in the right way, write moderately, and without ridiculing them?

I

I must dismiss this article with my address to the Papist Priests of *England* and *Ireland*. Some of them (immediately after my book was published and read by them) did command their parishoners in their respective Mass-houses (as I was told by a faithful friend) not to read my book, *sub pena excommunicationis*. Others made frivolous remarks on some of my observations and matters of fact; nay, a zealous Protestant having lent one of my books to a Roman-Catholic lady, she gave it to her Priest, and desired his opinion about it. The Priest read it over, and corrected only five passages with his hand in the same book, of which I shall speak in my second part. Above all, this article of Purgatory is the hardest thing to them: But they ought to consider, that I speak only of my country people, and if they complain, I must crave their leave to say, that by that, they make us believe that the *Spanish* contagion has reached to them, & want the same remedy with the *Spaniards*; namely, a narrow searching into the matter, &c.

PART IV.

Of the Inquisitors, and their practices.

IN the time of King *Ferdinand* the fifth, and Queen *Isabella*, the mixture of *Jews*, *Moors*, and *Christians* was so great, the relapses of the new converts so frequent, and the corruptions in matters of religion so bare-faced in all sorts and conditions of people, that the Cardinal of *Spain*, that thought the introducing the Inquisition could be the only way of stopping the course of wickedness and vice; so, as the sole remedy to cure the irreligious practices of those times, the Inquisition was established in the year 1471, in the court, and many other dominions of *Spain*.

The Cardinal's design in giving birth to this tribunal, was only to suppress Heresies, and chastise many horrible crimes committed against religion, viz. Blasphemy, Sodomy, Polygamy, Sorcery, Sacrilege, and many others, which are also punished in these kingdoms

doms by the prerogative court, but not by making use of so barbarous means as the Inquisition doth. The design of the Cardinal was not blamable, being in itself good, and approved by all the serious and devout people of that time; but the performance of it was not so, as will appear by and by.

I can only speak of the Inquisition of *Zaragosa*, for as I am treating of matters of fact, I may tell with confidence what I know of it, as an eye-witness of several things done there. This tribunal is composed of three Inquisitors, who are absolute judges; for, from their judgment there is no appeal, not even to the Pope himself, nor to a general council; as doth appear from what happened in the time of King *Philip* the second, when the Inquisitors having censured the Cardinal of *Toledo*, the Pope sent for the process and sentence, but the Inquisitors did not obey him, and though the council of *Trent* discharged the Cardinal, notwithstanding, they insisted on the performance and execution of their sentence.

The first Inquisitor is a divine, the second, a casuist, and the third, a civilian; the first and second are always Priests, and promoted from Prebends to the high dignity of being holy Inquisitors. The third sometimes is not a Priest, though he is drest in a clerical habit. The three Inquisitors of my time were, first, Don *Pedro Guerrero*. Second, Don *Francisco Torrejon*. Third, Don *Antonio Aliaga*. This tribunal hath a high sheriff, and God knows how many constables & under officers, besides the officers that belong to the house, and that live in it; they have likewise an executioner; or we may say, there are as many executioners, as officers and judges, &c. besides these, there are many *Qualificators* and *Familiares*, of which I will give an account by themselves.

The Inquisitors have a despotic power to command every living soul; and no excuse is to be given, nor contradiction to be made, to their orders; nay, the
people

people have not liberty to speak, nor complain in their misfortunes, and therefore there is a proverb which says, *Con la Inquisition Chiton*: Do not meddle with the Inquisition; or, as to the Inquisition, say nothing.— This will be better understood by the following account of the method they make use of for the taking up and arresting the people; which is thus:

When the Inquisitors receive an information against any body, which is always in private, and with such secrecy that none can know who the informer is (for all the informations are given in at night) they send their officers to the house of the accused, most commonly at midnight, and in a coach: They knock at the door, (and then all the family is in bed) and when some body asks from the windows who is there? The officers say, *the holy Inquisition*. At this word, he that answered, without any delay, or noise, or even the liberty of giving timely notice to the master of the house, comes down to open the door. I say, without the liberty of giving timely notice; for when the Inquisitors send the officers, they are sure, by the spies, that the person is within, and if they do not find the accused, they take up the whole family, and carry them to the Inquisition: So the answerer is with good reason afraid of making any delay in opening the street door. Then they go up stairs and arrest the accused without telling a word, or hearing a word from any of the family, and with great silence, putting him into the coach, they drive to the holy prison. If the neighbours by chance hear the noise of the coach, they dare not go to the window, for it is well known, that no other coach but that of the Inquisition is abroad at that time of the night; nay, they are so much afraid, that they dare not even to ask the next morning their neighbours any thing about it, for those that talk of any thing that the Inquisition doth, are liable to undergo the same punishment, and this, may be, the night following. So if the accused be the daughter, son, or

father,

father, &c. and some friends or relations go in the morning to see that family, and ask the occasion of their tears and grief, they do answer that their daugh- was stolen away the night before, or that the son, or father or mother (whoever the prisoner be) did not come home the night before, and that they suspect he was murdered, &c. This answer they give, because they cannot tell the truth, without exposing themselves to the same misfortune; and not only this, but they cannot go to the Inquisition to inquire for the prisoner, for they would be confined for that alone. So all the comfort the family can have in such a case, is to imagine that the prisoner is in *China*, or in the remotest part of the world, or in Hell, wherein *Nullus ordo sed sempiternus horror inhabitat.* This is the reason why no body knows the persons that are in the Inquisition till the sentence is published and executed, except those Priests and Friars summoned to hear the trial.

The *Qualificators* and *Familiaries* which are in the city and country, upon necessity, have full power to secure any person suspected with the same secrecy, and commit him to the nearest Commissary of the holy office of the Inquisition, and he is to take care to send him safely to the prison; which is all done by night, and without any fear that the people should deliver the prisoner, nay, or even talk of it.

Qualificators,

Are those, that by order from the Inquisitors, examine the crimes committed by the prisoners against the Catholic faith, and give their opinions or censures about it: They are obliged to secrecy, as well as other people; but as the number of them is great, the Inquisitors most commonly make use of ten or twelve of the most learned that are in the city, in difficult cases; but this is only a formality, for their opinions and censures are not regarded, the Inquisitors themselves being the absolute decisive judges. The distinguishing

mark

mark of a *Qualificator* is the Cross of the holy office, which is a medal of pure gold as big as a thirteen, with a Cross in the middle, half white, and half black, which they wear before their breast; but in public functions or processions, the Priests and Friars wear another bigger Cross of embroidery on their cloaks, or habits. To be *Qualificator* is a great honor to his whole family and relations, for this is a public testimony of the old Christianity, and pure blood (as they call it) of the family.

No Nobleman covets the honor of being a Qualificator, for they are all ambitious of the Cross of St. *James*, of *Alcantara*, of *Calatrava*, of *Malta*, and the *golden Fleece*, which are the five orders of the nobility; so the honor of a *Qualificator* is for those people, who though their families being not well known, are desirous to boast of their antiquity and Christianism, tho', to obtain such honor, they pay a great sum of money: For, in the first place, he that desireth to be a *Qualificator*, is to appear before the Holy Tribunal, to make a public profession of the Catholic faith, and to acknowledge the Holy Tribunal for the supreme of all others, and the Inquisitors for his own judges. This is the first step: After, he is to lay down on the table the certificate of his baptism, and the names of his parents for four generations; the towns and places of their former habitations; and two hundred pistoles for the expences in taking informations.

This done, he goes home till the Inquisitors send for him, and if they do not send for him in six months time he loseth the money, and all hopes of ever getting the Cross of *Qualificator*; and this happens very often for the reasons I shall give by and by.

The Inquisitors send their Commissaries into all the places of the new proponant ancestors, where they may get some account of their lives and conversations, and of the purity of their blood, and that they never were mixt with *Jewish* families, nor heretics, and that they were

were old Christians. These examinations are performed in the most rigorous and severe manner that can be; for if some of the informers and witnesses are in a falsity, they are put into the Inquisition; so every body gives the report concerning the family in question, with great caution, to the best of his knowledge and memory. When the commissaries have taken the necessary informations with witnesses of a good name, they examine the parish book, and take a copy of the ancestors names, the year and day of their marriages, and the year, day, and place of their burials. The commissaries then return to the Inquisitors with all the examinations, witnesses, proofs and convictions of the purity and ancient Christianity of the proponant's families, for four generations; and being again examined by the three Inquisitors, if they find them real and faithful, then they send the same commissaries to inquire into the character, life, and conversation of the *postulant*, or demanding person, but in this point the commissaries pass by many personal failings, so when the report is given to the holy Inquisitors, they send for the *postulant*, and exaxamine him concerning the matters of faith, the holy scriptures, the knowledge of the ancient fathers of the church, moral cases, all which is but mere formality, for the generality of the holy Fathers themselves do not take much pains in the study of those things, and therefore the *postulant* is not afraid of their nice questions, nor very solicitous how to resolve them.

When the examination is over, they order the secretary to draw the patent of the grant of the holy Cross to such an one, in regard to his families old purity of blood and Christianity, and to his personal parts and religious conversation, certifying in the patent, that for four generations past, none of his father's or mother's relations were at all suspected in points concerning the *holy Catholic Roman faith*, or mixt with *Jewish*, or Heretical blood.

The day following, the *postulant* appears before the assembly

Assembly of *Qualificators* in the Hall of the Inquisition, and the first Inquisitor celebrates the Mass assisted by two *Qualificators*, as Deacon and Subdeacon. One of the oldest Brethren preacheth a sermon on that occasion, and when the Mass is over, they make a sort of procession in the same Hall, and after it, the Inquisitor gives the book of the gospel to the *Postulant*, and makes him swear the usual oaths; which done, the *Postulant*, on his knees, receiveth the Cross, or Medal, from the hands of the Inquisitors, who, with a black ribbon, puts it on the *Postulant*'s neck, and begins to sing *Te Deum*, and the collect of thanks, which is the end of the ceremonies. Then all the assistant *Qualificators* congratulate the new brother, and all go up to the Inquisitor's apartment to drink chocolate, and after that, every one to his own dwelling place.

The new *Qualificator* dineth with the Inquisitors that day, and after dinner the Secretary brings in a bill of all the fees and expences of the informations; which he must clear before he leaves the Inquisition. Most commonly the whole comes to four hundred pistoles, including the two hundred he gave in the beginning; but sometimes it comes to a thousand pistoles, to those whose ancestors families were out of the kingdom, for then the Commissaries expend a great deal more: And if it happen they find the least spot of *Jewdaism*, or Heresy, in some relation of the family, the Commissaries do not proceed any further in the examinations, but come back again to the Inquisition immediately, and then the *Postulant* is never sent for by the Inquisitors, who keep the two hundred pistoles for pious uses.

Familiares

Are always lay-men, but of good sense and education. These wear the same Cross, and for the granting of it, the Inquisitors make the same informations and proofs as they make for *Qualificators*. The honor and privileges are the same; for they are not subject but to the tribunal of the Inquisition. Their businesses are not the same; for they are only employed in gathering together, and inquiring after all books against the Catholic faith, and to watch the actions of suspected people. They take a turn sometimes into the country, but then they do not wear their Cross openly till occasion requires it. They insinuate themselves into all companies, and they will even speak against the Inquisition, and against religion, to try whether the people are of that sentiment; in short, they are spies of the Inquisitors. They do not pay so much as the *Qualificators*, for the honor of the Cross, but they are obliged to take a turn now & then in the country, at their own expences. They are not so many in number as the *Qualificators*, for in a trial of the Inquisition, where all ought to be present, I did reckon once one hundred and sixty, and twice as many *Qualificators*. I saw the list of them both; i. e. of the whole kingdom of *Arragon*, wherein are *Qualificators*, of the secular Priests, 243, and of the regular, 406, *Familiares* 208.

The royal castle, formerly the palace of the King of *Arragon*, called *Aljaferia*, was given to the Inquisitors to hold their tribunal there, and prison too. The best apartments were for the three Inquisitors and their families, the rest for the Sheriff and subaltern officers. It is a musket shot distant from the city on the river side. But after the battle of *Almanza*, when the Duke of *Orleans* came as Generalissimo of the *Spanish* and *French* army, he thought that place necessary to put a strong garrison in; so he made the Marquiss *de Torsy* Governor of the fort of *Aljaferia*, and turned out the Inquisitors, who being obliged, by force, to quit their apartments, they took a large house near the *Carmelites* Convent; but two months after, finding that the place was not safe enough to keep the prisoners in, they removed to the palace of the Earl of *Tuentes*, in the great street

street called *Coso*, out of which they were turned by *Monsieur de Legal*, as I shall tell by and by.

A form of their public trial.

IF a trial is to be made publicly in the hall of the Holy Office, the Inquisitors summon two Priests out of every parish church, and two regular Priests out of every Convent: All the *Qualificators* and *Familiares* that are in the city: The Sheriff, and all the under officers: The Secretary, and three Inquisitors: All the aforesaid meet at the common hall on the day appointed for the trial, at ten in the morning. The hall is hung in black, without any windows, or light, but what comes in through the door. At the front there is an image of our Saviour on the Cross, under a black velvet canopy, and six candlesticks with six thick yellow wax candles on the altar's table: On one side there is a pulpit, with another candle, where the Secretary reads the crimes; three chairs for the three Inquisitors, and round about the hall, seats and chairs for the summoned Priests, Friars, Familiares, and other officers.

When the Inquisitors are come in, an under officer crieth out, *Silence, silence, silence; the holy Fathers are coming*, and from that very time, till all is over, nobody speaks, nay, nor spits, and the thought of the place puts every body under respect, fear, and attention.— The holy Fathers, with their hats on their heads, and serious countenances, go, and kneeling down before the altar, the first Inquisitor begins to give out, *Veni Creator Spiritus, Mentes tuorum visita*, &c. And the congregation sing the rest, and the collect being said by him also, every body sits down. The Secretary then goes up to the pulpit, and the holy Father rings a small silver bell, which is the signal for bringing in the criminal. What is done afterwards will be known by the following trials and instances, at which I was present

sent, being one of the youngest Priests of the Cathedral, and therefore obliged to go to these dismal tragedies; in which, the first thing, after the criminal comes in, and kneels down before the Inquisitors, who receives a severe, bitter corrrection from the first Inquisitor, who measures it according to the nature of the crimes committed by the criminal; of all which, to the best of my memory, I will give an account in the first trial.

Trial I.

OF the Reverend Father, *Joseph Silvestre*, *Franciscan* Friar; and the Mother *Mary* of *Jesus*, Abbess of the monastery of *Epila*, of *Franciscan* Nuns. Father *Joseph* was a tall lusty man, 40 years of age, and had been 12 years Professor of philosophy and divinity in the great Convent of St. *Francis*.[*] Sor *Mary* was 32 years old, mighty witty, and of an agreeable countenance. These two criminals were drest in brown gowns, painted all over with flames of fire, representing Hell, a thick rope tied about their necks, and yellow wax candles in their hands. Both, in this dull appearance, came and prostrated themselves at the Inquisitors feet, and the first holy Father began to correct them in the following words:

Unworthy creatures, how can our *Catholic Roman faith* be preserved pure, if those who, by their office and ministry, ought to recommend its observance in the most earnest manner, are not only the first, but the greatest transgressors of it? Thou that teachest another not to steal, not to commit fornication, dost thou steal, and commit sacrilege, which is worse than fornication? In these things we could shew you pity and compassion; but as to the transgressions of the express commandments of our church, and the respect due to us

the

---

[*] *Sor* is a title given to the Nuns, which answers to *Sister*, as coming from the Latin *Soror*.

the judges of the holy tribunal, we cannot; therefore your sentence is pronounced by these holy Fathers of pity and compassion, Lords Inquisitors, as you shall hear now, and afterwards undergo.

Sor Mary was in a flood of tears, but Father *Joseph*, who was a learned man, with great boldness and assurance, said, what, do you call yourselves holy Fathers of pity and compassion? I say unto you, that you are three devils on earth, Fathers of all manner of mischief, barbarity, and lewdness. No Inquisitors were ever treated at such a rate before, and we were thinking that Friar *Joseph* was to suffer fire, for this high affront to them. But Don *Pedro Guerrero*, first judge, though a severe, haughty, passionate man, ordered only a gag, or bit of a bridle to put in his mouth, but Friar *Joseph* flying into a fury, said, I despise all your torments, for my crimes are not against you, but against God, who is the only judge of my conscience, and you do yet worse things. &c.

The Inquisitors ordered to carry him to prison, while the crimes and sentence were reading. So he was carried in, and the Nun with great humility heard the accusation and sentence.

The Secretary, by order, begun to read, 1*st*. That Friar *Joseph* was made Father Confessor and *Sor Mary* Mother Abbess. That in the beginning they shewed a great example of humility and virtue to the Nuns; but afterwards, all this zeal of theirs did appear to be mere hypocrisy, and a cover for their wicked actions; for as she had a grate in the wall of Friar *Joseph*'s room, they both did eat in private, and fast in public: That the said Friar *Joseph* was found in bed with *Sor Mary* by such a Nun, and that she was found with child, and took a remedy to prevent the public proof of it. That both Friar *Joseph* and *Sor Mary* had robbed the treasure of the Convent, and that one day they were contriving how to go away into another country, and that they had spoken in an irreverent manner of the Pope and Inquisitors. This

This was the whole accufation againft them, which Friar *Jofeph* and *Sor Mary* had denied before, faying, it was only hatred and malice of the informers againft them, and defired the witnefles to be produced before them; but this being againft the cuftom of the holy office, the holy Fathers had pronounced the fentence; viz. That Friar *Jofeph* fhould be deprived of all the honors of his order, and of active and paffive voice, and be removed to a country Convent, and be whipped three times a week, for the fpace of fix weeks. That *Sor Mary* fhould be deprived of her Abbacy, and removed into another monaftry: This punifhment being only for their audacious and unrefpectful manner of talking againft the Pope and Inquifitors.

Indeed, by this fentence we did believe, that the crimes they were charged with, were only an invention of the malicious Nuns; but poor Friar *Jofeph* did fuffer for his indifcretion, for though the next day, the Inquifitors gave out that he efcaped out of the prifon, we did really believe he had been ftrangled in the Inquifition.

This was the firft trial I was prefent at, and the fecond was that of *Mary Guerrero* and Friar *Michael Navarro*, of which I have given an account in the chapter of *Auricular Confeffion*. After thefe two trials, the Inquifitors were turned out by Monfieur *de Legal*, and for eight months we had no Inquifition. How this thing happened, is worthy of obfervation, therefore I fhall give a particular account of it, that I may not deprive the public of fo pleafant a ftory.

In 1706, after the battle of *Almanza*, the *Spanifh* army being divided in two bodies, one of them thro' the kingdom of *Valencia*, to the frontiers of *Catalonia*, commanded by the Duke of *Berwick*, and other compofed of the *French* auxiliary troops, 14000 in number, went to the conqueft of *Arragon*, whofe inhabitants had declared themfelves for King *Charles* the 3d. The body of *French* troops was commanded by his highnefs the Duke of *Orleans*, who was the Generaliffimo of the whole

whole army. Before he came near the city, the magistrates went to meet him, and offered the keys of the city, but he refused them, saying, he was to enter it through a breach; and so he did, treating the people as rebels to their lawful King: And when he had ordered all the civil and military affairs of the city, he went down to the frontiers of *Catalonia*, leaving his Lieutenant General Monsieur *de Jofreville* Governor of the town. But this Governor being a mild tempered man, he was loth to follow the orders left with him, as to the contribution money: So he was called to the army, and the Lientenant General Monsieur *de Legal* came in his place. The city was to pay 1000 crowns a month, for the Duke's table, and every house a pistole, which by computation made up the sum of 18000 pistoles a month, which were paid eight months together, besides this, the Convents were to a pay a *Donative*, or gift proportionable to their rents. The college of *Jesuits* were charged 2000 pistoles; the *Dominicans* 1000, *Augustins* 1000, *Carmelites* 1000, &c. Monsieur *de Legal* sent first to the *Jesuits*, who refused to pay, saying, that it was against the ecclesiastical immunity: But *Legal* not acquainted with those sort of excuses, did send four companies of grenadiers to quarter in their college at discretion: The Father sent immediately an express to the King's Father Confessor, who was a *Jesuit*, with complaints about the case: But the grenadiers did make more expedition in their plundering, and mischiefs, than the *courier* did in his journey. So the Fathers seeing the damage all their goods had already received, and fearing some violence upon their treasure, went to pay Monsieur *Legal* the 2000 pistoles as a *Donative*.

Next to this he sent to the *Dominicans*. The Friars of this order are all *Familiares* of the holy office, and depending upon it, they did excuse themselves in a civil manner, saying, they had no money, and if Monsieur *de Legal*, had a mind to insist upon the demand of the

the 1000 piſtoles they could not pay them, without ſending to him the ſilver bodies of the ſaints. The Friars thought by this to frighten Monſieur *de Legal*, and if he was ſo reſolute, as to accept the offer, to ſend the ſaints in a proceſſion, and raiſe the people, crying out *Hereſy*, *Hereſy*. *De Legal* anſwered to the Friars, that he was obliged to obey the Duke's orders, and ſo he would receive the ſilver ſaints: So the Friars all in a ſolemn proceſſion, and with lighted candles in their hands, carried the ſaints to the Governor *Legal*: And as ſoon as he heard of this public devotion of the Friars, he ordered immediately four companies of grenadiers to line the ſtreets on both ſides, before his houſe, and to keep their fuzees in one hand, and a lighted candle in the other, to receive the ſaints with the ſame devotion and veneration. And though the Friars endeavoured to raiſe the people, no body was ſo bold as to expoſe themſelves to the army, there being left 8 regiments to keep the mob under fear and ſubjection. *Legal* received the ſaints, and ſent them to the mint, promiſing the Father Piror to give him what remained above the 1000 piſtoles. The Friars being diſappointed in their project of raiſing the people, went to the Inquiſitors to deſire them to releaſe immediately their ſaints out of the mint, by excommunicating Monſieur *de Legal*, which the Inquiſitors did upon the ſpot; and the excommunication being drawn and ſigned, they gave ſtrict orders to their ſecretary to go & read it before Monſieur *de Legal*, which he did accordingly: And Monſieur the Governor, far from flying into a paſſion, with a mild countenance took the paper from the Secretary, and ſaid; pray, tell your maſters, the Inquiſitors, that I anſwer them to-morrow morning. The Secretary went away fully ſatisfied with *Legal*'s civil behaviour. The ſame minute, as if he was inſpired by the holy ſpirit, without reflecting upon any conſequence, he called his own Secretary, he bid him draw a copy of the excommunication, putting out the name of *Legal*,

gal, and inserting in its place, *the holy Inquisitors*. The next morning he gave orders for four regiments to be ready, and sent them along with his Secretary to the Inquisition, with command to read the excommunication to the Inquisitors themselves, and if they made the least noise, to turn them out, open all the prisons, and quarter two regiments there. He was not afraid of the people, for the Duke took away all the arms from every individual person. And, on pain of death, commanded that noboby should keep but a short sword; and besides, four regiments were under arms, to prevent all sort of tumults and disturbance: So his Sacretary went and performed the Governor's orders.—The Inquisitors were never more surprised than to see themselves excommunicated by a man that had no authority for it, and resenting it, they began to cry out, *War against the Heretic de Legal*; this is a public insult against our *Catholic faith*. To which the Secretary answered, *Holy Inquisitors*, the King wants this house to quarter his troops in, so walk out immediately: And as they continued in their exclamations, he took the Inquisitors, with a strong guard, & carried them to a private house destined for them; but when they saw the laws of military discipline, they begged leave to take their goods along with them, which was immediately granted; and the next day they set out for *Madrid*, to complain to the King; who gave them this slight answer, I am very sorry for it, but I cannot help it; my crown is in danger, and my grandfather defends it, and this is done by his troops; if it had been done by my troops, I should apply a speedy remedy: But you must have patience till things take another turn. So the Inquisitors were obliged to have patience for eight months.

The Secretary of Monsieur *de Legal*, according to his orders, opened the doors of all the prisons, & then the wickednesses of the Inquisitors were detected, for four hundred prisoners got liberty that day, and among them sixty young women were found very well dreſt, who were, in all human appearance, the number of the three Inquiſitors *Seraglio*, as ſome of them did own afterwards. But this diſcovery, ſo dangerous to the holy tribunal, was in ſome meaſure prevented by the Archbiſhop, who went to deſire Monſieur *de Legal* to ſend thoſe women to his palace, and that his Grace would take care of them; and that in the mean time, he ordered an eccleſiaſtical cenſure to be publiſhed againſt thoſe that ſhould defame, by groundleſs reports, the holy office of the Inquiſition. The Governor anſwered to his Grace, he would give him all the aſſiſtance for it he could; but as to the young women it was not in his power, the officers having hurried them away; and indeed it was not; for as it is not to be ſuppoſed that the Inquiſitors, having the abſolute power to confine in their *Seraglio* whomſoever they had a fancy for, would chooſe ordinary girls, but the beſt and handſomeſt of the city: So the *French* officers were all ſo glad of getting ſuch fine miſtreſſes, that they immediately took them away, knowing very well they would follow them to the end of the world, for fear of being confined again. In my travels in *France* afterwards, I met with one of thoſe women at *Rotchfort*, in the ſame inn I went to lodge in that night, who had been brought there by the ſon of the maſter of the inn, formerly Lieutenant in the *French* ſervice in *Spain*, who had married her for her extraordinary beauty and good parts. She was the daughter of Counſellor *Balabriga*, and I knew her before ſhe was taken up by the Inquiſitors orders; but we thought ſhe was ſtolen by ſome officer; for this was given out by her Father, who died of grief and vexation, without the comfort of opening his trouble, nay, even to his Confeſſor; ſo great is the fear of the Inquiſitors there.

I was very glad to meet one of my country-women in my travels, and as ſhe did not remember me, and eſpecially in my then diſguiſe, I was then taken for nothing

thing but an officer. I resolved to stay there the next day, to have the satisfaction of conversing with her, and have a plain account of what we could not know in *Zaragosa*, for fear of incurring the ecclesiastical censure, published by the Archbishop. Now my conversation with her being *a propos*, and necessary to discover the roguery of the Inquisitors, it seems proper to divert the reader with it.

Mr. *Faulcaut*, my country-woman's husband, was then at *Paris*, upon some pretensions, and though her father and mother-in-law were continually at home, they did not mistrust me, I being a countryman of their daughter-in-law, who freely came to my room at any time, and as I was desiring her not to expose herself to any uneasiness on my account; she answered me, Captain, we are now in *France*, not in *Zaragosa*, and we enjoy here all manner of freedom without going beyond the limits of sobriety; so you may be easy in that point, for my father and mother-in-law have ordered me to be obliging to you, nay, and to beg the favour of you to take your repose here this week, if your business permit it, and to be pleased to accept this their small entertainment on freecost, as a token of their esteem to me, and my country-gentleman. If it had not been for my continual fear of being discovered, I would have accepted the proposition; so I thanked her, and begged her to return my hearty acknowledgment to the gentleman and lady of the house, and that I was very sorry, that my pressing business, at *Paris*, would prevent and hinder me to enjoy so agreeable company: But if my business was soon despatched at *Paris*, then, at my return, I would make a halt there, may-be for a fortnight. Mrs. *Faulcaut* was very much concerned at my haste to go away: But she did make me promise to come back again that way: So amidst these compliments, from one to another, supper came in, and we went to it, the old man and woman, their daughter and I; none but Mrs. *Faulcaut*

could

could speak *Spanish*, so she was my interpreter, for I could not speak *French*. After supper, the landlord and landlady left us alone, and I began to beg of her the favor to tell me the accident of her prison, of her sufferings in the Inquisition, and of every thing relating to the holy office, and fear not (said I) for we are in *France*, and not in *Zaragosa*; here is no Inquisition, so you may safely open your heart to a countryman of yours. I will, with all my heart, said she, and to satisfy your curiosity, I shall begin with the occasion of my imprisonment, which was as follows:

I went one day, with my mother to visit the Countess of *Attarafs*, and I met there Don *Francisco Torrejon*, her Confessor, and second Inquisitor of the holy office: After we had drunk chocolate, he asked me my age, and my Confessor's name, and so many intricate questions about religion, that I could not answer him: His serious countenance did frighten me, and as he perceived my fear, he desired the Countess to tell me, that he was not so severe as I took him to be; after which he caressed me in the most obliging manner in the world; he gave me his hand, which I kissed with great respect and modesty, and when he went away, he told me, my dear child, I shall remember you till the next time. I did not mind the sense of the words; for I was unexperienced in matters of gallantry, being only fifteen years old at that time. Indeed he did remember me, for the very night following, when we were in bed, hearing a hard knocking at the door, the maid that lay in the same room where my bed was, went to the window, and asking who is there? I heard say, The holy Inquisition. I could not forbear crying out: Father, father, I am ruined for ever. My dear father got up, and inquiring what the matter was; I answered him, with tears, the Inquisition; and he, for fear that the maid should not open the door as quick as such a case required, went himself, as another *Abraham*, to open the door, and to offer his dear

daughter

daughter to the fire of the Inquisitors, and as I did not cease to cry out, as if I was a mad girl, my dear father, all in tears, did put in my mouth a bit of a bridle, to shew his obedience to the holy office, and his zeal for the Catholic faith, for he thought I had committed some crime against religion; so the officers giving me but time to put on my petticoat and a mantle, took me down into the coach, and without giving me the satisfaction of embracing my dear father and mother, they carried me into the Inquisition: I did expect to die that very night; but when they carried me into a noble room, well furnished, and an excellent bed in it, I was quite surprised. The officers left me there, and immediately a maid came in with a salver of sweet meats and cinnamon-water, desiring me to take some refreshment before I went to bed: I told her I could not; but that I should be obliged to her, if she could tell me whether I was to die that night or not? Die (said she) you do not come here to die, but to live like a princess, and you shall want nothing in the world but the liberty of going out; and now pray mind nothing, but to go to bed, and sleep easy, for to-morrow you shall see wonders in this house, and as I am chosen to be your waiting-maid, I hope you will be very kind to me. I was going to ask her some questions, but she told me, madam, I have not leave to tell you any thing else till to-morrow, only that no body shall come to disturb you; and now I am going about some business, and I will come back presently, for my bed is in the closet near your bed: So she left me there for a quarter of an hour. The great amazement I was in took away all my senses, or the free exercise of them, for I had not liberty to think of my parents, nor of grief, nor of the danger that was so near me: So in this suspention of thought, the waiting-maid came and locked the chamber door after her, and told me, Madam, let us go to bed, and only tell me at what time in the morning you will have the chocolate ready? I ask-

ed

ed her name, and she told me it was *Mary*. *Mary*, for God's sake (said I) tell me whether I come to die or not? I have told you, madam, that you come, she said, to live as one of the happiest creatures in the world.— And as I observed her reservedness, I did not ask her any more questions: So recommending myself to God Almighty, and to our lady of *Pilar*, and preparing myself to die, I went to bed, but could not sleep one minute. I was up with the day, but *Mary* slept till six of the clock: Then she got up, and wondering to see me up, she said to me, pray madam, will you drink chocolate now? Do what you please (said I) then she left me half an hour alone, and she came back with a silver plate with two cups of chocolate and some biscuits on it. I drank one cup, and desired her to drink the other, which she did. Well, *Mary*, said I, can you give me any account of the reason of my being here? Not yet, madam, said she, but only have patience for a little while. With this answer she left me, and an hour after came again with two baskets, with a fine holland shift, a holland under petticoat, with fine lace round about it: Two silk petticoats and a little *Spanish* waistcoat, with a gold fringe all over it: With combs and ribbons, and every thing suitable to a lady of higher quality than I: But my greatest surprise was to see a gold snuff-box with the picture of Don *Francisco Torrejon* in it. Then I soon understood the meaning of my confinement. So I considered with myself, that to refuse the present would be the occasion of my immediate death, and to accept of it was to give him, even on the first day, too great encouragement against my honor. But I found, as I thought then, a medium in the case; so I said, *Mary*, pray give my service to Don *Francisco Torrejon*, and tell him, that as I could not bring my clothes along with me last night, honesty permits me to accept of these clothes which are necessary to keep me decent; but since I take no snuff, I beg his Lordship to excuse me, if I do not accept this box.

Mary

Mary went to him with this answer, and came again with a picture nicely set in gold, with four diamonds at the four corners of it, and told me, that his Lordship was mistaken, and that he desired me to accept that picture, which would be a great favour to him; and while I was thinking with myself what to do, *Mary* said to me, pray, madam, take my poor advice, accept the picture, and every thing that he sends to you; for consider, that if you do not consent and comply with every thing he has a mind for, you will soon be put to death, and no body will defend you; but if you are obliging and kind to him, he is a very complaisant and agreeable gentleman, and will be a charming lover, and you will be here like a Queen, and he will give you another apartment, with a fine garden, and many young ladies shall come to visit you: So I advise you to send a civil answer to him, and desire a visit from him; or else you will soon begin to repent yourself. O dear God, said I, must I abandon my honor without any remedy! If I oppose his desire, he by force will obtain it; so, full of confusion, I bid *Mary* to give him what answer she thought fit: She was very glad of my humble submission, and went to give Don *Francisco* my answer. She came back a few minutes after, all overjoyed, to tell me that his Lordship would honor me with his company at supper, and that he could not come sooner on the account of some business that called him abroad; but in the mean time desired me to mind nothing, but how to divert myself, and to give to *Mary* my measure for a suit of new clothes, and order her to bring me every thing I could wish for; *Mary* added to this, madam, I may call you now my mistress, and must tell you, that I have been in the holy office these fourteen years, and I know the customs of it very well, but because silence is imposed upon me under pain of death, I cannot tell you any thing but what concerns your person; so, in the first place, do not oppose the holy Father's will and pleasure: *Secondly*, if you see some young ladies here,

never

never ask them the occasion of their being here, nor any thing of their business, neither will they ask you any thing of this nature, and take care not to tell them any thing of your being here; you may come and divert yourself with them at such hours as are appointed; you shall have music, and all sorts of recreations; three days hence you shall dine with them, they are all ladies of quality, young and merry, and this is the best of lives, you will not long for going abroad, you will be so well diverted at home; and when your time is expired, then the holy Fathers will send you out of this country, and marry you to some nobleman. Never mention the name of Don *Francisco*, nor your name to any: If you see here some young ladies of your acquaintance in the city, they never will take notice of your formerly knowing each other, though they will talk with you of indifferent matters, so take care not to speak any thing of your family. All these things together made me astonished, or rather stupified, and the whole seemed to me a piece of enchantment; so that I could not imagine what to think of it. With this lesson she left me, and told me she was going to order my dinner, and every time she went out, she locked the door after her. There were but two high windows in my chamber, and I could see nothing through them, but examining the room all over, I found a closet with all sorts of historical and profane books, and every thing necessary for writing. So I spent my time till the dinner came in, reading some diverting amorous stories, which was a great satisfaction to me. When *Mary* came with the things for the table, I told her that I was inclined to sleep, and that I would rather sleep than go to dinner, so she asked me whether she should awaken me or not, and at what time? Two hours hence (said I) so I lay down and fell asleep, which was a great refreshment to me. At the time fixed she wakened me, and I went to dinner, at which was every thing that could satisfy the most nice appetite. After dinner

she

she left me alone, and told me, if I did want any thing I might ring the bell and call: So I went to the closet again, and spent three hours in reading. I think really I was under some enchantment, for I was in a perfect suspension of thought, so as to remember neither father or mother, for this run least in my mind, and what was at that time most in it, I do not know. *Mary* came and told me, that Don *Francisco* was come home, and that she thought he would come to see me very soon, and begged of me to prepare myself to receive him with all manner of kindness. At seven in the evening Don *Francisco* came, in his night-gown and night-cap, not with the gravity of an Inquisitor, but with the gaiety of an officer. He saluted me with great respect & civility, & told me he had designed to keep me company at supper, but could not that night, having some business of consequence to finish in his closet; and that his coming to see me was only out of the respect he had for my family, and to tell me at the same time, that some of my lovers had procured my ruin forever, accusing me in matters of religion; that the informations were taken, and the sentence pronounced against me, to be burnt alive, in a dry pan, with a gradual fire; but that he, out of pity and love to my family, had stopped the execution of it. Each of these words was a mortal stroke on my heart, and knowing not what I was doing, I threw myself at his feet, and said, *Seignior*, have you stopped the execution forever? That only belongs to you to stop it, or not, (said he) and with this he wished me a good night. As soon as he went away, I fell a crying, but *Mary* came and asked me what did oblige me to cry so bitterly? Ah! Good *Mary*, said I, pray tell me what is the meaning of the dry pan, and gradual fire? For I am in expectation of nothing but death, and that by it. O, pray never fear, you will see another day the pan and gradual fire; but they are made for those that oppose the holy Father's will, not for you, that are so ready to obey them. But, pray, was Don *Francisco* very civil and obliging? I do not know (said I) for his discourse has put me out of my wits; this I know, that he saluted me with respect and civility, but he has left me abruptly; well (said *Mary*) you do not know him, he is the most obliging man in the world, if people are civil with him, and if not, he is as unmerciful as *Nero*, and so for your own preservation, take care to oblige him in all respects; now, pray go to supper, and be easy. I was so much troubled in mind with the thoughts of the dry pan and gradual fire, that I could neither eat nor sleep that night. Early in the morning *Mary* got up, and told me, that no body was yet up in the house, and that she would shew me the dry pan and gradual fire, on condition, that I should keep it secret for her sake, and my own too; which I having promised her, she took me along with her, and shewed me a dark room with a thick iron door, & within it an oven, & a large brass pan upon it, with a cover of the same, & a lock to it, the oven was burning at that time, and I asked *Mary* for what use that pan was there? And she, without giving me any answer, took me by the hand, out of that place, & carried me into a large room, where she shewed me a thick wheel, covered on both sides with thick boards, and opening a little window, in the centre of it, desired me to look with a candle on the inside of it, and I saw all the circumference of the wheel set with sharp rasors. After that, she shewed me a pit, full of serpents and toads. Then she said to me, now, my good mistress, I'll tell you the use of these three things. The dry pan and gradual fire are for Hereticks, and those that oppose the holy Father's will and pleasure, for they are put all naked and alive into the pan, and the cover of it being locked up, the executioner begins to put in the oven a small fire, and by degrees he augmenteth it till the body is burnt into ashes. The second is designed for those that speak against the Pope, and the holy Fathers; and they are put within the wheel, and the door being locked,

the

the executioner turns the wheel till the person is dead. And the third is for those that contemn the images, and refuse to give the due respect and veneration to ecclesiastical persons, for they are thrown into the pit, & there they become the food of serpents & toads. Then *Mary* said to me, that another day she would shew me torments for public sinners, & transgressors of the five commandments of our holy Mother the Church; so I, in a deep amazement, desired *Mary* to shew me no more places, for the very thoughts of those three, which I had seen, were enough to terrify me to the heart.— So we went to my room, and she charged me again to be very obedient to all the commands Don *Francisco* should give me, or to be assured, if I did not, that I was to undergo the torment of the dry pan. Indeed I conceived such an horror for the gradual fire, that I was not mistress of my senses, nay, nor of my thoughts: So I told *Mary* that I would follow her advice, and grant Don *Francisco* every thing he would desire of me. If you are in that disposition (said she) leave off all fears and apprehensions, and expect nothing but pleasure and satisfaction, and all manner of recreation, and you shall begin to experience some of these things this very day. Now let me dress you, for you must go to wish a good-morrow to Don *Francisco*, and to breakfast with him. I thought really this was a great honor to me, and some comfort to my troubled mind; so I made all the haste I could, and *Mary* conveyed me through a gallery into Don *Francisco*'s apartment. He was still in bed, and desired me to sit down by him, and ordered *Mary* to bring the chocolate two hours after, and with this she left me alone with Don *Francisco*, who immediately, ardently declaring his inclinations, I had not the liberty to make any excuse, and so by extinguishing the fire of his passion, I was free from the gradual fire and dry pan, which was all that then troubled my mind. When *Mary* came with the chocolate, I was very much

ashamed

ashamed to be seen with him in bed, but she coming to the bed-side where I was, and kneeling down, paid me homage as if I was a queen; and served me first with a cup of chocolate, still on her knees, and bade me to give another cup to Don *Francisco* myself, which he received mighty graciously, and having drunk up the chocolate, she went out; we discoursed for a while of various things, but I never spoke a word but when he desired me to answer him: So at ten of the clock, *Mary* came again, and dressing me, she desired me to go along with her, and leaving Don *Francisco* in bed, she carried me into another chamber very delightful, and better furnished than the first; for the windows of it were lower, and I had the pleasure of seeing the river and gardens on the other side out of it. Then *Mary* told me, madam, the young ladies of this house will come before dinner to welcome you, and make themselves happy in the honor of your company, and will take you to dine with them. Pray remember the advices I have given you already, and do not make yourself unhappy by asking useless questions. She had not finished these words, when I saw entering my apartment (which consisted of a large anti-chamber and a bed-chamber with two large closets) a troop of young beautiful ladies, finely drest, who all, one after another, came to embrace me, and to wish me joy. My senses were in a perfect suspension, and I could not speak a word, nor answer their kind compliments: But one of them seeing me so silent, said to me, madam, the solitude of this place will affect you in the beginning, but when you begin to be in our company, and feel the pleasures of our amusements and recreations, you will quit your pensive thoughts: Now we beg of you the honor to come and dine with us to day, and henceforth three days in a week. I thanked them, and we went to dinner. That day we had all sorts of exquisite meats, and were served with delicate fruits and sweet-meats. The room was very long, with two tables on each side,

another

another at the front of it, and I reckoned in it that day 52 young ladies, the oldest of them not exceeding 24 years of age: Six maids did serve the whole number of us, but my *Mary* waited on me alone at dinner: After dinner we went up stairs into a long gallery, all round about with lattice-windows; where, some of us playing on instruments of music, others playing at cards, and others walking about, we spent three hours together. At last, *Mary* came up, ringing a small bell, which was the signal to retire into our rooms, as they told me; but *Mary* said to the whole company, Ladies, to day is a day of recreation, so you may go into what room you please, till eight of the clock, and then you are to go into your own chambers: So they all desired leave to go with me to my apartment, to spend the time there, and I was very glad, that they preferred my chamber to another; so all going down together, we found in my anti-chamber a table, with all sorts of sweet-meats upon it, iced cinnamon-water, and almonds-milk, and the like, every one did eat and drink, but no body spoke a word, touching the sumptuousness of the table, nor mentioned any thing concerning the Inquisition of the holy Fathers. So we spent our time in merry, indifferent conversation, till eight of the clock. Then every one retired to their own room, and *Mary* told me, that Don *Francisco* did wait for me, so we went to his apartment, and supper being ready, we both alone sat at table, attended by my maid only. After supper, *Mary* went away, and we to bed, and next morning, she served us with chocolate, which we drank in bed, and then slept till ten of the clock. Then we got up, and my waiting-maid carried me into my chamber, where I found ready, two suits of clothes, of a rich brocade, and every thing else, suitable to a lady of the first rank. I put on one, and when I was quite drest, the young ladies came to wish me a good morrow, all drest in different clothes, and better than the day before, and we spent the second and

third

third day in the same recreation; Don *Francisco* continuing also with me in the same manner. But the third morning, after drinking chocolate in bed, as the custom was for Don *Francisco* and me, *Mary* told me, that a lady was waiting for me in the other room, and desired me to get up, with an haughty look, and Don *Francisco* saying nothing, I then got up, and left him in bed. I thought that it was to give me some new comfort and diversion; but I was very much mistaken, for *Mary* conveyed me into a young lady's room not eight feet long, which was a perfect prison, and there, before the lady, told me, Madam, this is your room, and this young lady your bedfellow and comrade, and left me there with this unkind command. O Heaven's! Thought I, what is this that has happened to me? I fancied myself out of grief, and I perceived now the beginning of my vexation. What is this, dear lady? (said I) is this an enchanted palace, or an Hell upon earth? I have lost father and mother, and what is worse, I have lost my honor, and my soul forever. My new companion, seeing me like a mad woman, took me by the hands, and said to me, dear sister (for this is the name I will give you henceforth) leave off your crying, leave off your grief and vexation; for you can do nothing by such extravagant complaints, but heap coals of fire upon your head, or rather under your body. Your misfortunes and ours are exactly of a piece: You suffer nothing that we have not suffered before you; but we are not allowed to shew our grief, for fear of greater evils: Pray take good courage, and hope in God; for he will find some way or other to deliver us out of this hellish place; but above all things, take care not to shew any uneasiness before *Mary*, who is the only instrument of our torments, or comfort, and have patience till we go to bed, and then without any fear, I will tell you more of the matter. We do not dine with the other ladies to day, and may-be we shall have an opportunity of talking

before

before night, which I hope will be of some comfort to you. I was in a most desperate condition, but my new sister *Leonora* (this was her name) prevailed so much upon me, that I overcame my vexation before *Mary* came again, to bring our dinner, which was very different from that I had three days before. After dinner, another maid came to take away the platter and knife, for we had but one for us both, so locked up the door.

Now, my sister, said she, we need not fear being disturbed all this night: So I may safely instruct you, if you will promise me, upon the hopes of salvation, not to reveal the secret, while you are in this place, of the things I shall tell you. I threw myself down at her feet, and promised secresy. Then she begun to say: My dear sister, you think it a hard case that has happened to you, I assure you all the ladies in this house have already gone through the same, and in time you shall know all their stories, as they hope to know yours. I suppose that *Mary* has been the chief instrument of your fright, as she has been of ours, and I warrant she has shewn to you some horrible places, though not all, and that at the only thought of them, you were so much troubled in your mind, that you have chosen the same way we did to get some ease in our heart. By what has happened to us, we know that Don *Francisco* has been your *Nero*; for the three colours of our clothes are the distinguishing tokens of the three holy Fathers: The red silk belongs to Don *Francisco*, the blue to *Guerrero*, and the green to *Aliaga*. For they use to give the three first days these colours to those ladies that they bring for their use. We are strictly commanded to make all demonstrations of joy, and to be very merry three days, when a young lady comes here, as we did with you, and you must do with others: But after it we live like prisoners, without seeing any living soul but the six maids, and *Mary*, who is the housekeeper. We dine all of us, in the hall, three days a

week,

week, and three days in our rooms. When any of the holy Fathers have a mind for one of his flaves, *Mary* comes for her at nine of the clock, and conveyeth her to his apartment: But, as they have fo many, the turn comes, may-be, once in a month, except for thofe who have the honor to give them more fatisfaction than ordinary, thofe are fent for often. Some nights *Mary* leaves the door of our rooms open, and that is a fign that fome of the Fathers have a mind to come that night, but he comes in fo filent that we do not know whether he is our own patron or not. If one of us happen to be with child, fhe is removed to a better chamber, and fhe fees no perfon but the maid till fhe is delivered. The child is fent away, and we do not know where it is gone. *Mary* does not fuffer quarrels between us, for if one happens to be troublefome fhe is bitterly chaftifed for it: So we are always under a continual fear. I have been in this houfe thefe fix years, and I was not fourteen years of age, when the officers took me from my father's houfe, and I have been brought to bed but once. We are at prefent fifty-two young ladies, and we lofe every year fix or eight, but we do not know where they are fent; but at the fame time we get new ones, and fometimes I have feen here feventy-three ladies. All our continual torment is to think, and with great reafon, that when the holy Fathers are tired of one, they put her to death; for they never will run the hazard of being difcovered in thefe mifdemeanors: So, though we cannot oppofe their commands, and therefore we commit fo many enormities, yet we ftill fervently pray God and his bleffed Mother to forgive us them, fince it is againft our wills we do them, and to preferve us from death in this houfe. So, my dear fifter, arm yourfelf with patience, and put your truft in God, who will be our only defender and deliverer.

This difcourfe of *Leonora* did eafe me in fome meafure, and I found every thing as fhe had told me:

And

And so we lived together eighteen months, in which time we lost eleven ladies, and we got nineteen new ones. I knew all their stories, which I cannot tell you to-night, but if you will be so kind as to stay here this week, you will not think your time lost, when you come to know them all. I did promise her to stay that week, with a great deal of pleasure and satisfaction; but though it was very late, & the people of the house were retired, I begged her to make an end of the story concerning herself, which she did in the following manner: After the eighteen months, one night, *Mary* came & ordered us to follow her, & going down stairs, she bad us go into a coach, & this we thought the last day of our lives. We went out of the house, but where, we did not know, and were put in another house, which was worse than the first, where we were confined several months, without seeing any of the Inquisitors, or *Mary*, or any of our companions: And in the same manner we were removed from that house to another, where we continued till we were miraculously delivered by the *French* officers. Mr. *Faulcaut*, happily for me, did open the door of my room, and as soon as he saw me, he begun to shew me much civility, and took me and *Leonora* along with him, to his lodgings, and after he heard my whole story, and fearing that things would turn to our disadvantage, he ordered the next day, to send us to his father. We were drest in men's clothes, to go the more safely, and so we came to this house, where I was kept for two years, as the daughter of the old man, till Mr. *Faulcaut*'s regiment being broke, he came home, and two months after married me. *Leonora* was married to another officer, and they live in *Orleans*, which being in your way to *Paris*, I do not question but you will pay her a visit. Now my husband is at court, soliciting a new commission, and he will be very glad of your acquaintance, if he has not left *Paris* before you go to it. Thus ended our first entertainment the first night.

I stayed there afterwards twelve days, in which she told me the stories of all the young ladies, which *Leonora* did repeat to me, without any alteration, as to the substantial points of them: But these diverting accounts, containing some particular circumstances, touching the horrible procedure of that tribunal, but more especially, being full of amorous intrigues, I think fit not to insert them here, but to give them in a separate book, to the public, if desired; for as I have many other things to say, touching the corruptions of the *Romish* Priests, these accounts may be inserted there, to shew the ill practices and corruptions of the Inquisitors. So I proceed to speak of the new quarters of the *French* troops, in the Inquisition, and of the restoration of the holy Fathers into it, and afterwards I will go on with the instances of the public trials.

When the Marquiss *de Taurcey* was chosen Governor of the fort of *Aljaferia*, where formerly the holy office was kept, he put a strong garrison into it, the holy Fathers were obliged to remove and take away their prisoners, but they did wall all the doors of their secret prisons, where they used to keep the hellish engines, so we could not then know any thing of their barbarity in the punishing of innocents; and I think, that as they did consider themselves as unsettled, and being in hopes to recover again the former place, they did not move their inhuman instruments of torment, so there were none found in the last house, when they were turned out: Nay, among so great a number of prisoners, delivered out of it, we could converse with none of them: For as soon as they got out, for fear of a new order from the King, or Pope, they made their escape out of the country, and they were very much in the right of it, for the Inquisition is a place to be very much feared, and not to be tried a second time, if one can help it.

At last, after eight months reprieve, the same Inquisitors came again with more power than before, for

Don

Don *Pedro Guerrero*, first Inquisitor, was chosen by the Pope, at King *Philip*'s request, ecclesiastical Judge for Priests, Friars and Nuns, to examine and punish crimes of disaffection to his Majesty: So, for a while, he was Pope, King, and Tyrant. The first thing he did was to give the public an account of the crimes, for which all the prisoners, that had been delivered, were confined in the Inquisition, to vindicate this way the honor of the three Inquisitors, commanding, at the same time, all sorts of persons to discover, and secure any of the said prisoners, under pain of death. This proclamation was a thing never before heard of, and we may say, that *satisfactio non petita, generat suspicionem*: For really, by this, they did declare themselves guilty of what was charged on them, in relation to the Seraglio, in the opinion of serious, sensible people. But every body was terrified by the said proclamation, and none dared to say any thing about it.

The unmerciful *Guerrero*, like a roaring lion, begun to devour all sorts of people, shewing, by this, his great affection to the King, and fervent zeal for the Pope; for, under pretence of their being disaffected to his Majesty, he confined, and that publicly, near three hundred Friars, and one hundred and fifty Priests, and a great number of the laity. Next to this, he made himself master of their estates, which were sold publicly, being bought by the good loyal subjects. He did suspend, *ab officio & beneficio*, many secular Priests, and banished them out of the dominions of *Spain*; whipt others publicly, banished and whipt Friars, and took the liberty insolently to go into the monastery of the Nuns of St. *Lucia*, and whipt six of them, for being affected to *Charles* the III. and he imprisoned *Dona Catherina Cavero*, only for being the head of the imperial faction. But observe, that this whipping of the Nuns, is only giving them a discipline, i. e. so many strokes with a rod on the shoulders; but *Guerrero* was so impudent and barefaced a *Nero*, that commanding the poor

poor Nuns to turn their habits backwards, and discover their shoulders, he himself was the executioner of this unparalleled punishment.

As to the laity that were put into the Inquisition, and whose estates were seized, we did not hear any thing of them, but I am sure they did end their miserable lives in that horrid place. Many of them left a great family behind them, who all were reduced to beggery; for when the heads of them were confined, all the families must suffer with them: And this is the reason, why more than two thousand families left the city, and every thing they had, rather than undergo the miseries of that time, and the cruel persecution of *Guerrero*: So we may believe, that having so great authority as he had, he soon could recruit his *Seraglio*.

Though *Guerrero* was so busy in the affairs of the King, he did not forget the other business concerning the Catholic faith; so, to make the people sensible of his indefatigable zeal, he begun again to summon Priests and Friars to new trials, of which I am going to speak:

The trial of a Friar of St. Jerome, *organist of the convent in* Zaragosa.

ALL the summoned persons being together in the hall, the prisoner and a young boy were brought out, and after the first Inquisitor had finished his bitter correction, the secretary read the examinations and sentence, as followeth:

Whereas informations were made, and by evidences proved, that Fr. *Joseph Peralta* has committed the crime of Sodomy, with the present *John Romeo*, his disciple, which the said *Romeo* himself owned upon interrogatories of the holy Inquisitors: They having an unfeigned regard for the order of St *Jerome*, do declare and condemn the said Fr. *Joseph Peralta* to a year's confinement in his own convent, but that he may assist at the divine service, and celebrate Mass. *Item*, for an example to other like sinners, the holy Fathers declare that the said *John* is to be whipt through the public streets of the town, and receive at every corner, as it is a custom, five lashes; and that he shall wear a *Coroza*, i. e. a sort of a mitre on his head, feathered all over, as a mark of his crime. Which sentence is to be executed on *Friday* next, without any appeal.

After the secretary had done, Don *Pedro Guerrero* did ask Fr. *Joseph*, whether he had any thing to say against the sentence or not? And he answering, no, the prisoners were carried back to their prisons, and the company was dismissed. Observe the equity of the Inquisitors in this case: The boy was but fourteen years of age, under the power of Fr. *Joseph*, and he was charged with the penalty and punishment, Fr. *Joseph* did deserve. The poor boy was whipt according to sentence, and died the next day.

The trial of Father Pueyo, Confessor of the Nuns at St. Monica.

THIS criminal had been but six days in the Inquisition, before he was brought to hear his sentence, and every thing being performed as before, the Secretary read:

Whereas Father *Pueyo* has committed fornication with five spiritual daughters (so the Nuns, which confess to the same Confessor continually, are called) which is, besides fornication, sacrilege, and transgression of our commands, and he himself having owned the fact, we therefore declare, that he shall keep his cell for three weeks, and loose his employment, &c.

The Inquisitor ask'd him whether he had any thing to say against it: And Father *Pueyo* said, Holy Father, I remember that when I was chosen Father Confessor of the Nuns of our Mother St. *Monica*, you had a great value for five young ladies of the Monastery, and you

sent

sent for me, and begg'd of me to take care of them; so I have done, as a faithful servant, and may say unto you, *Domine quinque talenta tradidisti me, ecce alia quinque super lucratus sum.* The Inquisitors could not forbear laughing at this application of the scripture; and Don *Pedro Guerrero* was so well pleased with this answer, that he told him, *You said well*: Therefore, *Peccata tua remittuntur tibi, nunc vade in pace, & noli amplius peccare.* This was a pleasant trial, and *Pueyo* was excused from the performance of his penance by this impious jest.

The trial and sentence of the Licentiate Lizondo.

THE Secretary read the examinations, evidences and convictions, and the said *Lizondo* (who was a Licentiate, or Master of Arts) himself did own the fact, which was as followeth:

The said *Lizondo*, though an ingenious man, and fit for the sacerdotal function, would not be ordained, giving out that he thought himself unworthy of so high dignity, as to have every day the Saviour of the world in his hands, after the consecration. And by this feigned humility he began to insinuate himself into the people's opinion, and pass for a religious, godly man, among them. He studied physic, and practised it only with the poor, in the beginning; but being called afterwards by the rich, and especially by the Nuns, at last he was found out in his wickedness; for he used to give something to make the young ladies sleep, and this way he obtained his lascivious desires. But one of the evidences swore that he had done these things by the help of magic, and that he had used only an incantation, with which he made every body fall asleep: But this he absolutely denied, as an imposition and falsity. We did expect a severe sentence, but it was only that the Licentiate was to discover to the Inquisitors, on a day appointed by them, the receipt for making the people

sleep

sleep; and that the punishment to be inflicted on him, was to be referred to the discretion of the holy Fathers. We saw him afterwards every day walking in the streets; and this was all his punishment. We must surely believe that such crimes are reckoned but a trifle among them, for very seldom they shew any great displeasure or severity to those that are found guilty of them.

Of the order of the Inquisitors to arrest an HORSE, and to bring him to the holy office.

THE case well deserves my trouble in giving a full account of it; so I will explain it from the beginning to the end. The Rector of the university of *Zaragosa* has his own officers to arrest the scholars, and punish them if they commit any crime. Among their officers there was one called *Guadalaxara*, who was mighty officious and troublesome to the collegians or students; for upon the least thing in the world he did arrest them. The scholars did not love him at all, and contrived how they should punish him, or to play some comical trick upon him. At last, some of the strongest did agree to be at the bottom of the steeple of the university in the evening, and six of them in the belfry, who were to let down a lusty young scholar, tied with a strong rope, at the hearing of this word, *WAR*. So the scholars that were in the yard, and at the bottom of the steeple, did pick a quarrel purposely to bring *Guadalaxara* there, and when he was already among them, arresting one, they cried out, *WAR*. At which sign the six in the steeple let down the tied scholar, who taking in his arms *Guadalaxara*, and being pull'd up by the six, he carried him up almost 20 feet high, and let him fall down. The poor man was crying out, O Jesus! The Devil has taken me up. The students that were at the bottom had instruments of music, and put off their cloaks to receive him in, and as he cried out, *The Devil, **The Devil,*** the muficians anfwered him with the inftruments, repeating the fame words he did pronounce himfelf, and with this, gathering together great numbers of fcholars, they took him in the middle, continuing always the mufic and fongs, to prevent, by this, the people's taking notice of it, and every body believed that it was only a mere fcholaftical diverfion: So, with this melody and rejoicings, they carried the troublefome *Guadalaxara* out of the gates of the city into the field, call'd the *Burnt Place,* becaufe formerly the Heretics were burnt in that field. There was a dead horfe, and opening his belly, they tied the poor officer by the hands and legs, and placed him within the horfe's belly, which they fewed, leaving the head of *Guadalaxara* out, under the tale of the horfe, and fo they went back into the city. How difmal that night was, to the poor man, any body may imagine; but yet it was very fweet to him, in comparifon to what he fuffered in the morning; for the dog's going to eat of the dead horfe's flefh, he, for fear they fhould eat off his head, continually cried out, ho! ho! *perros,* i. e. dogs, and that day he found that not only the fcholars, but even the very dogs, were afraid of him, for dogs did not dare to approach the dead horfe. The labourers of the city, who are a moft ignorant fort of people, but very pleafant in their ruftic expreffions, going out to the field, by break of the day, faw the dogs near the horfe, and heard the voice, ho! ho! *perros.* They look'd up and down, and feeing nobody, drew near the horfe, and hearing the fame voice, frightened out of their fenfes, went into the city again, and gave out that a dead horfe was fpeaking in the *Burnt-Field,* and as they did affirm and fwear the thing to be true, crouds of people went to fee and hear the wonder, or, as many others faid, the miracle of a dead horfe fpeaking. A Public-Notary was among the mob, but nobody dared to go near the horfe: This Notary went to the Inquifitors to make affidavit of this cafe, and added,

added, that nobody having courage enough to approach the horse, it was proper to send some of the Friars, with holy water and *Stola*, to exorcise the horse, and find out the cause of his speaking. But the Inquisitors, who think to command beasts as well as reasonable creatures, sent six of their officers, with strict orders, to carry the horse to the holy office. The officers having an opinion that the Devil must submit to them, went, and approaching the horse, they saw the head under the tail, and the poor man crying out, help, take me out of this putrified grave; for God's sake, good people, make haste, for I am not the Devil, nor ghost, nor apparition, but the real body and soul of *Guadalaxara*, the Constable of the University; and I do renounce, in this place, the office of arresting scholars forever; and I do forgive them this wrong done to me, and thanks be to God, & to the Virgin of *Pilar*, who has preserved my body from being converted into a dead horse, that I am alive still.

These plain demonstrations of the nature of the thing did not convince, in the least, the officers of the Inquisition, who are always very strict in the performance of the orders given them; so they took the dead horse and carried it to the Inquisition. Never were more people seen in the streets and windows, than on that day, besides the great croud that followed the corps, which I saw myself; the Inquisitors having notice before-hand, went to the hall to receive the informations from the horse, and after they had asked him many questions, the poor man pushing up the tail with his nose, to speak, to see, and to be seen, still answering them; the wise holy Fathers trusting not to his information, gave order to the officers to carry the speaking horse to the *torture*, which being done accordingly, as they begun to turn the ropes through the horse's belly, at the third turning of them the skin of the belly broke, and the real body of *Guadalaxara* did appear in all his dimensions, and by the horse's torture, he

F f   saved

saved his life. The poor man died three weeks after, and he forgave the scholars who contrived this mischief, and an elegy was made on his death.

Thesis *defended by* F. James Garcia, *in the hall of the Inquisition.*

THE case of the Reverend Father *F. James Garcia* made a great noise in *Spain*, which was thus.

This same *James Garcia* is the learned man, of whom I have spoke several times in my book. His Father, though a shoe-maker by trade, was very honest and well beloved, and as God had bestowed on him riches enough, and having but one child, he gave him the best education he could in the college of *Jesuits*, where in the study of grammar, he signalized himself for his vivacity, and uncommon wit. After going to the university, he went through philosophy and divinity to the admiration of his masters; he entered St. *Augustin's* order, and after his noviciate was ended, desirous to obtain the degree of master of arts, he defended public thesis of philosophy, and after, other thesis of divinity, without any moderator to answer for him in case of necessity. The thesis and some propositions were quite new to the learned people: For among other propositions, one was, *Innocentium esse verum pontificem, non est de fide* i. e. It is not an article of faith, that Innocent is the true Pope. And next to this proposition, this other: *Non credere quod non video, non est contra fidem* It is not against the Catholic faith not to believe what I don't see.

Upon account of these two propositions, he was summoned by the Inquisitors, and ordered to defend the said propositions separately in the hall of the Inquisition, and answer for six days together to all the arguments of the learned *Qualificators*; which he did, and kept his ground, that instead of being punished for it, he was honored with the Cross of *Qualificator*, after the

the examinations were made of the purity of his blood.

Sentence given against Lawrence Castro, *Goldsmith, of* Zaragosa.

LAWRENCE *Castro* was the most famous and wealthy goldsmith in the city, and as he went one day to carry a piece of plate to Don *Pedro* Guerrero, before he paid him, he bad him to go and see the house along with one of his domestic servants; which he did, and seeing nothing but doors of iron, and hearing nothing but lamentations of the people within, having returned to the Inquisitors apartment, Don *Pedro* asked him, *Lawrence*, how do you like this place? To which *Lawrence* said, I do not like it at all, for it seems to me the very Hell upon earth. This innocent, but true answer, was the only occasion of his misfortune; for he was immediately sent into one of the hellish prisons, and at the same time many officers went to his house to seize upon every thing, and that day he appeared at the bar, and his sentence was read; he was condemned to be whipt through the public streets, to be marked on his shoulders with a burning iron, and to be sent forever to the gallies: But the good, honest, unfortunate man died that very day; all his crime being only to say, that the holy office did seem to him Hell on earth.

At the same time, a lady of good fortune was whipt, because she said in company, I do not know whether the Pope is a man, or a woman, and I hear wonderful things of him every day, and I do imagine, he must be an *animal* very rare. For these words she lost honor, fortune, and life, for she died six days after the execution of her sentence: And thus the holy Fathers punish trifling things, and leave unpunished horrible crimes.

The following instance will be a demonstration of this truth, and shew how the Inquisitors favour the ecclesiastics

ecclesiastics more than the laity, and the reason why they are more severe upon one than the other.

In the diocess of *Murcia* was a parish Priest in a village in the mountains. The people of it were almost all of them shepherds, and were obliged to be always abroad with their flocks, so the Priest being the commander of the shepherdesses, begun to preach every *Friday* in the afternoon, all the congregation being composed of the women of the town. His constant subject was the indispensable duty of paying the tithes to him, and this not only of the fruits of the earth, but of the seventh of their sacraments too, which is matrimony, and he had such great eloquence to persuade them to secrecy, as to thier husbands, and a ready submission to him, that he begun to reap the fruit of his doctrine in a few days, and by this wicked example, he brought into the list of the tithes all the married women of the town, and he did receive from them the tenth for six years together: But his infernal doctrine and practice was discovered by a young woman who was to be married, of whom the Priest asked the tithe before-hand; but she telling it to her sweet-heart, he went to discover the case to the next Commissary of the Inquisition, who having examined the matter, and found it true, he took the Priest and sent him to the Inquisition; he was found guilty of so abominable a sin, and he himself confessed it, and what was the punishment inflicted on him? Only to confine him in a Friar's cell for six months. The Priest being confined, made a virtue of necessity, and so he composed a small book, entitled, *The true Penitent*, which was universally approved by all sorts of people for solid doctrine and morality. He dedicated the work to the holy Inquisitors, who, for a reward of his pains, gave him another parish a great deal better than the first: But hardened wretch! There he fell again to the same trade of receiving the tithes; upon which the people of the parish complained to the Governor, who acquainted the King with

with the case, and his Majesty ordered the Inquisitors to apply a speedy remedy to it; so the **holy Fathers** did send him to the Pope's gallies for five years time.

I must own, it is quite against my inclination to give this and the like accounts, for it will seem very much out of the way of a clergyman: But if the reader will make reflections on them, and consider that my design is only to shew how unjustly the Inquisitors do act in this and other cases, he will certainly excuse me; for they really deserve to be ridiculed more than argued against, reasoning being of no force with them; but a discovery of their infamous actions and laws, may-be, will produce, if not in them, in some people at least a good effect.

The *Roman Catholics* believe there is a Purgatory, and that the souls suffer more pains in it than in Hell: But I think that the Inquisition is the only Purgatory on earth, and the holy Fathers are the judges and executioners in it. The reader may form a dreadful idea of the barbarity of that tribunal, by what I have already said, but I am sure it never will come up to what it is in reality, for it passeth all understanding, not as the *peace of God*, but as the war of the Devil.

So that we may easily know by this, and the aforesaid account, that they leave off the observance of the first precepts of the holy office, and chastise only those that speak either against the Pope, clergy, or the holy Inquisition.

The only reason of settling that tribunal in *Spain* was to examine and chastise sinners, or those that publicly contemned the Catholic faith: But now a man may blaspheme, and commit the most heinous crimes, if he says nothing against the three mentioned articles, he is free from the hellish tribunal.

Let us except from this rule the rich *Jews*, for the poor are in no fear of being confined there, they are the rich alone that suffer in that place, not for the crime of *Jewdaism*, (though this is the colour and pretence) but

but for the crime of having riches. *Francisco Alfaro*, a *Jew*, and a very rich one, was kept in the Inquisition of *Sevilla* four years, and after he had lost all he had in the world, was discharged out of it with a small correction: This was to encourage him to trade again, and get more riches, which he did in four years time: Then he was put again into the holy office, with the loss of his goods and money. And after three years imprisonment he was discharged, and ordered to wear, for six months, the mark of *San Benito*, i. e. a picture of a man in the middle of the fire of Hell, which he was to wear before his breast publicly. But *Alfaro* a few days after left the city of *Sevilla*, and seeing a pig without the gate, he hung the *San-Benito* on the pig's neck, and made his escape.. I saw this *Jew* in *Lisbon* and he told me the story himself, adding, now I am a poor *Jew*, I tell every body so, and though the Inquisition is more severe here than in *Spain*, nobody takes notice of me: I am sure, they would confine me for ever, if I had as much riches as I had in *Sevilla*. Really the holy office is more cruel and inhuman in *Portugal* than in *Spain*, for I never saw any publicly burnt in my own country, and I saw in *Lisbon* seven at once, four young women and three men; two young women were burnt alive, & an old man, and the others were strangled first. But being obliged to dismiss this chapter, and leave out many curious histories, I do promise to relate them in the second part of this work. Now let me entreat all true Protestants to join with me in my hearty prayer to God Almighty, thus:

O eternal God, who doft rule the hearts of Kings, and orderest every thing to the glory of the true religion, pour thy holy spirit upon the heart of *Lewis* the firft, that he may fee the barbarous, unchriftian practices of the Inquifitors, and with a firm refolution abolish all laws contrary to thofe given us by thy only fon, our Saviour, Jefus Chrift our Lord. *Amen.*

PART.

Of their prayers, adoration of images and relics.

ARTICLE I.

Of their Prayers.

THE prayers sung or said, in the church, are seven canonical hours, or the *seven services*, viz. *Tertia, Sexta, Nona, Vesperæ, Matutina & Completæ. Prima* is composed of the general confession, three psalms, and many other prayers, with the *Martyrologio Sanctorum*, i. e. with a commemoration of all the saints of that day. *Tertia*, is a prayer, or service of three psalms, anthem, and the collect of the day, &c. *Sexta, & Nona* are the same. *Vesperæ*, or evening songs, contain five anthems, five psalms, an hymn, *Magnificat*, or my soul doth magnify, &c. with an anthem, collect of the day, and commemorations of some saints. *Matutina*, or matins, is the longest service of the seven, for it contains, 1*st*. The psalm, O *come let us sing*. 2*d*. An hymn. 3*d*. Three anthems, three psalms, and three lessons of the old testament. 4*th*. Three anthems, three psalms, and three lessons of the day, i. e. of the life of the saint of that day, or of the mystery of it. 5*th*. Three anthems, three psalms, three lessons, of which the first beginneth with the gospel of the day, and two or three lines of it, and the rest is an homily, or exposition of the gospel. 6*th*. *Te Deum*. 7*th*. Five anthems, five psalms, an hymn, anthem of the day, the psalm, *Blessed be the Lord of Israel*, &c. The collect of the day, and some commemorations. *Completæ*, or complices, is the last service, which contains the general confession, an anthem, three or four psalms, and, *Lord now lettest thou*, &c. and some other adherent prayers

for

for the Virgin, the holy Cross, saints, &c. All these seven services are said, or sung in *Latin*, every day in cathedral churches, but not in all the parish churches.

In the cathedral churches on the festivals of the first class, or the greatest festivals, as those of Christ and the Virgin *Mary*, all the seven canonical hours are sung. *Prima*, at six in the morning, and a Mass after it. *Tertia*, at ten, the great Mass after, and after the Mass, *Sexta* and *Nona*. At two, or three in the afternoon, the *evening song*, at seven, *complices*, and half an hour after midnight the *matins*. In the festivals of the second class, as those of the Apostles, & some saints placed in that class by the Popes, *Tertia*, evening songs and matins are all that are sung, and likewise every day, though not with organ, nor music.

In the parish churches the Priests sing only *Tertia*, and *evening songs* on *Sundays* and festivals of the first class; except where there are some foundations, or settlements for singing *evening songs* on other private days. But the great Mass is always sung in every parish church, besides the Masses for the dead, which are settled to be sung.

In the Convents of the Friars, they do observe the method of the cathedrals, except some days of the week granted to them by the Prior, as recreation days, and then they say the service, and go to divert themselves all the day after. As to the Nuns, I have given an account in the first chapter of their lives and conversation.

The Priests and Friars that do not say, or sing the service with the community, are obliged in conscience to say those seven canonical hours every day, and if they do not, they commit a mortal sin, and ought to confess it among the sins of *omission*. Besides these seven services, they have, not by precept, but by devotion, the service, or small office of the Virgin *Mary*, the seven penitential psalms, and other prayers of saints, which are by long custom become services of precept, for

they

they never will dare to omit them, either for devotion's sake, or for fear that the laity would tax them with coldness and negligence in matters of exemplary devotion.

As to the public prayers of the laity, they all are contained in the beads or rosary of the Virgin *Mary*, and to give them some small comfort, there is a fixed time in the evening in every church for the rosary.—The sexton rings the bell, and when the parishioners, both men and women, are gathered together, the Minister of the parish, or any other Priest, comes out of the vestry, in his surplice, and goes to the altar of the Virgin *Mary*, and lighting two or more candles on the altar's table, he kneels down before the altar, makes the sign of the Cross, and begins the rosary with a prayer to the Virgin ; and after he has said half of the *Ave Maria*, &c. the people say the other half, which he repeats ten times, the people doing the same. Then he says *Gloria Patra*, &c. and the people answer, *As it was in the beginning*, &c. Then, in the same manner, the Priest says half of *Our Father*, and ten times half *Ave Maria*, and so he and the people do, till they have said them fifty times. This done, the Priest says another prayer to the Virgin, and begins her Litany, and after every one of her titles, or encomiums, the people answer, *Ora pro nobis*, pray for us. The Litany ended, the Priest and people visit five altars, saying, before each of them, one *Pater Noster*, and one *Ave Maria*, with *Gloria Patra* ; and, lastly, the Priest, kneeling down before the great altar, says an act of contrition, and endeth with *Lighten our darkness, we beseech thee*, &c. All the prayers of the rosary are in the vulgar tongue, except *Gloria Patra*, and *Ora pro nobis*, i. e. *Glory be to thee*, &c. and *Pray for us*.

After the rosary, in some churches, there is *Oratio mentalis*, i. e. a prayer of meditation, and for this purpose the Priest of the rosary, or some other of devout life and conversation, readeth a chapter in some devout book,

book, as *Thomas de Kempis*, or *Francis de Sales*, or *Father Eusebio*, of the difference between temporal and eternal things, and when he has ended the chapter, every one on their knees, begin to meditate on the contents of the chapter, with great devotion and silence. They continue in that prayer half an hour, or more, and after it, the Priests say a prayer of thanksgiving to God Almighty, for the benefits received from him by all there present, *&c.*

I must own, that I did always like this exercise of Christian devotion. For in the books, the good Priests make use of for that purpose, there is no superstitious doctrine, except touching the mystery of the Lord's supper, and even in this, the style is so ambiguous, that both Protestants, and Romans may use and understand it each in their own way. As for the rest of the meditation, it is only a sort of humiliation before God Almighty, contemplating his attributes, and our unworthiness, and asking his grace and holy spirit to better our lives, and to serve him with a pure and contrite heart. So if all their prayers, worship, and ceremonies, were as free from idolatry and superstition, as this of meditation is, I confess the church of *Rome* would have no corruptions at all.

I said *Public prayers of the laity*; for when they assist at the divine service, or hear Mass, they only hear what the Priest says in *Latin*, and answer *Amen*. Generally speaking, they do not understand *Latin*, and especially in towns of 300 houses and villages, there scarcely can be found one *Latinist*, except the curate, & even he very often doth not understand perfectly well what he reads in *Latin*: By this universal ignorance, we may say, that they do not know what they pray for; nay, if a Priest was so wicked in heart, as to curse the people in church, and damn them all in *Latin*, the poor idiots must answer *Amen*, knowing not what the Priest says. I do not blame the common people in this point, but I blame the Pope and Priests that forbid them to read

the

the scripture, and by this prohibition they cannot know what St. *Paul* says about praying in the vulgar tongue: So Pope and Priests, and those that plead ignorance, must answer for the people before the dreadful tribunal of God.

Besides this public prayer of the rosary, they have private prayers at home, as the *creed, the Lord's prayer, a prayer to the Virgin, the act of contrition,* and other prayers to Saints, Angels, and for souls in Purgatory. But this prayer of the rosary is not only said in church, but it is sung in the streets, and the custom was introduced by the *Dominican* Friars, who, in some parts of *Spain,* are called *The Fathers of the holy rosary.* Sundays and holy days, after *evening songs,* the Prior of the *Dominicans,* with all his Friars and corporation, or fraternity of the holy rosary, begins the Virgin's *evening songs,* all the while ringing the bells, which is a call for the procession, and when the evening songs are over, the Clerk of the Convent, drest in his *Alva* or surplice, taking the standard where the picture of the Virgin *Mary* is drawn with a frame of roses, and two novices in surplices, with candlesticks, walking on each side of the standard, the procession beginneth. First, all the brethren of the corporation go out of church, each with a wax candle in his hand; the standard followeth after, and all the Friars, in two lines, follow the standard. In this order the procession goes through the streets, all singing *Ave Maria,* and the laity answering as before. They stop in some public street, where a Friar, upon a table, preacheth a sermon of the excellency and power of the rosary, and gathering together the people, they go back again into the church, where the rosary being over, another Friar preacheth upon the same subject another sermon, exhorting the people to practice this devotion of the rosary, and they have carried so far this extravagant folly, that if a man is found dead, and has not the beads or rosary of the Virgin in his pocket, that man is not reckoned

oned a Christian, and he is not to be buried in consecrated ground till some body knoweth him, and certifieth that such a man was a Christian, and passeth his word for him. So every body takes care to have always the beads or rosary in his pocket, as the characteristic of a Christian. But this devotion of the rosary is made so common among bigots, that they are always with the beads in their hands, and at night round about their necks. There is nothing more usual in *Spain* and *Portugal*, than to see people in the markets, and in the shops, praying with their beads, and selling and buying at the same time; nay, the procurers in the great *Piazza* are praying with their beads, and at the same time contriving and agreeing with a man for wicked intrigues. So all sorts of persons having it as a law to say the rosary every day, some say it walking, others in company (keeping silent for a while) but the rest talking or laughing: So great is their attention and devotion in this indispensable prayer of the holy rosary.

But this is not the worst of their practices; for if a man, or Priest, neglects one day to say the rosary, he doth not commit a mortal sin, though this is a great fault among them: But the divine service, or seven canonical hours, every Priest, Friar, and Nun, is obliged to say every day, or else they commit a mortal sin, by the statutes of the church and Popes. This service, which is to be said in private, and with Christian devotion, is as much profaned among ecclesiastics and Nuns, as the rosary among the laity: for I have seen many ecclesiastics (and I have done it myself several times) play at cards, and have the breviary on the table, to say the divine service at the same time. Others walking in company, and others doing still worse things than these, have the breviary in their hands, and reading the service, when they at the same time are *in occasione proxima peccati*; and, notwithstanding, they believe they have performed exactly that part of the ecclesiastical duty. Next

Next to this abomination, is that practised between a Nun, and her Devoto, or gallant: I said, that the professed Nuns are obliged in conscience to say the divine service in *Latin*, every day, which requires more than an hour and a quarter to be said distinctly: But as they, and their Devotoes, spend all their time, while absent one from another, in writing letters of love to one another, they have no time to say the divine service, if it happens, that they did not assist that day at the public service. Then when they are at the grate in lascivious conversation, if some other company happens to come to the same grate, and interrupt them in their wicked practices, the Nun fetcheth two breviaries, one for herself, and one for her gallant, and alternatively they say the seven canonical hours, while the other company is there; and though they are saying, *We praise thee, O Lord,* &c. when the company goes away, they leave immediately, for a while, the breviary, and come again to their amorous expressions, and obscene actions, which ended, they go on with the divine service.

I know that modesty obligeth me to be more cautious in this account, and if it was not for this reason, I could detect the most horrible things of Friars and Nuns that ever were seen or heard in the world; but leaving this unpleasant subject, I come to say something of the profit the Priests and Friars get by their irreligious prayers, and by what means they recommend them to the laity.

The profits Priests and Friars get by their prayers, are not so great as that they get by absolution and Masses: For it is by an accident, if sometimes they are desired to pray for money. There is a custom, that if one in a family is sick, the head of the family sends immediately to some devout, religious Friar or Nun to pray for the sick, so, by this custom, not all Priests and Friars are employed, but only those that are known to live a regular life. But because the people are

are very much mistaken in this, I crave leave to explain the nature of those whom the people believe religious Friars, or in *Spanish*, *Gazmonnos*. In every convent there are eight or ten of those *Gazmonnos*, or devout men, who, at the examination for Confessors and preachers, were found quite incapable of the performance of the great duties, and so were not approved by the examiners of the convent. And though they scarcely understand *Latin*, they are permitted to say Mass, that by that means the convent might not be at any expence with them. These poor idiots, being not able to get any thing by selling absolutions, nor by preaching, undertake the life of a *Gazmonnos*, and live a mighty retired life, keeping themselves in their cells, or chambers, and not conversing with the rest of the community: So their brethren *Gazmonnos* visit them, and among themselves, there is nothing spared for their diversion, and the carrying on their private designs.

When they go out of the convent, it must be with one of the same *farandula*, or trade: Their faces look pale; their eyes are fixed on the ground, their discourse all of heavenly things, their visits in public, and their meat and drink but very little before the world, though in great abundance between themselves, or, as they say, *Inter privatos parietes*. By this mortifying appearance, the people believe them to be godly men, and in such a case as sickness, they rather send to one of these to pray for the sick, than to other Friars of less public fame. But those hypocrites, after the apprenticeship of this trade is over, are very expert in it, for if any body sends for one of them, either without money, or some substantial present, they say that they cannot go, for they have so many sick persons to visit and pray for, that it is impossible for them to spare any time. But if money or a present is sent to him, he is ready to go and pray every where.

So these ignorant, hypocritical Friars are always
followed

followed by the ignorant people, who furnish them with money and presents for the sake of their prayers, and they live more comfortably than many rich people, and have 100 pistoles in their pockets, oftener than many of the laity who have good estates.

Some people will be apt to blame me for giving so bad a character of those devout men in appearance, when I cannot be a judge of their hearts: But I do answer, that I do not judge thus of all of them, but only of those that I knew to be great hypocrites and sinners; for I saw seven of them taken up by the Inquisitors, and I was at their public trial, as I have given an account in the former chapter: So, by those seven, we may give a near guess of the others, and say, that their outward mortifying appearance is only a cloak of their private designs.

There are some Nuns likewise, who follow the same trade as I have given one instance in the chapter of the Inquisition: And though the ignorant people see every day some of those *Gazmonnos* taken up by the Inquisitors, they are so blinded, that they always look for one of them to pray. These hypocrites do persuade the heads of families, that they are obliged in conscience to mind their own business, rather than to pray, and that the providence of God has ordered every thing for the best for his creatures, and that he (foreseeing that the heads of families would have no time to spare for prayers) has chosen such religious men to pray for them, so they are well recompensed for their prayers, and God only knoweth whether they pray or not. Most commonly, when they are wanted, they are at the club, with their brethren *Gazmonnos*, eating and drinking, afterwards painting their faces with some yellow drug, to make themselves look pale and mortified. O good God! How great is thy patience in tolerating such wicked men?

Besides these monastical persons, there are many blind people, who can repeat some prayers to saints by heart,

heart, and get money for them. They walk the streets day and night, and they carry a lanthorn by night, not to see with, but to be seen by others. The people call them, and give a penny for saying the prayer of such a saint, and this way they make their lives very merry and easy.

As to the means the Priests and Friars make use of, and the doctrines they preach to recommend this exercise of praying to the people, I can give but one instance of them as matter of fact, for I was the author of it. Being desired to preach upon the subject of prayer, by the Mother Abbess of the Nuns of St. *Clara*, who had told me in private, that many of her Nuns did neglect their prayers, and were most commonly at the grate with their Devotoes, and the good mother, out of pure zeal, told me, that such Nuns were the Devils of the monastery; so to oblige her, I went to preach, and took my text out of the gospel of St. *Matthew*. Chap. xvii. v. 21. *Howbeit this kind goeth not out but by prayer and fasting*, but in our vulgar, the text is thus, *Howbeit this kind of Devils*, &c. And after I had explained the text, confining myself wholly to the learned *Silveira*'s commentaries, I did endeavour to prove, that the persons devoted to God by a public profession of monastical life, were bound in conscience to pray without ceasing, as St. *Paul* tells us, and that if they neglected this indispensable duty, they were worse than Devils: And after this proposition, I did point out the way and method to tame such Devils, which was by prayer and fasting: And lastly, the great obligation laid upon us by Jesus Christ and his Apostles, to make use of this exercise of prayer, which I did recommend as a *medium* to attain the highest degree of glory in Heaven, and to exceed even Angels, Prophets, Patriarchs, Apostles, and all the Saints of the heavenly court.

I do not intend to give a copy of the sermon, but I cannot pass by the proof I gave to confirm my proposition,

tion, to shew by it, the trifling method of preaching, most generally used among the Roman-catholic preachers.

The historiographers and chronologers of St. *Augustine*'s order, say, (said I) that the great Father *Augustine* is actually in Heaven, before the throne of the Holy Trinity, as a reward for the unparelleled zeal and devotion he had on earth, for that holy mystery, & because he spent all his free time on earth in praying, which makes him now in Heaven greater than all sorts of saints. They say more, viz. that in the Heaven of the Holy Trinity, there are only the *Father*, the *Son*, the *Holy Ghost*, the *Virgin Mary*, St. *Joseph*, and, the last of all, St. *Augustine*. Thus Father *Gracia*, in his *Santoral*, printed in *Zaragosa*, in 1707, vide sermon on St. *Augustine*.

To this, I knew would be objected the 11th verse of the xi. chap. of St. *Matthew*, *Among them that are born of women, there hath not risen a greater than* John *the Baptist*. To which I did answer, that there was no rule without an exception, and that St. *Augustine* was excepted from it: And this I proved by a maxim received among divines, viz. *Infimum supremi excedit supremum infimi*, the least of a superior order exceeds the greatest of an inferior. There are three Heavens, as St. *Paul* says, and, as other expositors, three orders. They place in the first Heaven, the three divine persons, the Virgin *Mary*, St. *Joseph*, and St. *Augustine*; in the second, the spiritual intelligences; and in the third, St. *John Baptist*, at the head of all the celestial army of saints. Then, if St. *Augustine* is the last in the highest Heaven, though St. *John* is the first in the lowest, we must conclude, by the aforementioned maxim, that the great Father *Augustine* exceeds in glory all the saints of the heavenly Court, as a due reward for his fervent zeal in praying, while he was here below among men.

With this instance, I did recommend the exercise of prayer to the Nuns, assuring them of the same reward in Heaven, if they did imitate so glorious a saint: Nay, I did corroborate this with the historical account of St. *Augustine*'s heart, in the city of *Pavia*, which is kept separate from the body, which is in that town also, in a crystal box. The chronologers say, that every year, on *Trinity Sunday*, the heart is continually moving within the box, as if it was alive, and that this is a testimony of the great devotion of that Saint, for the Trinity, and a proof that he is before that holy mistery, praising continually the blessed *Trias*, and so his heart, by its continual motion on that day, shews the great reward of his soul in Heaven.

The more I remember this, and the like nonsensical proofs and methods of preaching, the more I thank God for his goodness, in bringing me out of that communion into another, where, by application, I learn how to make use of the scripture, to the spiritual good of souls, and not to amusements, which are prejudicial to our salvation.

Thus I have given you an account of the public and private prayers of Priests, Friars, Nuns, and Laity; of the profits they have by it, and of the methods they take to recommend this exercise of praying, to all sorts and conditions of people. Sure I am, that after a mature consideration of their way of praying, and of that we make use of in our reformed congregations, every body may easily know the great difference between them both, and that the form and practice of prayers among Protestants, are more agreeable to God, than those of the *Romish* Priests and Friars can be.

ARTICLE II.

Of the adoration of Images.

THE adoration of images was commanded by several general councils, and many Popes, whose commands and decrees are obeyed as articles of our
Christian

Christian faith, and every one that breaketh them, or, in his outward practice, doth not conform to them, is punished by the Inquisitors as an Heretic; therefore it is not to be wondered at, if people, educated in such a belief, without any knowledge of the sin of such idolatrous practices, do adore the images of the Saints with the same, and sometimes more devotion of heart, than they do God Almighty in spirit.

I begin, therefore, this article with myself, and my own forgetfulness of God. When I was in the college of *Jesuits*, to learn grammar, the teachers were so careful in recommending to their scholars devotion to the Virgin *Mary* of *Pilar*, of *Zarogosa*, that this doctrine, by long custom, was so deeply impress'd in our hearts, that every body, after the school was over, used to go to visit the blessed image, this being a rule and a law for us all, which was observed with so great strictness, that if any student, by accident, missed that exercise of devotion, he was the next day severely whipped for it. For my part, I can aver, that during the three years I went to the college, I never was punished for want of devotion to the Virgin. In the beginning of our exercises, we were bidden to write the following words, *Dirige tu calamum Virgo* Maria, *meum*; Govern my pen, O Virgin *Mary*! And this was my constant practice in the beginning of all my scholastical and moral writings, for the space of ten years, in which, I do protest before my eternal Judge, I do not remember whether I did invoke God, or call on his sacred name or not. This I remember, that in all my distempers and sudden afflictions, my daily exclamation was, *O Virgin del Pilar!* Help me, O Virgin! *&c.* so great was my devotion to her, and so great my forgetfulness of our God and Saviour Jesus Christ. And indeed a man that does not inquire into the matter, hath more reason, according to the doctrine taught in those places, to trust in the Virgin *Mary*, than in Jesus Christ: For these are common expressions in their sermons: *That neither*

neither God, nor Jesus Christ can do any thing in Heaven, but what is approved by the blessed Mary, that she is the door of glory, and that nobody can enter into it, but by her influence, &c. And the preachers give out these propositions as principles of our faith, insomuch, that if any body dares to believe the contrary, he is reputed an Heretic, and punished as such.

But because this article requireth a full examination, and an account to be given of the smallest circumstances belonging to it, I shall keep the class and order of Saints, and of the adoration they are worshipped with, by most people in the *Roman catholic* countries. And first of all, the image of Jesus Christ is adored as if the very image of wood was the very Christ of flesh and bones. To clear this, I will give an instance or two of what I saw myself.

In the cathedral church of St. *Salvator*, there was an old image of Jesus Christ, crucified, behind the choir, in a small unminded chapel; nobody took notice of that crucifix, except a devout Prebend, or canon of the church, who did use every day to kneel down before that image, and pray heartily to it. The Prebend (though a religious man in the outward appearance) was ambitious in his heart of advancement in the church; so, one day, as he was on his knees before the old image, he was begging that, by its power and influence, he might be made a Bishop, & after a Cardinal, and lastly, Pope; to which earnest request the image gave him this answer, *Et tu que me ves a qui, que hazes pormi?* i. e. *And thou seest me here, what do you do for me?* These very words are written, at this present day, in gilt letters, upon the crown of thorns of the crucifix: To which the Prebend answered, *Domine peccavi, & malum coram te feci,* i. e. *Lord I have sinned, and done evil before thee.* To this humble request, the image said, *Thou shalt be a Bishop,* & accordingly he was made a Bishop soon after. These words, spoken by the crucifix of the cathedral church, made such a noise, that

crowds

crowds of well disposed, credulous people used to come every day to offer their gifts to the miraculous image of our Saviour, and the image, which was not minded at all before, after it spoke, was, and has been ever since, so much reverenced, that the offerings of the first six years were reckoned worth near a million of crowns. The history of the miracle reports, that the thing did happen in the year 1562, and that the chapter did intend to build a chapel in one corner of the church, to put the crucifix in with more veneration and decency; but the image spoke again to the Prebend, and said, *My pleasure is to continue where I am till the end of the world:* So the crucifix is kept in the same chapel, but richly adorned, and nobody ever since dare touch any thing belonging to the image, for fear of disobliging the crucifix. It has an old wig on its head, the very sight of which is enough to make every one laugh; its face looks so black & disfigured, that nobody can guess whether it is the face of a man or a woman, but every body believes that it is a crucifix, by the other circumstances of the Cross, and crown of thorns.

This image is so much adored, and believed to have such a power of working miracles, that if they ever carry it out in a procession, it must be on an urgent necessity: For example, if there is want of rain in such a degree that the harvest is almost lost, then, by the common consent of the Archbishop and chapter, a day is fixed to take the crucifix out of its chapel in a public procession, at which all the Priests and Friars are to assist without any excuse, and the devout people too, with marks of repentance, and public penances. Likewise the Archbishop, Viceroy, and magistrates, ought to assist in robes of mourning; so when the day comes, which is most commonly very cloudy, and disposed to rain, all the communities meet together in the cathedral church: And in the year 1706, I saw, upon such an occasion as this, 600 disciplinants, whose blood run

from

from their shoulders to the ground, many others with long heavy Crosses, others with a heavy bar of iron, or chains of the same, hanging at their necks; with such dismal objects in the middle of the procession, 12 Priests drest in black ornaments, taking the crucifix on their shoulders, and with great veneration carry it through the streets, the eunuchs singing the Litany.

I said, that this image is never carried out but when there is great want of rain, and when there is sure appearance of plenteous rain; so they never are disappointed in having a miracle published after such a procession: Nay, sometimes it begins to rain before the crucifix is out of his place, and then the people are almost certain of the power of the image: So that year the chapter is sure to receive double tithes: For every body vows and promises two out of ten to the church for the recovery of the harvest.

But what is more than this, is, that in the last wars between King *Philip* and King *Charles*, as the people were divided into two factions, they did give out by a revelation of an ignorant, silly *Beata*, that the crucifix was a *Butiflero*, i. e. affectionate to King *Philip*, and at the same time there was another revelation, that his mother, the Virgin of *Pilar*, was an *Imperialist*, i. e. for King *Charles*; and the minds of the people were so much prejudiced with their opinions, that the partizans of *Philip* did go to the crucifix, and those of King *Charles* to the Virgin of *Pilar*. Songs were made upon this subject: One said, *When* Charles *the Third mounts on his Horse, the Virgin of* Pilar *holds the Stirrup.* The other said, *When* Philip *comes to our Land, the Crucifix of St.* Salvator *guides him by his Hand.* By these two factions, both the Virgin and her son's image began to lose the presents of one of the parties, and the chapter, having made a bitter complaint to the Inquisitors, these did put a stop to their sacrilegious practices; so high is the people's opinion of the image of the crucifix, and so blind their faith, that all the world
would

would not be able to perfuade them that that image did not fpeak to the canon, or prebendary, and that it cannot work miracles at any time. Therefore our cuftom was, after fchool, to go firft to vifit the crucifix, touch its feet with our hands, and kifs it, and from thence go to vifit the image of the Virgin of *Pilar*, of which I am going to fpeak, as the next image to that of Jefus Chrift, though, in truth, the firft as to the people's devotion.

And becaufe the ftory, or the hiftory of the image, is not well known, at leaft, I never faw any foreign book treat of it, it feems proper to give a full account of it here, to fatisfy the curiofity of many that love to read and hear new things, and this I think is worth every body's obfervation,

The book, call'd *The Hiftory of our Lady of Pilar, and her Miracles*, contains, to the beft of my memory, the following account: The Apoftle St. *James* came, with feven new converts, to preach the gofpel in *Zaragofa* (a city famous for antiquity, and for its founder, *Cæfar Auguftus*; but more famous for the heavenly image of our Lady) and as they were fleeping on the river *Ebro*'s fide, a celeftial mufic awakened them at midnight, and they faw an army of Angels, melodiously finging, come down from heaven, with an image on a pillar, which they placed on the ground, forty yards diftant from the river, and the commanding Angel fpoke to St. *James*, and faid, This image of our Queen fhall be the defence of this city, where you come to plant the Chriftian religion; take therefore good courage, for, by her help and affiftance, you fhall not leave this city without reducing all the inhabitants in it to your Mafter's religion; and as fhe is to protect you, you alfo muft fignalize yourfelf in building a decent chapel for her. The Angels leaving the image on the earth, with the fame melody and fongs, went up to Heaven, and St. *James*, with his feven converts, on their knees, began to pray, and thank God for this ineftimable estimable treasure sent to them; and the next day they began to build a chapel with their own hands. I have already given an account of the chapel, and the riches of it, now I ought to say something of the idolatrous adoration given to that image, by all the Roman-catholics of that kingdom, and of all that go to visit her.

This image has her own chaplain, besides the chapter of the prebends and other Priests, as I have told before. The Virgin's chaplain has more privilege and power than any King, Archbishop, or any eclesiastical person, excepting the Pope; for his business is only to dress the image every morning, which he doth in private, and without any help: I say in private, that is, drawing the four courtains of the Virgin's canopy, that nobody may see the image naked. Nobody has liberty, but this chaplain, to approach so near the image, for, as the author of the book says, *An Archbishop (who had so great assurance as to attempt to say Mass on the altar table of the Virgin) died upon the spot, before he began Mass.* I saw King *Philip* and King *Charles*, when they went to visit the image, stand at a distance from it. With these cautions it is very easy to give out, that no body can know of what matter the image is made, that being a thing referred to the Angels only: So all the favour the Christians can obtain from the Virgin, is only to kiss her *Pillar*, for it is contrived, that by having broke the wall backwards, a piece of pillar as big as two crown-pieces is shewn, which is set out in gold round about, and there Kings, and other people, kneel down to adore and kiss that part of the stone. The stones and lime that were taken, when the wall was broke, are kept for relics, and it is a singular favour, if any can get some small stone, paying a great sum of money.

There is always so great a crowd of people, that many times they cannot kiss the pillar; but touch it with one of their fingers, and kiss afterwards the part of
the

the finger that did touch the pillar. The large chapel of the lamp is always, night & day, crowded with people; for, as they say, that chapel was never empty of Chriftians, fince St. *James* built it; fo the people of the city, that work all day, go out at night to vifit the image, and this blind devotion is not only among pious people, but among the moft profligate & debauched too, infomuch, that a lewd woman will not go to bed without vifiting the image; for they certainly believe, that no body can be faved, if they do not pay this tribute of devotion to the facred image.

And to prove this erroneous belief; the chaplain, who dreffes the image (as he is reckoned to be a heavenly man) may eafily give out what ftories he pleafes, and make the people believe any revelation from the Virgin to him, as many of them are written in the book of the Virgin of *Pilar, viz.* Dr. *Auguftine Ramirez,* chaplain to the image, in 1542, as he was dreffing it, it talked with him for half a quarter of an hour, and faid, My faithful and well beloved *Auguftine*, I am very angry with the inhabitants of this my city for their ingratitude. Now, I tell you as my own chaplain, that it is my will, and I do command you to publifh it, and fay the following words, which is my fpeech to all the people of *Zaragofa:* Ungrateful people, remember, that after my fon died for the redemption of the world, but more efpecially for you the inhabitants of this my chofen city, I was pleafed, two years after I went up to Heaven, in body and foul, to pitch upon this felect city for my dwelling place; therefore I commanded the Angels to make an image perfectly like my body, and another of my fon Jefus, on my arms, and to fet them both on a pillar, whofe matter nobody can know, and when both were finifhed, I ordered them to be carried in a proceffion, round about the Heavens, by the principal Angels, the heavenly Hoft following, and after them the Trinity, who

took me in the middle, and when this procession was
over in Heaven, I sent them down with illuminations
and music to awake my beloved *James*, who was a-
sleep on the river side, commanding him, by my ambassador *Gabriel*, to build, with his own hands, a chapel for my image, which I did accordingly, and ever
since I have been the defence of this city, against the
Saracen army, when, by my mighty power, I killed, in
one night, at the breach, 50,000 of them, putting the
rest to a precipitate flight.

After this visible miracle (for many saw me in the
air fighting) I have delivered them from the oppres-
sion of the *Moors*, and preserved the faith and religion
unpolluted for many years, in this my city. How
many times have I succoured them with rain, in time
of need? How many sick have I healed? How much
riches are they masters of by my unshaken affection to
them all? And what is the recompence they give me
for all these benefits? Nothing but ingratitude: I
have been ashamed, these 15 years, to speak before
the eternal Father, who made me Queen of this city:
Many and many times I am at court, with the three
persons, to give my consent for pardoning several sinners, and when the Father asketh me about my city, I
am so bashful that I cannot lift up my eyes to him.
He knoweth very well their ingratitude, and blameth
me for suffering so long their covetousness: And this
very morning, being called to the council of the Trinity,
for passing the divine decree, under our hands and seal,
for the Bishoprick of *Zaragofa*, the Holy Spirit has affronted me, saying, I was not worthy to be of the private council in Heaven, because I did not know how
to govern and punish the criminals of my chosen city,
and I have vowed not to go again to the heavenly court
till I get satisfaction from my offenders: So I do thun-
der out this sentence, against the inhabitants of *Zaragofa*, that I have resolved to take away my image from
them, and resign my government to *Lucifer*, if they do
not

not come, for the space of 15 days, every day with gifts, tears, and penances, to make due submission to my image, for the faults committed by them these 15 years: And if they come with prodigal hands, and true hearts, to appease my wrath, which I am pleased with, they shall see the rain-bow for a signal, that I do receive them again into my favour. But, if not, they may be sure that the Prince of Darkness shall come to rule and reign over them; and further, I do declare, that they shall have no appeal, from this my sentence, to the tribunal of the Father; for this is my will and pleasure.

These are the words of the revelation (I mean) this is the substance of it; for, perhaps, I leave out many words, and add many others, to give sense to the English: But as to the substance I am not mistaken, as may be found in the *Virgin*'s book, published by authority and leave of the Inquisitors, in 1688, in *Zaragosa*, by *Peter Dormer*. I had the book, which, for my extraordinary devotion to the Virgin, I used to read every day, and I may give a full account of it better than of the bible, having read it six or eight times every year. But I do not design to give a translation of it now, nor to be tedious upon one subject; therefore I only say, that after this revelation was published, all the inhabitants of the city were under such a concern, that the magistrates, by the Archbishop's order, did publish an ordinance for all sorts of people to fast three days every week, and not to let the cattle go out those days, and to make the cattle fast, as well as the reasonable creatures; and as for the infants, not to suckle them but once a day. All sorts of work were forbidden for fifteen days time, in which the people went to confess and make public penances, and offer whatever money and rich jewels they had, to the Virgin.

Observe now, that this publishing of the revelation was in the month of *May*, and it is a customary thing for

for that country to see almost every day the rainbow at that time: So there was, by all probability, certain hopes that the rain bow would not fail to shew its many colour'd faces to the inhabitants of *Zaragosa*, as did happen the eleventh day, but it was too late for them, for they had bestowed all their treasures on the image of the Virgin. Then the rejoicings began, and the people were almost mad for joy, reckoning themselves the most happy, blessed people in the universe. Then they vow'd solemnly to build her the largest and most capacious church in the world; but their want of money did hinder the beginning of it for ten years. Then the magistrates (thinking that the wealth of the city was sufficient to begin the temple) bestowed 50000 pistoles for the laying the foundations of it. A subscription was made among the private persons, which did amount to 150000 pistoles; and Don *Francisco Ibannez de la Riva de Herrera*, then Archbishop of *Zaragosa*, and afterwards of *Toledo*, and general Inquisitor, commanded all the people, ecclesiastical and secular, to go on Sundays, and holy days in the afternoon, and carry materials for the work of the week following. I went myself many holy days and Sundays, and I saw his Grace, and all his family, with baskets, carrying stones from the river to the open foundations, and, by his example, gentlemen and ladies, old and young, Priests and Friars, were excited to do the same, till the first stone of the foundation was laid by his Grace, drest in his pontifical; and after that, giving his blessing to the building, he recommended the finishing of it to the people's care. They are at work ever since every day, and in 14 years, since the foundation of the temple, there is yet but the third part built up, by 500 workmen constantly at it, and I believe that if ever it is finished, it will be twice bigger and larger than St. *Paul*'s church in *London*. So great and blind is the bigotry and devotion of that people for the Virgin of *Pilar*.

By

By these and the like revelations, given out every day by the Virgin's chaplain, the people are so much infatuated, that they certainly believe there is no salvation for any soul without the consent of the Virgin of *Pilar*, so they never fail to visit her image every day, and pay her due homage, for fear that if she is angry again, *Lucifer* should come to reign over them: And this is done by the Virgin's crafty chaplain, to increase her treasure and his own too. As to him, I may aver, that the late chaplain, Don *Pedro Valanzuela* was but six years in the Virgin's service; yearly rent is 1000 pistoles, and when he died, he left, in his testament, 20000 pistoles to the Virgin, and 10000 to his relations; now, how he got 30000 pistoles clear in six years, every body may imagine.

As to the miracles wrought by this image, I could begin to give an account, but never make an end; and this subject requiring a whole book to itself, I will not trouble the reader with it, hoping in God, that if he is pleased to spare my life some years, I shall print a book of their miracles and revelations, that the world may, by it, know the inconsistent grounds and reasons of the *Romish* communion.

Now, coming again to the adoration of images, I cannot pass by one or two instances more of the image of Jesus Christ, adored by the Roman catholics.

The first is that of the crucifix in the monument, both on *Thursday* and *Friday* of the holy week. The *Roman catholics* have a custom on holy *Thursday*, to put the consecrated Host in the monument, till *Friday* morning, at eleven of the clock, as I have already said, treating of the estation of the holy Calvary.

Now I will confine myself wholly to the adoration paid to the crucifix, and all the material instruments of our Saviour's passion, by Priests, Friars, and magistrates. In every parish church and convent of Friars and Nuns, the Priests form a monument, which is of

the

the breadth of the great altar's front, consisting of 10 or 12 steps, that go gradually up to the *Ara*, or altar's table, on which lies a box, gilt, and adorned with jewels, wherein they keep, for 24 hours, the great Host, which the Priest, that officiates, has consecrated on *Thursday*, between eleven and twelve. In this monument, you may see as many wax-candles as parishioners belonging to that church, and which burn 24 hours continually. At the bottom of the monument there is a crucifix laid down on a black velvet pillow, and two silver dishes on each side. At three of the clock, in the afternoon, there is a sermon preached by the *Lent* preachers, whose constant text is, *Mandatum novum du vobis, ut diligatis invicem, Sicut dilexi vos.* Expressing in it, the excessive love of our Saviour towards us. After it, the Prelate washeth the feet of 12 poor people, and all this while the people that go from one church to another, to visit the monuments, kneel down before the crucifix, kiss it's feet, and put a piece of money into one of the dishes. The next day, in the morning, there is another sermon, of the passion of our Saviour, wherein the preacher recommendeth the adoration of the Cross according to the solemn ceremony of the church. That day, *i. e.* Good *Friday*, there is no Mass in the *Romish* church, for the Host, which was consecrated the day before, is received by the Minister, or Prelate, that officiates, and when the passion is sung, then they begin the adoration of the crucifix, which is at the bottom of the monument; which is performed in the following manner: First of all, the Priest that officiates, or the Bishop, when he is present, pulling off his shoes, goes, and kneels down three times before the crucifix, kisseth its feet, and in the same manner comes back again to his own place. All the Priests do the same, but without putting any thing into the dish, this being only a tribute to be paid by the magistrates and laity. This being done by all the magistrates, the Priest biddeth them to come at four in the

the afternoon, to the defcent of Jefus Chrift, from the Crofs, and this is another idolatrous ceremony and adoration.

The fame crucifix, that was at the bottom of the monument, is put on the great altar's table, veiled or covered with two curtains, and when the people are gathered together in the church, the chapter, or community comes out of the veftry, and kneeling down before the altar, begins, in a doleful manner, to fing the pfalm, *Miferere*, and when they come to the verfe, *Tibi foli peccavi*, &c. they draw the curtains, and fhew the image of Chrift crucified to the people. Then the preacher goes up to the pulpit, to preach of the pains and afflictions of the Virgin *Mary* (whofe image fhedding tears is placed before the image of her fon.) I once preached myfelf upon this occafion in the convent of St. *Auguftine*, in the city of *Huefca*, and my text was, *Animam meam pertranfivit gladius*. After the preacher has exaggerated the unparelleled pains of the Virgin *Mary*, feeing her fon fuffer death, in fo ignominious a manner, he orders *Satellites* (fo they call thofe that ftand with the nails, hammer, and other inftruments ufed in the crucifixion) to go up to the Crofs, and take the crown of thorns off the crucifix's head, and then he preacheth on that action, reprefenting to the people his fufferings as movingly as poffible. After the *Satellites* have taken the nails out of the hands and feet, they bring down the body of Jefus, and lay him in a coffin, and when the fermon is over, the proceffion beginneth all in black, which is called the burying of Chrift. In that proceffion, which is always in the dark of the evening, there are vaft numbers of difciplinants that go along with it, whipping themfelves, and fhedding their blood, till the body of Jefus is put into the fepulchre. Then every body goes to adore the fepulchre, & after the adoration of it, beginneth the proceffion of the eftations of the holy Calvary,

vary, of which I have spoken already in the 2d chapter of this book.

I will not deprive the public of another superstitious ceremony of the *Romish* Priests, which is very diverting, and by which their ignorance will be more exposed to the world; and this is practised on the Sunday before *Easter*, which is called *Dominica Palmarum*, in which the church commemorateth the triumphant entry of Jesus Christ into *Jerusalem*, sitting on an ass, the people spreading their clothes and branches of olive trees on the ground: So, in imitation of this triumph, they do the same in some churches and convents.

The circumstance of one being representative of Jesus, on an ass, I never saw practised in *Zaragosa*, and I was quite unacquainted with it, till I went to *Alvalate*, a town that belongs to the Archbishop in *temporalibus* and *spiritualibus*, whither I was obliged to retire with his Grace in his precipitate flight from King *Charles*'s army, for fear of being taken prisoner of state. We were there at the *Franciscan* convent on that Sunday, and the Archbishop being invited to the ceremomony of the religious triumph, I went with him to see it, which was perform'd in the following manner.

All the Friars being in the body of the church, the Guardian placing his Grace at the right hand, the procession began, every Friar having a branch of olive-trees in his hand, which was blessed by the Rev. Father Guardian; so the Cross going before, the procession went out of the church to a large yard before it: But, O God! What did we see at the door of the church, but a fat Friar, drest as a *Nazareen*, on a clever ass, two Friars holding the stirrups, and another pulling the ass by the bridle. The representative of Jesus Christ took place before the Archbishop. The ass was an he one, though not so fat as the Friar, but the ceremony of throwing branches and clothes before him, being quite strange to him, he began to start and caper, and at last threw down the heavy load of the Friar.—

The

The aſs ran away, leaving the reverend on the ground, with one arm broken. This unuſual ceremony was ſo pleaſant to us all, that his Grace, notwithſtanding his deep melancholy, did laugh heartily at it. The aſs was brought back, and another Friar, making the repreſentative, did put an end to this aſs-like ceremony.

But the ignorance and ſuperſtition beginneth now; when the ceremony was over, a novice took the aſs by the bridle, and began to walk in the cloiſter, and every Friar made a reverence, paſſing by, and ſo the people kneeling down before him, one ſaid, *O happy aſs*, others (eſpecially the old women) cried out, *O burro de Chriſto*, i. e. O aſs of Chriſt! But his Grace diſpleaſed at ſo great a ſuperſtition, ſpoke to the guardian, and deſired him not to ſuffer his Friars to give ſuch an example to the ignorant people, as to adore the aſs. The guardian was a pleaſant man, and ſeeing the Archbſhop ſo melancholy, only to make him laugh, told his Grace that it was impoſſible for him to obey his Grace, without removing all his Friars to another convent, and bring a new community. Why ſo, ſaid his Grace? Becauſe (replied the guardian) all my Friars are he aſſes. And you the guardian of them (anſwered his Grace.)

Thus Prieſts and Friars excite the people, not only to adore the image of Jeſus Chriſt, but irrational creatures too; nay, the very inſenſible (though vegetable, as they ſay) things. They give out, that the nails of the feet of Chriſt's image of *Calatrao* grow every week, and the Clerk of the chapel keeps a box full of them, to give the pairings to the people, as a great relic, which they kiſs and adore as if they were little gods, and I kept myſelf, when I was young, a piece of thoſe nails ſet in gold, hanging night and day on my neck. So great is the ſtupidity of the people, and ſo great the ignorance of the Prieſts and Friars, or rather their craftineſs and covetouſneſs, for I cannot believe they credit themſelves the ſtories which they give out,

K k

There is another image of the Virgin *Mary*, called *la Aurora*, i. e. the morning day break, in the convent of *Franciscan* Friars, called Jesus of the bridge, because it is near the wooden bridge of the city. This image was in great veneration some years ago, and the lay-brethren of that convent were very much respected by all the people of that city, because they had given out that there was always one lay-brother in that convent so godly that he was in high esteem and favour with the Virgin *de la Aurora*, but unhappily for that image, for the convent, and for the lay-brethren of it; for one of them, who was clerk of the chapel of the Virgin, gave out in the city, that on her festival day, which was the *Tuesday* after *Easter*, the image was to dance with him after evening songs were over. This uncommon miracle excited the curiosity of almost all the inhabitants of the city to meet there at the fixed day; but the crafty Friars knowing that the 20th part of the people could not see it, upon second thoughts, spread in the city that the miracle was to be continued for eight days, or, as they say, all the days of the *Octava* of the Virgin. So the first and second days were appointed for the noblemen and ladies, and the rest for tradesmen and common people.

When the day was come, and the evening songs were over, the image of the Virgin was in the middle of the altar of her chapel, in a gilt small chapel, richly drest, and all the altar round about full of wax-candles: Before the altar a scaffold was set up for the music, and for the lay-brother, so when the church was full of people, the father guardian made the signal to the brother to begin to dance, *las folias*, i. e. the follies, with the *Castannetes*, or cracking of the fingers. The Friar danced a long while without being accompanied by the image: The people began to say that the lay-brother was a cheat, which being heard by him, he fell down upon his knees, and began to cry bitterly, and say to the image in an innocent stile; hear, young *Madona*,

de

do not make me pass for a cheat; you know very well what you promised me one night, when I was combing the wig that my cousin gave you: Hear, do you remember? You say nothing? Then, by this holy cross, you shall pay for it. Now I will ask you to be as good as your word, twice more, and if you will expose me to be laughed at, by the people here present, by my faith, I will swear that you are the cheat, and every body will believe me, and none for the future will care for you. O what joy was it to the Friar, and the people, to see the image make a reverence to the brother! Now (said he) you are an honest woman, come let us dance the *Folias*, and let every one here present know that you perform whatever you promise. The image really began to turn round about, for the space of three minutes. A reverend silence was kept in the church, all were surprised to see so wonderful a miracle, and no body dared to say a word, but the good brother, who (when the image ceased from her motions) turning to the people, said, Now you see the great esteem this image hath for me, and because I love the inhabitants of *Zaragosa*, as my own life, I will ask a favour from my image for them; which, if she refuseth, I have done with her, there are the keys of her treasure, and let her hire another servant, for I am sure no body can be so faithful as I have been to her. Ay, she will think on it before she loseth me! Now the favour that I beg of you, for my fellow-citizens of *Zaragosa*, (turning to the image) is, that you will take the name of every one that comes, and offers you the charity of one Mass only (for I would not have them pay too dear for this favour) and enter it in the book of eternal life. My old country friends, do not think this to be a small favour, for with it you may give a fig for the Devil, and laugh at him. Now let me see what answer she gives me. Will you grant them this favour? Then the image lifted up, and bowed down its head; at which signal, the people cried out, *Viva, viva la Virgin de la Aurora.* Let the Virgin of the morning live: Or long live the Virgin of *Aurora.* This miracle was immediately divulged through the whole city, and for the six following days the church was crowded with people from morning till the dance of *Folias* was ended: But the Inquisitors finding the thing something odd, they sent the Secretary to the convent at midnight, with order to take up the lay-brother, and search the image; which being done accordingly, he found an instrument to move the image with, which did come down under the altar's table, where another lay-brother did turn the instrument: So the cheat was found out, but too late, for in the six days the image harlaquin danced, the Friars got four thousand pieces of eight for Masses, as the Father guardian of the convent owned to the Inquisitors, and all that was inflicted on the two lay-brothers, for this crime, was to send them into another convent in the country. The convent lost a great deal by this discovery, for the people never went near it since, and the community that was formerly composed of an hundred Friars, is now reduced to thirty in all. This dance of the *Spanish* follies, or the follies of that dance (for one made many fools with it) did happen in 1705, of which I was an eye-witness, for I went twice to see the wonder of wonders, as the Friars used to call it.

The adoration of St. *Mames* in the Parish church of St. *Mary Magdalene*, is another instance of the Priests superstition or covetousness. The Priests of the parish with the minister, Doctor *Parras*, seeing that their church was not haunted as many others, for want of a new miraculous saint, pretended they found out in a rock the corps of St. *Mames*, who was a shepherd, and so making a gilt box, they put this saint, drest like a shepherd, into it, with a pastoral hook, and many lamps and sheep made of silver: The box was placed on the altar's table under the feet of a crucifix, and they exhorted every one to worship and adore him, celebrating

lebrating his singular virtues with an *Octava*, or eight days of festival, and eight panegyric sermons. This invention was in 1709, and I was the first year the seventh preacher in his *Octava*. The novelty of a new saint brought all the people of the city, and many of the country to adore him. Music, illuminations, ringing of bells, and public processions, were in the most solemn and magnificent manner observed, and performed during eight days, in which, many miracles were published as tokens of St. *Mames*'s power, and the affection he had for the people. I was, as well as the other preachers, very much embarrassed, having no history, nor public account of the new saint's life; but at last we found a new way to satisfy the Priests of the parish, and to extol the virtues of their saints; for we eight preachers, among ourselves, agreed to take for our text, every one of us, the *Athenians* motto: *Ignoto Deo*, and to alter it for the division of the heads, thus: *Ignoto Pastori*, and to imitate St. *Paul*, who persuaded the *Athenians* that the unknown God by them was the very God; and persuaded the people that the unknown shepherd of St. *Mames*, whom we began to adore, was the very shepherd, who was to take care of his chosen flock in *Zaragosa*. So, upon this foundation, every one endeavoured to publish the encomiums of the new saint, which were all fictions out of our heads. These sermons were very much praised by Doctor *Parras*, minister of the parish, and by all his Priests, and being printed afterwards by the heirs of *Pedro Dormer*, every body bought them, in order to be acquainted by them with the unknown shepherd St. *Mames*. All the while I was there after, I observed all sorts and conditions of people going to worship and adore the corner of the box of the saint, and when I left *Zaragosa*, the church and chapel was very much improved by the miracles wrought daily by St. *Mames*.

But the bigotry of Priests and Friars is so great, that
they

they are not satisfied with adoring and worshiping images of saints, and their relics, but they make the very beasts to worship them also; this will appear by the daily custom they have on St. *Martin*'s day. They publish, and the people believe, what is written in the life of St. *Antonio Abbot*, viz. that he was an advocate for the cattle with God, and therefore, in the church of St. *Martin*, in *Zaragosa*, his image is in the middle of the great altar, with a pig at his feet: For the history says, that he cured many pigs. In memory then, and veneration of this saint (whom we may call the saint of the beasts) the magistrates of the city assist at the great Mass, and the sermon preached on his festival day, & every body recommends his beasts to him, and puts them under his care and protection, and they have not only this faith, but they give a public testimony of it; for that day, in the morning, and in the afternoon, every one, from the Archbishop to the carrier, sends his horses, mules, asses, and pigs, to make three turns round about the church of St. *Martin*: The coachmen and servants do endeavour to dress the beasts with the best mantles, collars of small bells, and the necks & tails full of such ribbons as they can get; so when they have finished the third turn, they stop before the church's door, and make a sort of a bow, and the clerk of the church, who is a Priest, gives them the blessing, and a bit of blessed bread. Every beast is to pay to his advocate half a real of plate, which is very much, every year, and not only the beasts or cattle of the city pay that tribute, but all, or almost all the cattle of the country, except the sheep, for 20 sheep pay only the sum aforesaid. There are four Priests belonging to that church, which are called, *Commisarios de Bestias de St. Antonio Abad*, Commissaries of St. *Anthony*'s beasts; and after his festival, they take their circuits through the whole kingdom; they do not preach, but in every town they go through all the inhabitants of it bring their cattle and sheep into a large field, and

the

the Priest of the circuit gives them St. *Antonio*'s blessing, and receives the tribute; afterwards he blesseth the waters, grass, earth, and the very straw the people keep to feed their cattle: So if a mule or horse is sick, they pray to St. *Antonio*, and many go to the Priest and desire him to say a Mass for the beast, that it may, by the help of it, recover its health. The four ignorant Priests tell such stories of St. *Antonio* and his pig to the country people and idiots, that many poor silly women, thinking themselves unworthy to approach near, or pray to the glorious saint himself, pray before the pig, make their requests to it, and generously give it ribbons and trinkets, that by its intercession, their beasts and themselves may be preserved from all evil and mischief in all times of their tribulation, in the hour of death, and in the day of judgment. These are their practices, their corruptions, and their abominations, before the Lord.

But because this article of images, and the next of relics, contribute very much to the discovery of the idolatries, and of the bigotries and superstitions of all those of that communion, I shall not leave this subject, without giving an account of some remarkable images which are worshiped and adored by them all.

They have innumerable images of Christ, the Virgin *Mary*, the Angels and Saints in the streets, in small chapels built within the thickness of the walls, and most commonly in the corners of the streets, which the people adore, kneel down before, and make prayers and supplications to. They say, that many of those images have spoke to some devout persons, as that of St. *Philip Nery* did to a certain ambitious Priest, who, walking through the street where the image was, was talking within himself, and saying, Now I am a Priest, next year I hope to be Dean, after Bishop, then Cardinal, and after all *Summus Pontifex*, to which soliloquy, the image of St. *Philip* answered: *And after all those* **honors, comes death,** *and after death,* Hell and

and damnation for ever. The Priest being surprised at this answer, so much *a propos,* and looking up and down, he saw the mouth of the image open, by which he concluded that the image had given him the answer, and so, taking a firm resolution to leave all the thoughts of this deceitful world, with his own money he purchased the house where the image was, and built a decent chapel in honor of St. *Philip,* which now, by the gifts of pious people, is so much enlarged, that we reckon St. *Philip*'s church and parish to be the third in the city for riches, and the number of beneficiate Priests being 46, besides the Rector.

In St. *Philip*'s church there is a miraculous crucifix, called *El santa Christo delas peridas :* The holy Christ of child-bed women ; which is very much frequented by all people, but chiefly by the ladies, who go there to be churched, and leave the purification offerings mentioned in the ceremonial law of *Moses.* And as there is this image, which is an advocate of women delivered of child, there are also two images, who are advocates of barren women, one of the Virgin in the convent of *Recolet* Friars of St. *Augustine,* and another of St. *Antonio de Paula :* The first is called *the Virgin of the barren women* ; the second, *the intercessor of the barren ladies.* This second image is in the convent of *Victorian Friars,* and is kept in a gilt box, in a chapel within the cloister, and the door is always lock'd up, and the key kept by the Father corrector, i. e. the superior of the convent.

These two images, or rather the stewards of them, work undeniable miracles every year, for no barren woman goes to pray and adore these images, without coming home with child, for they are so sure by faith, or action, that they give out, and make the poor husbands believe, that they find themselves very much altered, *&c.* So if the *Victorian* Friars publish one or two miracles, one week, the *Recolets* do publish three or four the week following, and so they make good the

physicians

physicians, saying, that there is no such thing as barrenness, where there are such images, and that *exitus acta probat*, &c. For no woman, who goes to make three turns round the box of St. *Antonio de Paula*, or adore the girdle of the Virgin, is barren afterwards. But the *Victorians* get more profit by it than the *Recolets*; for all the ladies that are, or pretended to be barren, go to St. *Antonio*, and the common people to the *Recolets*. The truth is, that the *Victorians* are well drest, and most commonly, handsome fellows, merry, and fit for company, polite, and great gamesters, which are good qualifications to please intriguing women.

Another instance of their ignorant practices is, their adolatrous adoration of the Virgin *Mary* in bed, on her ascension-day, the fifteenth of *August*. All the ladies of the parish join all their jewels and ribbons, on the fourteenth of that month, and go to church in the afternoon, where the parish minister, with his clergy, or the Prior of the convent, with his Friars, are waiting for them; then the ladies, to take a refreshment (or, as they call it, *The collation of the Virgin*) go all together to the vestry, or to a private room for visits, and all are very merry for an hour or two: Then the superior chooses one of the richest ladies for waiting lady to the blessed *Mary*, and six assistants under her, which must be unmarried young ladies, and this honorable employment is for one year. The waiting-lady and her assistants are to dress the Virgin, and order the bed with great nicety, and assist every day, morning and evening, during the eight days of the festival at church, and pay for a splendid dinner the eight days for the clergy, or community, and they are obliged to serve at the table, as an act of humility. So, when every thing is settled between them and the superior, they go into the church, and every thing being ready, they set up the bed, which is made very neat, and with curtains of the best brocade; the image of the Virgin, in a clean fine shift, is laid down on the bed by the waiting lady and her assistants, and cover'd with a quilt, which is very richly laced round about. The bed is under a canopy, and twenty-four large, thick wax candles are burning round it. When all is in order, the evening songs begin, and after them every Priest or Friar, and the people after them, draw near the bed, kneel down, say a prayer, and kiss one of the Virgin's hands with great devotion. The next day is the great festival, which is celebrated with music, High-Mass, a sermon, evening songs, and a general procession through the streets. After which the same religious ceremony, of praying and kissing her hand, is devoutly repeated by the clergy and laity; and these public demonstrations of zeal and devotion (except the procession) are continu'd every day during the *Octava*.

Another practice like this, of paying worship and adoration to the Virgin Mother, and her child Jesus in a manger, is observed on *Christmas*, and eight days after: But especially the Nuns do signalize themselves on this festival, and that on which Jesus was lost and found again in the Temple; for they hide the child in some secret place under the altar's table, and after evening songs they run up and down thro' the garden, cloisters, and church, to see whether they can find the innocent child, and the Nun that finds him out, is excus'd, for that year, from all the painful offices of the convent, but she is to give, for 3 days together, a good dinner to all the Nuns and Father Confessor; and that year she may go to the grate at any time, without any leave or fear, for she doth not assist at the public service of prayers: In short, she has liberty of conscience that year, for finding the lost child, and she is often lost too at the end of the year, by following a licentious sort of life.

These

These are, in some measure, voluntary devotions and adorations, but there are many others by precept of the church, and ordinances of several Popes, who have granted proper services to several images, with which Priests and Friars do serve and adore them, or else they commit a mortal sin, as well as if they neglected the divine and ecclesiastical service, and the due observance of the ten commandments of the law of God. I will give a few instances of these adorations by precept, and with them I shall dismiss this present article.

There are, in the church of *Rome*, proper services granted by the Popes for the invention or finding out of the Cross, and for the exaltation of it, and every Priest, Friar and Nun, is obliged, in conscience, to say these services in honor of the Cross; and after the great Mass they adore the Cross, and this is properly adoration, for they say in the hymn, *Let us come and adore the holy Cross*, &c. and the people do the same after them. They carry the Cross on the 3d of *May*, and on the great Litany-days, in a solemn procession, to some high place out of the town, and after the officiating Priest has lifted up the Cross towards the south, north, west, and east, blessing the four parts of the world, and singing the Litany, the procession comes back to the church. These festivals are celebrated with more devotion and veneration, as to the outward appearance, than pomp and magnificence, except in the churches dedicated to the holy Cross, where this being the titular festival, is constantly perform'd with all manner of ceremonies, as the days of the first class.

Again, There is another superstitious (tho' profitable to the clergy) ceremony in their church, which they call the adoration of the peace of God, for which purpose they keep in every church two flat pieces of silver, like a smoothing-iron, with an handle whereon are engraved the figure of the Cross, and the images

of

of the Apostles *Peter* and *Paul*; so in the great Mass, when the Priest comes to break the consecrated Host, and puts the small part within the chalice, and says, *Pax Domini sit semper vobiscum*: That is, *The peace of the Lord be always with you*, and this he says, making the sign of the Cross on the chalice, then the deacon gives him the silver piece, which he kisseth, and the deacon doing the same, gives it to the subdeacon, and so it goes round to the incenser, and one of the acoliti, *i. e.* those that carry the two candlesticks. The other acolitus, who hath the second piece, comes to join both pieces together, and having a silken towel on his neck, he goes to give the piece to the magistrates all on their knees, and to the rest of the people, and every body gives the peace offering in money, which is for the Priest that officiates. But the greatest offering to the Cross, of money and eatable things, is on the Sunday next before Easter. That day Priests and Friars bless the palms, or olive branches, and make of them small Crosses, which, as they make the people believe, are the best relics against lightnings and thunders: So the people, willing to have so great a safeguard, together with the blessed branch of olive-tree, go to church, and (especially the children) carry another branch furnished with sweet meats, tied up with all sorts of ribbons, and some pieces of silver too; and when they receive the blessed branch and the Cross from the hand of the Priest (after the benediction is over) they leave the rich branch; so in some parish churches the minister gets by it, eatable things, ribbons, money, and wood for firing for a whole year; and the people think themselves very happy and safe for that year with the small blessed Cross: But, for all that, many and many are killed every summer by flashes of lightning.

There are proper services granted to the Virgin *Mary*, under the following names: The Virgin of the
rose

rose of St. *Dominick*, of the girdle of St. *Augustine*, or the rope of St. *Francis*, and of the scapulary of Mount *Carmel*. All these distinguishing signs of the Virgin *Mary*, are celebrated by the church and fraternities of devout people, and adored by all Christians, being all images and relics to be worshipped by the special command of the Pope: Of which precepts I will speak shortly, at the end of this book, if there be room for it. Now, by what has been said, where can we find expressions fit to explain the wickedness, of the Romish Priests, the ignorance of the people, committed to their charge, and the idolatrous, nonsensical, ridiculous ceremonies, with which they serve, not God, but saints, giving them more tribute of adoration, than to the Almighty? I must own, that the poor people who are easily persuaded of every thing, are not to be blamed, but only the covetous, barbarous clergy; for these (though many of them are very blind) are not to be supposed ignorant of what sins they do commit, and advise the people to commit: So, acting against the dictates of their own consciences, they, I believe, must answer for their ill guided flock, before the tribunal of the living God.

ARTICLE III.

Of their relics, and their trust in them.

THE council of *Trent* laid a curse on all those that should not give the honor due to the saints, their sepulchres and relics; but Priests and Friars, as divine expositors of the council, explain the word honor to be godly worshiping and adoration; and this is to set the greater value on the relics, and get more riches by them: And though the same council did command not to receive any new relic, without the consent of the Bishop of the diocess, they do not mind councils in matters of self-interest, and they make every day, as they

they have occasion for them, new relics of the bones of a dead horse or dog, &c. as we shall see by and by: So, it will likewise appear, that all the relics are only a colour and pretence for Priests and Friars to get money.

As to the famous celebrated Virgin of *Pilar*, the greatest relic is to have none, by which they preserve the admiration of the people for the holy image, made of heavenly matter, which was never touch'd till this day: But they give (as I have said already) for relics, the dust, & small bits of the stones they took from the wall, when they made an hole to shew, through it, the holy pillar, on which the image stands. But here we must observe, that the hole being no bigger than the circumference of a small plate, and being made these 1600 years & more, all which time they have been bestowing relics of the dust and stones to every good benefactor, it is a wonder that the stock of the Virgin's chaplain is not exhausted: But the people are not surprised at it, for the chaplain gives out, and it is printed in her book, that the dust and stones are always kept up in in the same quantity by a miracle, and that the image will continue this miracle, for the comfort of all Christians, to the end of the world; and that then the same Angels that brought the image from Heaven, shall come to take it up again; for no heavenly thing can be expos'd to the final conflagration.

Besides those sort of relics, the Popes have granted free and full indulgence, and pardon of sins, to all those that should have either a rosary or medal touch'd by the image of *Pilar*, and such an indulgence serves once in the life of the person that keeps one of those relics, and once more at the point of death; so the chaplain has business enough every day, for there is not one living person in all *Spain*, I verily believe, that has not a relic of this sort, for the chaplain receives a voluntary gift for the trouble of touching the medal or

beads

beads, or any other thing with the image, so that he makes relics of every thing. But, as to the rich people, the chaplain useth them with more respect, in order to get the more from them; for he gives them a piece of an old mantle of the Virgin, I mean of one that has been once on the image; and such a piece is esteemed highly by the rich, as a thing that has touch'd the image a long time. And when any of the rich people are sick, they send for a whole mantle, to put it on the bed, and if the sick recovers, 'tis thought that 'tis a miracle wrought by the mantle; and they pay a pistole for every day they keep the mantle in the house.

As to the *lignum crucis*, or the wood of the Cross, on which our Saviour suffered death, I suppose every body knows the common opinion of the *Romans*, which is, that it groweth every year; so no wonder if there is so great a quantity of it in the world; and I am sure, if all the bits and relics of the holy wood could be gathered together in one place, there would be firing enough for a whole year, for a great many families: But this is so well known, by all people, that I need say no more of it; and I shall treat only of the relics that I saw myself, or read of in the book called *Flos Sanctorum*: Where an historical account is given of the lives and relics of saints, and of the miracles wrought by them.

In the cathedral church of St. *Salvator*, the chapter keeps, with great veneration, the bodies of St. *Peter Argues*, and St. *Dominguito*. The first was born in a town called *Epila*, distant 21 miles from *Zaragosa*, and by his learning was promoted to one of the prebends of the cathedral, and was murthered within the church, after *matins* or midnight songs, as he was going to the vestry. This sacrilegious murther was the occasion of a long *interdictum*: For some said, it was committed by order from the Governor of the city, for jealousy;

for

for the said saint was at that time Confessor of his lady, and more than Confessor too, as malicious people said. The reputation of the whole chapter being stained and lessened by this accident, the prebends give out, that *Peter Argues* was a pious godly minister of J. C. and that he was murthered by some Infidels, that were *incognito* in the city, and that he had wrought many miracles after his death, as appeared by certificates from the persons healed by his influence in heaven. The chapter found great opposition among the nobility, and to stop, at once, the mouths of the people, they resolved to send one of the prebendaries to *Rome*, to solicit the canonization of St. *Peter Argues*, and give 100000 crowns to the Pope, which is the sum settled by his Holiness for the making of a saint; which was accordingly done, and the brief of his canonization being come to the chapter, and with it a bridle for malicious and blasphemous tongues; the chapter, all the clergy, secular and regular, and the whole city, celebrated the first festival of their new saint. His body having been embalmed and preserved, was shewn to the people. Many earnestly begged some relic, but the body being whole, the thing could not be granted: But many bigots went to scratch the ground on which the saint was murthered, and kept the dust for a great relic. The town of *Epila* did contribute for the building of a magnificent chapel to the saint, and the chapter built a noble monument for his body. The silver box wherein the body is kept, is placed under the altar; there are three keys, one is kept by the Dean, another by the Archbishop, and the third by the Viceroy, and no body can see the glorious body without the concurrence of the three key-keepers, and though I was three years and some months in ecclesiastical duty, in the cathedral, I could not have the satisfaction of seeing the body of our *Concolega*, as the chapter calls him: And I presume there must be something extraordinary in the case, for all relics

relics and bodies of canoniz'd persons are generally shewn to the people; But, to satisfy the public, there is, behind the altar, a statue of the saint, made of marble, and the people use to take three turns round the altar, and kiss the pole of the statue's neck, and kneeling before the altar they pray, by faith, to the incorrupted body of the glorious Martyr St. *Peter Argues*.

As to St. *Dominguito*, he was a singing boy of the cathedral, and his whole life was full of wonders in working miracles; so, after his death, he was beatified, and after canoniz'd; but this saint is not much in veneration, and he has only a private festival, solemnized only by the singing boys of the church. His body (as they say) is still uncorrupted, and I saw it, thro' the glass of his box, several times.

In the parish church of St. *Lawrence*, the beneficiates have in great veneration the head of that Martyr, who (as the history of his life reports) was born in the city of *Huesca*, distant 36 miles from *Zaragosa*, and afterwards suffer'd martyrdom at *Rome*. How many bodies St. *Lawrence* had, I do not know, for (tho' it is certain he had but one body and one head) there are two whole bodies of the same saint, one at *Rome*, and another at *Huesca*, and seven heads in the city of *Zaragosa*: He is call'd the courteous and civil *Spaniard*, because, when St. *Vincent* (who was also a *Spaniard*, born in the city of *Valencia*) suffer'd martyrdom at *Rome*, many years after St. *Lawrence*, as he had been a great devoto of *Lawrence*, his body being order'd to be put in the same sepulchre and coffin with St. *Lawrence's*, as the people were going to put it at the left hand, St. *Lawrence's* body mov'd to the left, and left the right to St. *Vincent*, which was a piece of great civility and good manners; therefore, ever since, he has been call'd *El Cortes Espannol*. To the honor of this saint, a magnificent church was built, and dedicated to his name at *Rome*, *extra muros*, or without the wall; which at this present is call'd St. *Lawrence extra muros*: His body is kept there with great veneration, and many indulgences are granted to those that visit that church, as may be seen in the Pope's yearly Bull: And because this saint suffered death in so cruel a manner, as to have his body roasted upon an iron grate, and when one side was roasted, he said to the Tyrant, *Come eat of this side, for it is ready roasted*; therefore, as he underwent the flames of fire on earth, the Popes granted a privilege to his church, that all those that go to visit his sepulchre, may take a soul out of purgatory, and redeem it from the tormenting flames of that dreadful place. There is one whole body of his at *Rome*, as the history of his life, and the *Martyrologium* of that church, testify.

St. *Polonia* is the patroness of all those that have the tooth-ach, and there is not one church nor convent without a tooth of this saint; so that if all her teeth were gathered together, I believe they would make half a million.

I could give so many other instances of the multiplicity of legs, teeth, arms, &c. of one and the same saint in different places, that the reader must needs be surprised, unless I give him an account of the custom the Popes have in making all sorts of relics of whatever saint they please.

When a church, convent, &c. begs of his Holiness a relic of any saint, and it cannot be found, or is already granted to some other church, he sends for an head, or an arm, to some church-yard, and baptizes it with the name of the desired saint; as we see it in the multiplicity of St. *Lawrence*'s heads, and many others, which are well known among the Roman-catholics

tholics, and which were baptized by the Pope, to please only the petitioners. It is reported, and attested in the life of St. *Lucia*, that refusing to satisfy the brutal desire of the Tyrant, he commanded her eyes to be plucked out, and so she died, and therefore all blind people in a body, or fraternity, acknowledge her for their patroness. In the convent of the Nuns, call'd St. *Bernardo*'s ladies, there is to be seen the two eyes of this saint, and in almost every parish church and convent, there is the same relic kept, not only to comfort the blind, but to blind others too, who want no such comfort.

I might have said much more upon each of these articles, and there are some others I have not yet touched on: But for all these things, I shall refer the reader to another book, which I intend to write on this subject (as I before hinted) if my poor endeavours, in this one, be so fortunate as to please the public, and if they do not (as I have too much reason to fear) I have said more than enough already: So, I conclude all, beseeching the supreme disposer of all things, to grant that all who take this piece into their hands, may read it with as much candour and piety as I have written it with sincerity, truth, and a desire of doing them good; that those of this nation, who as yet lie blinded with *Romish* errors, may see the great difference between popery discountenanced in *Ireland*, & triumphant in *Spain*, and know what imperious Lords they would soon find their humble Priests metamorphosed into, if they should ever be so unhappy as to have this kingdom in the condition they wish it; and lastly, that all among us, that are already enlightened with the truth, may seriously ponder with themselves the extraordinary blessings they enjoy above their neighbouring countries, and piously acknowledge, with the prophet, *That their lines are fallen to them in pleasant places.* Here none are afraid of being hurried out of their houses to loathsome dungeons and horrible death, without any reason given to themselves, or any body else: Here gentlemen are under no uneasy apprehensions of having the sanctity of their nuptial beds violated by the secret intrigues, or their children reduced to poverty by the rapacious avarice of profligate men; here the innocent Virgins may contentedly enjoy themselves, without fear of being drawn, by the sanctified out-side of debauched hypocrites, into dishonor in this world, and endless misery in the next. And what is the crown of all, the gospel, that fountain of living waters, is open to all that please to come and drink, and our divine religion clearly explained to the meanest capacity, and the truth of it evidently demonstrated by the greatest genius the world has ever seen: And all these blessings, supported by a Prince, and defended by an army that thoroughly understand the value of those liberties, and the excellency of that religion they protect; for, surely, if, in spite of all these mercies, we plot our own destruction, & force our way to Hell, through all the bars God has set in our passage, our punishments in the next world will be as much superior to those of other nations, as the Almighty's care, to prevent our ever suffering any, has been.

FINIS.

www.ingramcontent.com/pod-product-compliance
Lightning Source LLC
Chambersburg PA
CBHW032045230426
43672CB00009B/1472